SPANISH REVIEW GRAMMAR

Plaza de Doña Elvira, Seville, Spain

SPANISH REVIEW GRAMMAR

THIRD EDITION

CON TEMAS ORALES Y ESCRITOS

Vincenzo Cioffari
BOSTON UNIVERSITY

Emilio González
GRADUATE CENTER
THE CITY UNIVERSITY OF NEW YORK

D. C. HEATH AND COMPANY
Lexington, Massachusetts   Toronto   London

International Standard Book Number: 0-669-62760-7

Library of Congress Catalog Card Number: 79-151634

Preface to the Third Edition

In preparing the original edition of the Spanish Review Grammar the authors had a twofold purpose in mind: first, to review all the basic essentials of vocabulary and grammatical construction; second, to provide material for a solid foundation in self-expression, both oral and written. Consequently the book is divided into two parts, each of which is designed to accomplish the stated purpose.

Part One, consisting of fourteen lessons, reviews briefly and concisely all those essentials which are assumed to have been covered before entering a course in review grammar. The selections, written in current style and controlled vocabulary, furnish a core for reviewing the most basic rules of construction. The Word Reminder makes sure that the student does not overlook the words of highest frequency. These words, together with items related to the subject matter, provide material for self-expression. They are incorporated in the exercises.

Part Two, consisting also of fourteen lessons, provides a complete course in conversation and composition, based on a wide range of topics of permanent cultural interest. One outstanding feature of Hispanic civilization is developed at a time, in relation to the country where it is best represented. The student is provided with enough information on a given theme to maintain his interest and develop an intelligent discussion. The authors have purposely avoided disconnected data in order to maintain human interest while providing a substantial background.

The book is intended for students who have completed a beginning course in Spanish. In view of the success of the two previous editions, the authors have preserved these basic features in the Third Edition. On the basis of the experience shared with us by the many users of the book, we have recast grammatical rules to achieve greater clarity. We have equalized lessons which were too long. We have brought all information up to date and introduced the latest current expressions. We have added an Appendix which provides terms for discussions on careers, professions, and daily foods. We felt it necessary to provide food for the body as well as the mind. We have summarized the ideas presented in each cultural selection, so that students will not feel frustrated and bewildered.

v

The Third Edition increases the emphasis on self-expression in Spanish and decreases the dependence on translation. Many new pattern drills have been introduced in the body of the text in order to induce the student to use Spanish all the time. Translation has been retained only as a check for exactness and clarity. Professor and Mrs. Cioffari have created a completely new accompanying course for the laboratory, geared to promote individual progress. Both the Workbook and the tapes provide the type of drills which not only train the speech and the ear, but train the mind to acquire new language. We tried in every way to overcome the shortcomings of mechanical repetition.

For college classes we suggest one of two procedures:

I. Present each lesson of Part One orally in class, one complete lesson a day.

Present each lesson of Part Two in three assignments: FIRST DAY, grammar and reading selection. SECOND DAY, *Expresiones Útiles*, *Resumen Práctico*, and *Ejercicio I* (*Conversación*). THIRD DAY, the rest of the *Ejercicios*.

II. Skip Part One entirely and let the students use it only for reference. The Review at the beginning of each lesson in Part Two covers adequately all the essentials. Present each lesson of Part Two in three assignments, as outlined above.

For high school classes we suggest the following procedure:

Present each lesson of Part One in two assignments: FIRST DAY, grammar, reading selection, Useful Expressions, and Word Reminder. SECOND DAY, *Conversación* and *Ejercicios*.

Present each lesson of Part Two in four assignments: FIRST DAY, grammar and a first reading of the selection. SECOND DAY, a second reading of the selection, *Expresiones Útiles*, and *Resumen Práctico*. THIRD DAY, *Ejercicios I, II,* and *III.* FOURTH DAY, the rest of the *Ejercicios*.

Naturally the instructor is the best judge of the procedure which will bring the desired results. These suggestions are intended as a guide for the less experienced, or as a procedure for classes composed of various sections.

We wish to express our gratitude to our many friends who have favored us with constructive criticism through the various stages of this work, from the first mimeographed edition through the manuscript of this Third Edition. Our particular thanks on this edition go to Vincent G. Cioffari, who carefully checked all grammatical explanations and exercises for clarity and consistency; to Prof. Angelina G. Cioffari, whose critical experience with the two previous editions has amounted to collaboration; and to the Modern Language Department of D. C. Heath and Company, whose painstaking care and personal interest have contributed immensely to the improvements which we hope we have achieved.

Vincenzo Cioffari
Emilio González

Contents

Preface   *v*

PART ONE

Lección 1   NUESTRA CALLE

Gender of Nouns. Definite Articles   3
Plural of Nouns. Uses of the Definite Articles   4
Conjugations. Present Tense of the Indicative. English Equi-
    valents of the Present Tense. Negative Sentences   5
Interrogative Sentences   6

Lección 2   UNAS VECINAS

Indefinite Articles. Adjectives   11
Position of Adjectives. Agreement of Adjectives   12
Present Indicative of **ser**. Present Indicative of **tener**. Seasons,
    Months, and Days   13

Lección 3   LOS SOMBREROS

Personal Pronouns (Subject). Omission of the Subject Pronoun   19
Present Indicative of **estar**. Uses of **ser** and **estar**   20
Para to Express Purpose. The Impersonal Forms **hay** and **hace**   21

Lección 4   EN LA TIENDA DE ROPA

Syllabication   27
Practical Rule for Dividing Words into Syllables. Rule of
    Accents   28
Present Indicative of **dar, querer, ir, venir**   29
Numerals   30

ix

Lección 5 ¿QUÉ HORA ES?

Hours of the Day	35
Omission of the Indefinite Article. Prepositions. **Poder, deber,** and **tener que** with the Infinitive	36
Present Indicative of **poder, volver, encontrar, jugar**	37

Lección 6 PLANES PARA EL VERANO

Interrogative Words. Future Tense	43
Future of Irregular Verbs. Numerals	44

Lección 7 UNA CARTA ENTRE AMIGAS

Direct Object Personal Pronouns	49
Position of Object Pronouns. Command Forms	50
Position of Object Pronouns with a Command Form. Present Indicative of **poner, hacer, decir**	51

Lección 8 EL PRIMER VIAJE EN AVIÓN

Possession. Possessive Adjectives	57
Possessive Pronouns. The Verb **gustar**	58
Present Indicative of **caer, saber, ver**	59

Lección 9 EN LA TIENDA DE ABARROTES

Demonstrative Adjectives. Demonstrative Pronouns	65
Negative Words and Expressions. The Preposition **a**	66
Indirect Object Personal Pronouns	67

Lección 10 UNA ENTREVISTA

Past Tenses. Past Participles	73
Present Tense of **haber**. Present Perfect Tense: Formation. Present Perfect Tense: Uses. Relative Pronouns	74

Lección 11 EL IMPERFECTO GRAMATICAL

The Imperfect Tense: Formation and Uses 81
Irregular Imperfects. The Conditional. Personal Pronouns after
 Prepositions. Present Indicative of **conocer, oír, reír, salir, traer** 82

Lección 12 UN VIAJE A XOCHIMILCO

Reflexive Verbs. Reflexive for the Passive 87
Preterite Tense: Formation and Uses. **Acabar de** + Infinitive 88
Hacer + Infinitive. Some Common Verbs Irregular in the Pre-
 terite 89

Lección 13 UN VIAJE EN AUTOMÓVIL

Radical-changing Verbs of the First Class 95
Volver a + Infinitive. Orthographic Changes in Verbs 96

Lección 14 EL CAFÉ

Present Subjunctive: Formation. Uses of the Subjunctive 103
Present Subjunctive of **ser, tener, ir, venir.** Idiomatic Present and
 Idiomatic Past 104

PART TWO

Lección 15 LOS INCAS DEL PERÚ

Gender of Nouns (Cont.). Plural of Indefinite Articles. Neuter
 Articles and Pronouns 113
Uses of **¿ no es verdad?** and **¿verdad?** Uses of **por** and **para** 114

Lección 16 EL TURISMO EN MÉXICO

Double Object Pronouns. Table of Personal Pronouns 121
Position of Object Pronouns. Negative Commands 122
¿Dónde? and **¿A dónde (Adónde)?** 123

Lección 17   EL TEATRO EN ESPAÑA

Present Participle and Progressive Construction   129
Present Participle Alone. Infinitive after Prepositions. Com-
    pound Prepositions. **Hay que, tener que,** and **deber**   130
Haber de and **deber de**   131

Lección 18   EL PAISAJE DE CHILE

Relative Adjectives, Pronouns, and Adverbs   137
Interrogative Adjectives and Pronouns   139

Lección 19   LOS JARDINES DE ESPAÑA

Possessives   145
Verbs Reflexive in Spanish but Not in English. Reciprocal Verbs   146

Lección 20   EL PETRÓLEO Y VENEZUELA

Position of Adjectives   153
Formation of Adverbs. Common Words Used as Adjectives and
    Adverbs. Comparison of Adjectives   154
Comparison of Adverbs. Irregular Comparison of Adjectives and
    Adverbs   155
Comparison of Equality. Absolute Superlative. Translation of
    "than" in Comparisons   156
"In" after a Superlative   157

Lección 21   EL NORTE DE ESPAÑA

Imperfect Subjunctive. Uses of the Subjunctive (Cont.)   163
The Subjunctive in Adjective Clauses. The Subjunctive in Ad-
    verbial Clauses   164

Lección 22   LAS FALLAS DE VALENCIA Y LA SEMANA
               SANTA EN SEVILLA

Compound Tenses of the Indicative. Compound Tenses of the
    Subjunctive   173
Uses of the Compound Tenses. Sequence of Tenses   174

Lección 23   LA AVIACIÓN EN COLOMBIA

Augmentatives and Diminutives   181
Indefinite Adjectives   182
Indefinite Pronouns   183

Lección 24   LA CULTURA EN EL URUGUAY

Summary of Radical-changing Verbs   189
Summary of Orthographic Changes in Verbs   192
Impersonal Expressions   193

Lección 25   LOS BAILES ESPAÑOLES

Conditions   201
Aun and **aún. Acá** and **allá**   202

Lección 26   BUENOS AIRES, LA METRÓPOLI COMERCIAL
                 DE HISPANOAMÉRICA

Ojalá or **tal vez** with the Subjunctive. The Independent Subjunctive   209
Subjunctive in Modified Assertions. Probability. **Sino** and **sino
  que**   211
Future Subjunctive   212

Lección 27   LA CIVILIZACIÓN ÁRABE EN ESPAÑA

Inverted Word Order. Exclamations   217
Interjections. Intonation   218

Lección 28   UNA CARTA DE PANAMÁ

Family Names. Letter Writing   225

Appendix I: SELECCIONES INFORMATIVAS

La elección de una carrera: Carreras y profesiones liberales   234
Comida en un restaurante. Lista de comestibles   242

Appendix II: VERBS

Regular Verbs	248
Radical-changing Verbs	252
Orthographic-changing Verbs	253
Irregular Verbs	256

Vocabulary

Spanish-English	265
English-Spanish	299

Index 319

Photograph Credits 322

Maps

Spain	9
Mexico, Central America and the Caribbean	101
South America	109

T A P E S	NUMBER OF REELS:	8 7″ full track
	SPEED:	3 3/4 ips
	RUNNING TIME:	8 hours (approximate)

PART ONE

LECCIÓN 1

Nuestra calle

1. Gender of Nouns

Nouns ending in –o are generally masculine. Nouns ending in –a are generally feminine. Nouns ending in –e or a consonant may be either masculine or feminine and the gender has to be learned together with the noun. There are no neuter nouns in Spanish.

el chico the boy (*masculine*)   **el hombre** the man (*masculine*)
la chica the girl (*feminine*)   **la mujer** the woman (*feminine*)
el juego the game (*masculine*)
la escuela the school (*feminine*)

Two common words ending in –o are feminine: **la mano** *the hand* and **la radio** *the radio*.

A fair number of words ending in –a (especially –ma and –ta) are masculine: **el poema** *the poem*, **el pianista** *the pianist*, **el mapa** *the map*, **el cura** *the priest*, **el día** *the day*. (Notice that words ending in –ta frequently have both the masculine and feminine forms: **el pianista, la pianista; el artista, la artista.**)

2. Definite Articles

The definite article corresponds to the English word *the*. The forms are as follows:

el *before masc. sing. nouns*   **el niño** the boy
la *before fem. sing. nouns*   **la escuela** the school
los *before masc. pl. nouns*   **los jardines** the gardens
las *before fem. pl. nouns*   **las casas** the houses

3

Street scene in Córdoba, Spain

The article **el** is used before feminine singular nouns beginning with a stressed **a** sound. In such cases the plural is the regular feminine article **las.**

el agua the water, **las aguas**

The article **el** combines with prepositions **a** and **de** to form **al** and **del.**

Juegan al fútbol.	They play football.
El automóvil del padre.	The father's car.

3. Plural of Nouns

To form the plural of a noun ending in a vowel, add **–s** to the singular.

campo field, **campos**   **vecina** neighbor, **vecinas**   **calle** street, **calles**

Nouns endings in a consonant add **–es.**

ciudad city, **ciudades**   **automóvil** car, **automóviles**

Nouns with an accented vowel before the final consonant in the singular drop the written accent in the plural.

jardín, jardines   **sección, secciones**

4. Uses of the Definite Articles

The definite article is generally repeated before each noun, especially if the nouns are of different genders.

Vemos las casas, los jardines y los árboles.	We see the houses, gardens, and trees.

The definite article is used in Spanish but not in English before nouns used in a generic sense, that is when a general quality of persons or objects is expressed.

La hierba es verde.	Grass is green.
Me gusta la música.	I like music.

5. Conjugations

All Spanish verbs are listed in the infinitive, which is the general form, without indication of person or tense. These infinitives end in **–ar, –er,** or **–ir.** Verbs ending in **–ar** are first conjugation; verbs ending in **–er,** second; and verbs ending in **–ir,** third. These classifications or conjugations simplify the learning of the proper endings of verbs.

6. Present Tense of the Indicative

Verbs which simply make statements or ask questions are in the indicative mood. The indicative is the normal form in which Spanish verbs occur unless there is a reason for the use of another mood. Following are the forms of the present for the three conjugations.

	1ST CONJ.	2ND CONJ.	3RD CONJ.
yo	hablo	aprendo	vivo
tú	hablas	aprendes	vives
él, ella, Vd.	habla	aprende	vive
nosotros, –as	hablamos	aprendemos	vivimos
vosotros, –as	habláis	aprendéis	vivís
ellos, ellas, Vds.	hablan	aprenden	viven

7. English Equivalents of the Present Tense

The present tense in Spanish may express not only the fact that an action is taking place in the present time, but also that an action is actually in progress, or that the speaker is emphatic about his statement. **Yo hablo** corresponds to *I speak, I am speaking,* or *I do speak.*

Es verdad, los hombres trabajan mucho.	It is true, men do work a great deal.

8. Negative Sentences

To turn a sentence into the negative the adverb **no** is placed before the verb and nothing can come between **no** and the verb except personal object pronouns.

La calle es muy tranquila.	The street is very quiet.
La calle no es muy tranquila.	The street is not very quiet.

9. Interrogative Sentences

To turn a sentence into the interrogative form the subject is placed after the verb and the question is introduced by an inverted question mark at the beginning, as well as the regular question mark at the end. Sometimes the question is asked just by the inflection of the voice. The English words *do*, *does*, or *did* are not translated when they introduce a question.

Los hombres trabajan mucho.	The men work a great deal.
¿Trabajan mucho los hombres?	Do the men work a great deal?
Hay flores en el jardín.	There are flowers in the garden.
¿ Hay flores en el jardín?	Are there flowers in the garden?

Nuestra calle

La calle en que vivimos es ancha y bonita. Tiene árboles a cada lado. Las casas tienen jardines con flores y césped. En esta parte de la ciudad no hay apartamentos grandes; todas las casas son pequeñas. Los apartamentos se encuentran en otra parte, lejos de
5 aquí. Y no hay mucho tránsito porque no hay ni tiendas ni escuelas. Así que la calle es muy tranquila.

Los niños pasan muchas horas en la calle. Los chicos juegan al fútbol; las chicas miran el juego o charlan con otras muchachas. Las mujeres charlan con sus vecinas. Los hombres trabajan en los
10 jardines cuando vuelven a sus casas. De vez en cuando lavan sus automóviles. Cuando están cansados, se sientan al aire libre y fuman sus pipas.

USEFUL EXPRESSIONS

a cada lado on each side	**de vez en cuando** from time to time
el césped (*used in the sing.*) the lawn	**al aire libre** in the open air

No hay ni tiendas ni escuelas.   There are neither stores nor schools.

WORD REMINDER

acera sidewalk
andar to walk
callarse to become quiet
casarse to get married
cerca de near
cigarrillo cigarette
cuarto room
delante de in front of
descansar to rest
detrás de behind
largo long
levantarse to get up

limpiar to clean
piso floor, story
ruido noise
ventana window
a menudo often, frequently
como (por) regla general as a general
   rule
hace calor it is warm
hace frío it is cold
por el día during the day
por la noche in the evening
por la tarde in the afternoon

CONVERSACIÓN

1. ¿Es ancha y larga la calle donde viven Vds.? 2. ¿Tienen flores los jardines en la primavera? 3. ¿En qué mes están verdes los árboles? 4. En una ciudad moderna, ¿hay mucho tránsito en las calles? 5. ¿Cuántos cuartos tiene un apartamento pequeño, como regla general? 6. Si Vd. se casa, ¿qué cuartos quiere en su apartamento? 7. ¿Hay aceras en las calles principales de una ciudad? 8. ¿Tiene Vd. que andar mucho para ir de su casa a la universidad? 9. ¿Qué hay a cada lado de una calle? 10. ¿Limpian las calles en el invierno en la ciudad en que Vd. vive? 11. ¿Descansa Vd. cuando está cansado? 12. ¿Charlan a menudo los hombres con sus vecinos?

EJERCICIOS

I. Repeat the following sentences, using the words given in parentheses and making the appropriate changes:

1. El apartamento (apartamentos) en que yo (nosotros) vivo es grande.
2. La ciudad (ciudades) tiene una tienda (tiendas) y una escuela (escuelas). 3. El niño (niños) pasa el día (días) jugando al fútbol en la calle (calles). 4. La vecina (vecinas) charla con el vecino (vecinos). 5. Cuando estoy (estamos) cansado, descanso y fumo mi (nuestras)

pipa. 6. La chica (chicas) está contenta sólo cuando se casa. 7. Hay un árbol (árboles) grande en su jardín (jardines). 8. El coche (coches) está detrás de la casa (casas). 9. La primavera (primaveras) es bonita en este país (países). 10. Cuando el hombre (hombres) se casa, se calla también.

II. PRÁCTICA ORAL. Listen to each sentence as given by the instructor. Then when he cues in the phrase in parentheses, supply a complete sentence:

1. José tiene que trabajar (María, yo, Vd., las chicas, nosotros). 2. De vez en cuando hace calor (frío, fresco, viento, mucho calor). 3. Nosotros vivimos lejos de aquí (yo, ellos, los amigos, tú, Alberto). 4. Delante de la casa no hay ni árboles ni hierba (ni césped ni flores, ni acera ni automóviles, ni chicos ni chicas). 5. Los niños juegan al fútbol (nosotros, yo, Vd., los hombres). 6. Por regla general yo no fumo cigarrillos (ellos, Vds., las mujeres, mis padres). 7. Las calles tienen aceras anchas (apartamentos pequeños, tiendas bonitas, mucho tránsito, muchos jardines). 8. En el verano me gusta descansar (en la primavera, en el otoño, en el invierno).

III. Supply the correct definite articles and read fluently:

1. Tengo —— mapa en —— mano. 2. Hace calor por —— día y frío por —— noche. 3. —— artista está en —— jardín, jugando con —— niños y —— muchachas. 4. —— hombres y —— mujeres viven en —— casas en —— invierno. 5. —— flores en —— campos son bonitas. 6. —— automóviles están en —— calles de —— ciudad. 7. Aprendemos —— poemas en —— escuelas. 8. Él fuma —— cigarrillos y —— pipa. 9. En —— verano y en —— primavera —— árboles son bonitos. 10. —— casa de —— pianista no es muy tranquila.

IV. Prepare at home and read fluently in Spanish:

1. The neighbors work in the afternoon. 2. There are neither schools nor apartments near here. 3. We live in the city from time to time. 4. He is learning Spanish with a teacher. 5. Is it warm in the summer in front of the house? 6. I have to study my lesson; you have to keep (become) quiet. 7. He is washing the windows on (**de**) the first floor. 8. Do you rest when you are tired? 9. There is a great deal of traffic when the men return to their homes. 10. The gardens are in another part of the city.

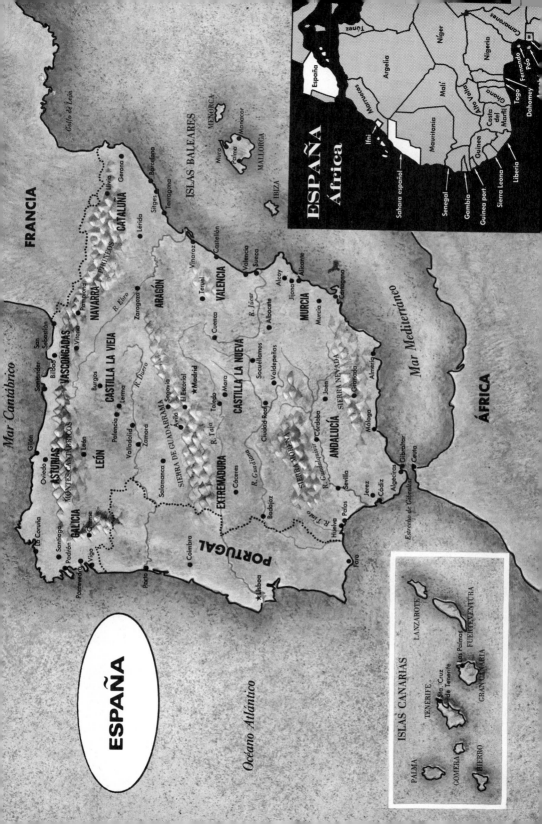

Movie theatre in Madrid, Spain

LECCIÓN 2

Unas vecinas

10. Indefinite Articles

The indefinite article corresponds to the English *a* or *an*. The plural form in Spanish is translated by the word *some* in English. The indefinite article has the following four forms:

un *before masc. sing. nouns*	**un marido** a husband
una *before fem. sing. nouns*	**una esposa** a wife
unos *before masc. pl. nouns*	**unos días** some days
unas *before fem. pl. nouns*	**unas mujeres** some women

11. Adjectives

With descriptive adjectives, when the masculine singular ends in **-o,** the feminine singular ends in **-a,** the masculine plural in **-os,** and the feminine plural in **-as.** However, when the masculine singular ends in **-e** or a consonant (except for adjectives of nationality), the feminine singular is the same as the masculine, and the plural ends in **-es** for both genders.

Adjectives of nationality which end in a consonant in the masculine singular add **-a** to form the feminine; if they have a written accent on the last vowel they lose it. Moreover, they add **-es** to the masculine singular to form the masculine plural and **-as** to form the feminine plural, and again they lose the accent.

> **el señor español, la señora española**
> **un amigo francés, unos amigos franceses**
> **una amiga inglesa, unas amigas inglesas**

Except for **uno** and its compounds, cardinal numbers do not vary in form until after the hundreds. Ordinal numbers have four forms, the same as any other adjective whose masculine singular ends in **-o.**

tres calles three streets   **veinte y unas casas** twenty-one houses
doscientos (-as) alumnos (-as) two hundred pupils
la primera noche the first night   **el segundo día** the second day

Other adjectives, such as demonstratives, possessives, and interrogatives, will be treated under their respective headings.

12. Position of Adjectives

Descriptive adjectives generally come after the noun they modify. We call descriptive those adjectives which denote a physical quality such as color, size, shape, etc., or nationality. Moreover, any adjective which is long or is modified by an adverb generally comes after the noun.

la calle tranquila the quiet street
un chico muy inteligente a very intelligent boy

Adjectives denoting a characteristic generally associated with a word, some short adjectives, and some common adjectives such as **grande, bueno, malo,** and **santo,** generally come before the noun, unless the quality itself is stressed. The Spanish speaker can give different shades of meaning by placing adjectives before or after the noun.

la blanca nieve the white snow	**la casa blanca** the white house
una gran ciudad a great city	**una ciudad grande** a large city
el pobre marido the poor husband (*pitiable*)	**el marido pobre** the poor husband (*not much money*)
una buena comida a good meal (*ample*)	**una comida buena** a fine meal (*as opposed to a bad one*)

Limiting adjectives such as articles, numbers, demonstratives and indefinite adjectives always come before the noun.

13. Agreement of Adjectives

An adjective agrees in gender and number with the noun or pronoun to which it applies. An adjective modifying two or more words of different genders is masculine plural in form.

| la misma línea | the same line |
| **el padre y la madre españoles** | the Spanish father and mother |

14. Present Indicative of *ser*

There are two verbs in Spanish which mean *to be*, namely **ser** and **estar**. Each has its own definite uses, which will be reviewed in due course. The present indicative of **ser** is as follows:

yo	**soy**	nosotros, –as	**somos**
tú	**eres**	vosotros, –as	**sois**
él, ella, Vd.	**es**	ellos, ellas, Vds.	**son**

15. Present Indicative of *tener*

The verb **tener** means *to have* in the sense of *hold*, *possess*, or *own*. It is not used to form compound tenses. Its forms are as follows:

yo	**tengo**	nosotros, –as	**tenemos**
tú	**tienes**	vosotros, –as	**tenéis**
él, ella, Vd.	**tiene**	ellos, ellas, Vds.	**tienen**

16. Seasons, Months, and Days

The names of months and days are generally written with small letters. The days of the week and the months of the year are all masculine. The definite article is generally used with days of the week except after **ser**.

(las estaciones)

la primavera the spring
el verano the summer
el otoño the autumn
el invierno the winter

(los días)

domingo Sunday
lunes Monday
martes Tuesday
miércoles Wednesday
jueves Thursday
viernes Friday
sábado Saturday

(los meses)

enero January
febrero February
marzo March
abril April
mayo May
junio June
julio July
agosto August
septiembre September
octubre October
noviembre November
diciembre December

Unas vecinas

— Buenas tardes, señora Morales. ¡Qué bonita está la tarde!

— Sí, muy bonita. Hace un poquito de fresco, ¿no es verdad?

— Es verdad, pero así me gusta el tiempo. No me gusta cuando hace calor.

5 — A mí tampoco. Ni tampoco me gusta el frío del invierno. ¿Qué tal la familia?

— Muy bien, gracias. Traté de telefonearle esta mañana, pero la línea estaba ocupada.

— Claro que estaba ocupada. Tenemos a la señora Moncado
10 y a la señora López en la misma línea. Están siempre al teléfono.

— No sé qué trabajo hacen durante el día.

— ¿Trabajo? ¿Las ha visto Vd. nunca trabajar?

— Tiene Vd. razón. Sus pobres esposos en cambio trabajan siempre. Cuando el señor Moncado llega a su casa, aunque can-
15 sado, tiene que ir de compras. El pobrecito no descansa nunca.

— El señor López vuelve a su casa a las siete de la noche. Antes de cenar tiene que preparar la comida. Su esposa es una mujer muy bonita, pero perezosa.

— Es lástima, pero así pasa con las bonitas. Están siempre al
20 teléfono o en el cine.

— Es verdad. Cada día por la tarde encuentro a la señora Moncado en el cine. No pasa un día que no la vea allí.

— Hay unas mujeres que nunca hacen nada. Pero mire que allí vienen nuestras vecinas. ¡Buenas tardes, amigas! ¿Cómo
25 están Vds.? ¡Qué lindas están Vds. esta tarde! Ahora mismo hablábamos de Vds. ¡Qué gusto en verlas!

USEFUL EXPRESSIONS

buenas tardes good afternoon, good evening

hace un poquito de fresco it is a bit cool

a mí tampoco neither do I

¿qué tal? how is? how are you?

tratar de to try to

claro que of course

tener razón to be right

en cambio instead, on the other hand

ir de compras to go shopping

es lástima it's too bad

así pasa con that's how it is with

WORD REMINDER

adiós good-bye (*for good*)
almorzar to have lunch
almuerzo lunch
comer to eat
desayunarse to have breakfast
desayuno breakfast
esposo husband, bridegroom
fruta fruit
matrimonio (married) couple

pagar to pay
sacar to take out
salir to go out
en casa at home
hasta luego, hasta la vista good-bye
  (*until I see you again*)
pasar tiempo to spend time
perder el tiempo to waste time

CONVERSACIÓN

1. ¿Le gusta a Vd. el tiempo cuando hace calor? 2. ¿Cuáles son las mejores estaciones del año para Vd.? 3. ¿Compra Vd. muchas frutas en el otoño? 4. ¿Paga Vd. mucho por ellas? 5. ¿Descansa Vd. después de un día de trabajo? 6. ¿Hacen preguntas en español los estudiantes? 7. ¿Qué hacen por lo general los esposos cuando llegan a sus casas? 8. ¿Va Vd. al cine de vez en cuando? 9. ¿Tiene Vd. sueño después de almorzar? 10. ¿A qué hora prefiere Vd. desayunarse? 11. ¿Cuál viene primero en el día, el almuerzo o el desayuno? 12. ¿Quién prepara la comida en su casa? 13. ¿Conoce Vd. a algún matrimonio español?

EJERCICIOS

I. Repeat the following sentences, using the words given in parentheses and making the appropriate changes:

1. Encuentro una mujer (mujeres) en el mercado (mercados). 2. Él (Ellos) come mucha fruta en su casa (casas). 3. ¿Trabaja Vd. (Vds.) a menudo en el verano (veranos)? 4. ¿Pasa Vd. (Vds.) todo el día (días) en el cine (cines)? 5. Vd. (Vds.) tiene razón; la vecina (vecinas) es muy vieja. 6. Cuando hace fresco voy (vamos) a la ventana (ventanas) y charlo (charlamos) con un amigo (amigos). 7. Antes de comer tengo (tenemos) que ayudar a mi hermana (hermanas). 8. El marido (maridos) pobre no puede ir de compras con su esposa (esposas). 9. El pobre

esposo (esposos) sólo tiene que pagar. 10. El alumno (alumnos) aprende bien si tiene un buen libro (libros). 11. Puede Vd. (Vds.) sacar otra cosa (cosas). 12. No quiere (quieren) almorzar porque no tiene (tienen) hambre.

II. PRÁCTICA ORAL. *Listen to each sentence as given by the instructor. Then when he cues in the phrase in parentheses, supply a complete sentence:*

1. No me gusta el invierno tanto como el verano (nos gusta, le gusta, te gusta, les gusta). 2. Trató de telefonearle (trataré, tratarán, tratamos, han tratado). 3. ¿Quiere Vd. ir de compras por la tarde? (por la mañana, esta tarde, a las diez de la mañana). 4. No había fruta en nuestro jardín este verano (en su jardín, en mi jardín, en nuestra casa, en su tienda). 5. Yo aprendo mucho en la clase (ellos, Vds., María, tú, nosotros). 6. Deseamos cenar pronto (lavarnos las manos, leer una novela, desayunarnos, salir de casa). 7. No me gusta comer sólo (ir de compras, perder el tiempo, almorzar temprano, preparar la comida). 8. Juan es perezoso (la señora López, Vd., yo, nosotros). 9. ¿Trabaja toda la semana su padre? (su madre, Juan, sus hermanos, los alumnos).

III. *Supply indefinite articles and read aloud:*

1. —— buena palabra es —— poema. 2. Es —— libro excelente; tiene —— cosas muy interesantes. 3. —— libro y —— pluma son necesarios para los estudiantes. 4. —— apartamentos son grandes. 5. —— cuartos son pequeños. 6. —— mujeres son bonitas y —— mujeres son feas. 7. —— esposos tienen que ir de compras antes de cenar. 8. Tenemos teléfono en nuestra casa, pero —— vecina está siempre en la línea. 9. —— día hace calor y —— día hace frío. 10. —— hombres no descansan nunca.

IV. *Prepare at home and read fluently in Spanish:*

1. When it is a bit cold we stay at home. 2. Frequently we have breakfast at seven, but today we are having breakfast at eight. 3. Some men have to prepare their meals when they get home. 4. The poor wives are tired because they too work during the day. 5. That's how it is

with children; they never rest. 6. Do you see them every time you go
to the movies? 7. What a beautiful morning! I like spring very much.
8. We were just talking about you. Paul says he doesn't like winter.
9. I don't like winter either, and besides the winters are too long.
10. We don't have money to travel during the summer. 11. Our
neighbors say they are very busy. 12. Did you ever see them work?

A colorful hat seller
in Acapulco, Mexico

LECCIÓN 3

Los sombreros

17. Personal Pronouns (Subject)

The personal pronouns used as subjects of a verb are as follows:

	SINGULAR			PLURAL	
1st person	yo	I		nosotros, –as	we
2nd person	tú	you (*fam.*)		vosotros, –as	you (*fam.*)
3rd person	él	he		ellos	they (*m.*)
	ella	she		ellas	they (*f.*)
	Vd. (usted)	you		Vds. (ustedes)	you

The familiar forms **tú** and **vosotros** are used in addressing a member of one's family (such as brother, sister, mother, father, etc.), a close friend or an animal. **Tú** is widely used in poetry and in prayers.

The polite forms **usted** and **ustedes** are the forms used in conversation, except with close friends. The foreigner seldom finds any need for anything but the polite form, but if he really mixes with Spanish-speaking people he will hear the familiar form constantly. **Usted** is generally abbreviated **Vd.** or **Ud.**, and **ustedes** is abbreviated **Vds.** or **Uds.**

18. Omission of the Subject Pronoun

The subject pronoun is generally omitted in Spanish, especially in conversation.

> **Están siempre en el cine.**   They are always at the movies.

The subject pronoun is not omitted when the speaker places emphasis on it, when the subjects in the same construction are different, or when

19

a contrast between subjects is desired. Moreover, the pronoun **usted** is generally not omitted, except to avoid repetition.

Él tiene la cara delgada, pero ella tiene la cara ancha.	He has a thin face, but she has a full face.
¿ Trata Vd. de aprender mucho cuando está en clase?	Do you try to learn a great deal when you are in class?

19. Present Indicative of *estar*

yo	**estoy**	*I am*	nosotros, –as	**estamos**	*we are*	
tú	**estás**	*you are*	vosotros, –as	**estáis**	*you are*	
él	**está**	*he is*	ellos}	**están**	*they are*	
ella	**está**	*she is*	ellas}			
Vd.	**está**	*you are*	Vds.	**están**	*you are*	

The verb **estar** means *to be*, the same as the verb **ser**. However, the two cannot be used interchangeably, as shown in the next section.

20. Uses of *ser* and *estar*

ser	*estar*
1. Expresses a *permanent* or *inherent* quality. **La mujer es baja.** The woman is short.	1. Expresses an *accidental* or *temporary* quality, or a quality which can easily be changed. **La línea está ocupada.** The line is busy.
2. Expresses possession. **El sombrero es de mi hermano.** The hat is my brother's.	2. Expresses place or location. **Están siempre al teléfono.** They are always on the telephone.
3. Expresses origin, or material from which an object is made. **Juan es de Puerto Rico.** John is from Puerto Rico. **El sombrero es de paja.** The hat is made of straw.	3. Used when speaking of the state of health. **¿ Cómo está Vd.?** How are you?

4. Always used with a predicate noun or pronoun.

Alberto es un hombre maduro.
Albert is a mature man.

5. Used with the adjectives *young, old, rich, poor.*

¿Quiere Vd. ser rico? Do you want to be rich?

4. Expresses the result of an action.

La puerta está cerrada. The door is closed.

5. Used with present participle to express progressive action.

Estoy escribiendo una carta. I am writing a letter.

With certain adjectives either **ser** or **estar** may be used, according to the idea which the speaker wants to convey. They are not interchangeable when used in this way. **Ser** expresses a permanent or inherent quality; **estar** expresses the same quality as temporary or transitory.

Los árboles son verdes.   Trees are green (*by nature*).
Los árboles están muy verdes en el   Trees are very green in the summer.
verano.

21. *Para* to Express Purpose

To express the purpose of an action Spanish uses the preposition **para** followed by an infinitive. It is translated by *in order to* or just *to.*

Para vivir bien hay que comer bien.   One has to eat well (in order) to live well.

22. The Impersonal Forms *hay* and *hace*

The impersonal form **hay** is the third person singular of the verb **haber** and is used to introduce a statement of fact. It is translated by the English *there is* or *there are* (*is there* or *are there* when used in a question).

¿Hay muchas prendas de vestir?   Are there many articles of clothing?

The impersonal form **hace** is the third person singular of the verb **hacer** and is used in many idiomatic expressions, such as expressions about the weather (**hace buen tiempo, hace mal tiempo, hace frío, hace calor,** etc.).

Cuando hace frío el sombrero nos   When it is cold the hat warms our
calienta la cabeza.   heads.

Los sombreros

Como prenda de vestir el sombrero tiene varios usos. En los países de mucho sol, el sombrero protege la cabeza en los días en que el sol quema. Cuando llueve, el sombrero sirve de paraguas. Cuando hace viento, el sombrero nos protege el peinado. Cuando
5 hace frío, nos calienta la cabeza. Cuando hace calor, el sombrero permite refrescarnos, quitándonoslo. A los jóvenes les da el aspecto de hombres maduros. A los hombres maduros les da el aspecto de jóvenes serios. A los que tienen mucho pelo, el sombrero se lo conserva. A los que no tienen pelo, el sombrero les esconde la
10 calvicie. ¿Qué prenda de vestir podría ser más útil, como no sean los pantalones o las faldas?

Como artículo de ornamento, el sombrero puede ser el tesoro de las mujeres. Si la mujer es baja, el sombrero alto le añade diez centímetros de altura. Si la mujer es alta, el sombrero plano la
15 entona con el paisaje. Si la mujer tiene la cara ancha, el sombrero grande le hace más finas las facciones. Si tiene la cara delgada, el sombrero pequeño le da cierto encanto. Los sombreros tienen más colores que el arco iris. Pueden armonizar con cualquier paisaje, con cualquier mueble, con cualquier temperamento.
20 Es lástima que los sombreros de mujer ya no estén de moda. Ahora las mujeres sólo llevan pelucas de toda clase. Es difícil distinguir las jóvenes de las viejas porque todas tienen pelo rubio o castaño, y el pelo blanco no se encuentra más.

USEFUL EXPRESSIONS

prenda de vestir article of clothing
país de sol sunny country
servir de to serve as
da cierto encanto lends a certain charm

como no sean unless it be
hace más finas las facciones makes her features more delicate
de toda clase of all types
no ... más not ... any more

WORD REMINDER

blusa blouse
cambiar to change
camisa shirt
clima *m.* climate
chaqueta jacket, coat
dejar to leave behind; allow, let
entonces then
espejo mirror
falda skirt
llevar to wear
media stocking
pantalones *m. pl.* trousers
¿Cuántos años tiene Vd.? How old are you?

peinarse to comb one's hair
peluca wig
ponerse a to start
ropa interior underwear
sombrerería hat shop
suéter *m.* sweater
a mediados de toward the middle of
a pesar de in spite of
en lugar de instead of
en vez de instead of
valer la pena to be worth while

¿A cuántos estamos? What is the date today?

CONVERSACIÓN

1. ¿Tiene muchos usos el sombrero? 2. ¿Deja Vd. a menudo su sombrero en su casa? 3. ¿Es importante el peinado para el aspecto de una muchacha? 4. ¿Tiene mucho pelo el profesor de español? 5. ¿Qué prendas de vestir lleva Vd.? (No es preciso mencionar la ropa interior.) 6. ¿Cuándo decimos que un hombre tiene calvicie? 7. ¿Llevan sombreros anchos las señoras que tienen la cara delgada? 8. ¿Lleva Vd. un sombrero nuevo cuando hace mal tiempo? 9. A pesar de lo que cuestan, ¿vale la pena llevar sombreros bonitos? 10. En lugar de faldas, ¿qué llevan las señoritas en las universidades? 11. ¿Qué se compra en una sombrerería? 12. En vez de sombreros, ¿qué llevan las mujeres ahora?

EJERCICIOS

I. Make up questions containing each of the following expressions and ask someone to answer your question:

1. prenda de vestir
2. los días en que el sol quema
3. hace viento
4. permitir

5. hombre maduro
6. calvicie
7. cansarse mucho
8. después del verano

9. vale la pena
10. el arco iris
11. un paisaje bonito
12. ¿cuántos años?

II. PRÁCTICA ORAL. The instructor will give two separate phrases. Combine them to make a complete sentence.

MODEL: ¿Qué se compra? Una sombrerería. RESPONSE: ¿Qué se compra en una sombrerería?

1. Hay varios usos. El sombrero. 2. Protege la cabeza. Hace frío. 3. Tiene muchos muebles. Su casa. 4. Sirve de paraguas. Llueve. 5. Nada puede ser más útil. Un sombrero. 6. No somos españoles. Comprendemos bien. 7. Los hombres maduros. El aspecto de jóvenes serios. 8. Cualquier temperamento. Los sombreros pueden armonizar. 9. ¿No quiere Vd. contestar? Mi pregunta. 10. No tiene mucho pelo. Tiene calvicie. 11. Las señoras. Pelucas de toda clase. 12. El pelo castaño. Muy bonito.

III. Make up original sentences in Spanish around the following situations, but do not just translate the words given:

1. Someone wants to buy a hat in a hat store. 2. The street where you live is attractive. 3. The neighbors are always on the telephone. 4. Men work in their gardens during the summer. 5. Ladies like to go shopping. 6. Trousers are more necessary than hats. 7. No one likes to go out when it's cold and windy. 8. The various uses of hats. 9. Wigs are now in style. 10. Gray hair has disappeared.

IV. DIÁLOGO. Present the following dialogue in class:

Linda: ¡Qué sombrero tan bonito, Clara!
Clara: Eres muy amable, Linda. Me gusta más tu sombrero de paja.
Linda: Llevo siempre sombreros de paja cuando hace calor. Pero hoy hace frío.
Clara: Es que estamos a mediados de octubre. Ya empieza el invierno.
Linda: El clima es perfecto aquí. Siempre hace sol, pero no hace demasiado calor.

Clara: Los árboles están verdes hasta noviembre. Los días son perfectos y las noches son agradables.

Linda: Lo que no me gusta en el otoño es que no hay tantos días de fiesta. En el verano hay muchos días de descanso.

Clara: Pues, el sábado y el domingo son días de descanso. ¿No te parece bastante?

Linda: Ya que no podemos tener tres sábados y cuatro domingos por semana, me contento así.

V. Prepare at home and read fluently in Spanish:

1. There are many men who do not wear hats in the winter. 2. If the weather is bad we take an umbrella. 3. The trousers are long and the skirts are short. 4. A small hat lends her charm, don't you think so? 5. When it is windy it is cold also. 6. We came in the store in order to buy a hat. 7. If a man is rich he can go shopping frequently. 8. Can one expect more from a hat? 9. He has the opportunity to cool off when he goes into a movie. 10. A wig hides baldness but it does not hide the years.

Men's clothing shop in Madrid, Spain

LECCIÓN 4

En la tienda de ropa

23. Syllabication

A syllable is the part of a word which can be pronounced with a single impulse of the voice. In Spanish it always contains a vowel sound and may in addition contain one or more consonant sounds. The vowel sound may consist of a single vowel, a diphthong, or a triphthong. A diphthong is a group of two vowels pronounced with a single impulse; it is made up of a strong vowel (**a, e, o**) and a weak vowel (**i, u**), or two weak vowels. When a weak vowel has a written accent it is pronounced separately and forms a separate syllable. A triphthong is a combination of three vowels pronounced with one impulse.

In dividing words into syllables the following rules should be observed (they are different from English):

1. A single consonant between two vowels goes with the vowel following. Since **ch, ll,** and **rr** are letters of the alphabet, they are considered single consonants and are treated as such. (Remember that **ch** comes after all the **c**'s and **ll** after all the **l**'s in the dictionary.)

   ma-ri-do   **de-ma-sia-do**   **lle-ga-mos**   **de-re-cho**

2. Except as explained in 3, two consonants between vowels are separated so that one goes with the preceding and one with the following syllable.

   cua-ren-ta   **mis-mo**   **al-gu-nos**   **en-se-ñar-nos**

3. Two consonants of which the second is **l** or **r** are not separated, except the combinations **rl, sl, tl, sr,** and **nr,** which are separated.

   ma-dre   **ten-dre-mos**   **im-po-si-ble**   **Car-los**   **is-la**

27

4. When there are more than two consonants between vowels, just one consonant or one of the inseparable combinations mentioned in 3 goes with the second syllable.

som-bre-ro   siem-pre   nues-tra   trans-por-tar

24. Practical Rule for Dividing Words into Syllables

1. Write separately the vowel or combination of vowels contained in a word.

automóvil   au - o - ó - i

2. If the combination contains two strong vowels (**a, e, o**) or a weak vowel (**i, u**) with a written accent, the vowels should be listed separately.

María   a - í - a

3. Beginning with the last vowel, put each single consonant (including **ch, ll, rr**) with the vowel following, and separate two consonants, one with the preceding and one with the following vowel, unless you have an inseparable combination.

automóvil	**au-o-ó-i**	**au-to-mó-vil**
callarse	**a - a - e**	**ca-llar-se**
cuarenta	**ua-e-a**	**cua-ren-ta**

4. A prefix forms a separate syllable.

explicar   ex-pli-car   distinguido   dis-tin-gui-do

25. Rule of Accents

Spanish words are accented according to specific rules set down by the Spanish Academy and modified according to usage.[1] Once these general rules are learned there is very little difficulty in knowing where to stress a word in pronunciation or where to place the accent in writing.

---

[1] The written accent was used on a few monosyllabic forms of irregular verbs such as **fuí, fué, dió, vió.** It was used by some writers on the past participle of verbs ending in **-uir,** such as **construído, concluído,** etc. A 1952 ruling of the Spanish Academy has eliminated accents in such words.

The only written accent generally used in Spanish is the acute ('). The rules are as follows:

1. Words ending in a vowel, or in the consonants **n** or **s,** are stressed on the next to the last syllable and require no written accent.

    que-ri-do   es-pa-ño-les

2. Words ending in any consonant other than **n** or **s** are stressed on the last syllable and take no written accent.

    ol-vi-dar   ciu-dad

3. Words which are not stressed according to these two rules bear a written accent on the syllable that is stressed in pronunciation.

    jar-dín   jó-ve-nes

4. The written accent is used to distinguish certain words, as for example all interrogative pronouns and adjectives, demonstrative pronouns other than neuters, the accented form of the adjective which is compounded to form an adverb in –**mente,** and the following words.

mí me, myself	**mi** my
sí yes, himself, etc.	**si** if
más more	**mas** but
él he	**el** the
dé (*pres. subjve. of* **dar**)	**de** of
sólo only	**solo** alone, single
tú you	**tu** your
té tea	**te** you (*object*)

26. Present Indicative of *dar, querer, ir, venir*

Many verbs are irregular in one or more tenses and the forms must be learned individually. Some of the commonest ones are as follows:

dar to give	**doy, das, da, damos, dais, dan**
querer to wish	**quiero, quieres, quiere, queremos, queréis, quieren**
ir to go	**voy, vas, va, vamos, vais, van**
venir to come	**vengo, vienes, viene, venimos, venís, vienen**

27. Numerals

The cardinal numbers from 1 to 21 are as follows:

1 **uno (un), una**	8 **ocho**	15 **quince**	
2 **dos**	9 **nueve**	16 **diez y seis (dieciséis)**	
3 **tres**	10 **diez**	17 **diez y siete (diecisiete)**	
4 **cuatro**	11 **once**	18 **diez y ocho (dieciocho)**	
5 **cinco**	12 **doce**	19 **diez y nueve (diecinueve)**	
6 **seis**	13 **trece**	20 **veinte**	
7 **siete**	14 **catorce**	21 **veinte y un(o) (veintiuno [veintiún])**	

The numbers from 30 to 100 by tens are as follows:

30 **treinta**		70 **setenta**	
40 **cuarenta**		80 **ochenta**	
50 **cincuenta**		90 **noventa**	
60 **sesenta**		100 **ciento (cien)**	

Uno before a masculine singular noun is **un**. **Ciento** becomes **cien** before a noun or before **mil**. Cardinal numbers generally come before the word they modify and, except for the words **uno** and **ciento,** do not change in form. Some numbers above **ciento** do change in form, as we shall see later.

En la tienda de ropa

— Buenos días, señores González. ¿En qué puedo servirles?

— Mi marido quiere comprar un traje.

— Muy bien. Tenemos una buena selección este mes. ¿Qué color quiere Vd., señor?

5 — Pues, me parece que un traje azul sería bueno.

— No, querido, tú no quieres un traje azul. Ya tienes dos.

— Tal vez un traje marrón. ¿Hay trajes marrones?

— ¿Marrón? ¡Imposible, Pedro! El marrón no va bien con tu pelo rubio. ¿Quiere enseñarnos un traje gris, por favor?

10 — ¿Quiere Vd. gris claro o gris oscuro, señor?

— Él quiere gris oscuro. Ya tienes uno gris claro, ¿no es verdad?

— Sí, María, pero no quiero otro traje gris.

— No seas tonto, Pedro. El gris es lo que más te conviene.

— Bueno. Tráiganos algunos trajes grises, tenga la bondad.   15

— ¿De qué medida, señor? ¿cuarenta y dos?

— Sí, señor, cuarenta y dos.

— ¿Cuarenta y dos? Es demasiado grande para ti. Mejor sería el cuarenta y uno.

— El cuarenta y uno me aprieta, María. Tú lo sabes.   20

— Si tú no comieras tanto, no estarías tan gordo. ¿Hay trajes cuarenta y uno, por favor?

— Lo siento mucho, señora, pero ahora mismo no tenemos cuarenta y uno en este color. Sólo hay cuarenta y dos.

— Es lástima. Tendremos que buscar en otra tienda. ¡Hasta   25 luego!

USEFUL EXPRESSIONS

¿En qué puedo servirles? What can I do for you?
no va bien con it does not match
lo que más te conviene what suits you best
tenga la bondad please, if you will
me aprieta (it) fits me tightly, it is snug
ahora mismo right now
tendremos que buscar we shall have to look

WORD REMINDER

abrigo overcoat
acompañar to accompany
además (de) besides, moreover
barato cheap
bastar to be sufficient
camisa shirt
camisería shirt store
cliente *m.* customer
corbata necktie
dependiente *m.* clerk

necesitar to need
olvidarse to forget
zapato shoe
a la derecha to the right
a la izquierda to the left
cambiarse de ropa to change clothes
desde luego of course
lo más pronto posible as soon as possible
tener prisa to be in a hurry

CONVERSACIÓN

1. Cuando un marido quiere comprar un traje, ¿lo acompaña a menudo su esposa? 2. ¿Bastan dos trajes azules para un hombre? 3. Además de azul, ¿qué otros colores son buenos para trajes de hombre? 4. ¿Busca Vd. generalmente un traje bonito o un traje barato? 5. ¿Se cambia Vd. de ropa a menudo durante el día? 6. ¿Tiene Vd. muchos trajes y muchas corbatas en su casa? 7. ¿Le aprieta a Vd. un traje de medida treinta y siete? 8. ¿Le gustaría comprar zapatos nuevos lo más pronto posible? 9. Si una persona es muy gorda, ¿necesita comer mucho? 10. ¿Qué hay a la derecha del profesor en la clase? ¿a la izquierda?

EJERCICIOS

I. Divide into syllables and pronounce each word by syllables:

1. tráiganos. 2. seas. 3. abrigo. 4. izquierdo. 5. acompañar. 6. cualesquiera. 7. serios. 8. oportunidad. 9. paraguas. 10. calvicie. 11. artículo. 12. comprender. 13. entonces. 14. paisaje. 15. después. 16. camisería.

II. Make up questions for each of the following expressions and ask someone to answer them:

1. desde luego	7. ir bien con algo
2. en seguida	8. estar ocupado
3. lo más pronto posible	9. cada vez que
4. ahora mismo	10. hasta luego
5. tener prisa	11. cambiarse de ropa
6. lo que más te conviene	12. tenga la bondad

III. PRÁCTICA ORAL. Listen to each sentence as given by the instructor. Then when he cues in the words in parentheses, supply the complete sentence:

1. Yo salgo de mi casa y doy un paseo (Vd., Pedro, María y Pablo, nosotros). 2. Ellos quieren trabajar ahora mismo (yo, ella, Vds., tú).

3. Llegaré pronto a mi casa (a la escuela, a la tienda, a la sombrerería, al teatro). 4. Esta tarde queremos visitarle (quiero, quieren, quieres). 5. Tú tienes que venir lo más pronto posible (Vds., Vd., nosotros, ella). 6. Nosotros nos cambiamos de ropa cada dos días (los niños, yo, Vd., el profesor). 7. La corbata va bien con el traje (la camisa, el sombrero, los guantes, los zapatos). 8. Yo voy a buscarlo por todas partes (nosotros, ella, los hombres, Felipe). 9. Si ellos van ahora, sin duda estará en casa (nosotros, Vd., yo, Juan). 10. ¿Puedo contar con Vd. para ir a la fiesta? (podemos, pueden, puede, podría). 11. Me dijo que volvería en seguida (lo más pronto posible, mañana por la mañana, mañana por la tarde). 12. Yo no puedo olvidarme (tú, ella, Vds., nosotros).

IV. Prepare at home and read fluently in Spanish:

1. Do you wish to have a good suit for the winter? 2. Will you show us some cheap neckties, please? 3. We have to buy two shirts as soon as possible. 4. Why are you in a hurry? Can't you wait for a half hour? 5. Don't be foolish, my friend. A half hour is too long. 6. This shirt does not go well with this suit. Bring me a white one, please. 7. Does he always forget when it is time to eat? 8. We come here often, but you are never here. 9. She is right. There is no shirt store on this street if we go to the right. 10. What size does she wear, fifty-six?

LECCIÓN 5

¿ Qué hora es ?

28. Hours of the Day

In expressing the hour of the day the feminine article is used before the hour (modifying the word **hora** understood). If the hour is *one*, the verb and the article are singular; otherwise they are both plural. In expressions where the number of the hour is not given, the verb and the article are singular **(es mediodía, es medianoche)**. The fraction past the hour is added by using the word **y.** The fraction before the hour is subtracted by using the word **menos.**

Es la una.	It's one o'clock.
Es la una y media.	It's half past one.
Son las dos.	It's two o'clock.
¿ Qué hora es?	What time is it?
Son las dos y cuarto.	It's a quarter past two.
A las cinco.	At five o'clock.
A las cinco menos veinte (minutos).	At twenty to five.

Media is an adjective and agrees with the word **hora** understood; in **mediodía** it agrees with **día. Cuarto** is a noun and does not agree with anything else. The numerals expressing minutes do not change in form.

Son las seis y veintisiete (minutos).   It's six twenty-seven.

When the hour is given, the expression for *in the morning* is **de la mañana;** the expression for *in the afternoon* is **de la tarde;** and for *in the evening* or *at night*, it is **de la noche.**

Son las nueve de la mañana.   It is nine in the morning.

35

Church of Los Santos Juanes, Valencia, Spain

When the hour is not given, the corresponding expressions are **por la mañana, por la tarde,** and **por la noche.**

Por la tarde mi esposa va de compras.	In the afternoon my wife goes shopping.

29. Omission of the Indefinite Article

The indefinite article is used in English but omitted in Spanish before a predicate noun denoting a profession, trade, or nationality, and not qualified by an adjective.

Yo soy médico y él es abogado.	I am a doctor and he is a lawyer.

If the predicate noun is qualified in any way, the indefinite article is required.

¿Es él un buen abogado?	Is he a good lawyer?

The indefinite article is omitted before **otro** *another,* **cien** *one hundred,* **mil** *one thousand*; and after **medio** *half a,* **tal** *such a,* and **qué** *what a.*

Cien alumnos en una clase son demasiados.	One hundred pupils in one class are too many.

30. Prepositions

Some of the common simple prepositions are: **a** *to*; **con** *with*; **de** *of, from*; **en** *in, on*; **para** *for*; **por** *through.* Only two of these prepositions combine with the definite article: **a + el = al; de + el = del.**

Parte del día y de la noche.	Part of the day and night.

31. *Poder, deber,* and *tener que* with the Infinitive

Poder and **deber** are followed by the infinitive without a preposition. **Poder** means *to be able* or *can.* **Deber** means *ought to, should,* or *to be obliged to.* **Tener que** followed by the infinitive means *to have to* or *must.* **Deber** in this sense means the moral obligation of performing an action, whereas **tener que** denotes the personal need of performing an action. Other uses of these verbs will be taken up in Section 90.

Tengo que preocuparme por todo.	I have to worry about everything.
Vd. debe trabajar todo el día.	You are obliged to work the whole day.

32. Present Indicative of *poder, volver, encontrar, jugar*

poder to be able	**puedo, puedes, puede, podemos, podéis, pueden**
volver to go back, return	**vuelvo, vuelves, vuelve, volvemos, volvéis, vuelven**
encontrar to meet; find	**encuentro, encuentras, encuentra, encontramos, encontráis, encuentran**
jugar to play	**juego, juegas, juega, jugamos, jugáis, juegan**

¿ Qué hora es ?

¿Qué hora es? ¿Quién lo sabe y a quién le importa?

Para mí la hora no existe. Cuando tengo hambre como, y cuando tengo sed bebo. Cuando tengo sueño me acuesto y cuando no quiero dormir más, me levanto. Cuando me da la gana de pasearme, me paseo, y cuando estoy cansado de pasearme, me 5 siento. Y cuando quiero trabajar ... pues, la verdad es que no quiero trabajar.

La hora es parte del día, y el día es parte del año. El año no es más que una vuelta de la tierra alrededor del sol. Pues, si a la tierra le da la gana de girar alrededor del sol, ¿a mí qué me puede 10 importar?

Lo que me gusta es levantarme en un día de primavera y mirar los árboles y las flores, escuchar el canto de los pájaros, y respirar el aire fresco de la mañana. Lo que me gusta es sentarme con los amigos y oír la música de la radio, mirar la televisión y tomar café 15 y comer dulces. Para mí la vida es un encanto y ¿por qué tengo que preocuparme por la hora?

Sin embargo la vida es dura y hay que trabajar para vivir. Quien no trabaja no come, y a mí me gusta comer. Es lástima, pero es la hora de volver al trabajo. 20

USEFUL EXPRESSIONS

¿Qué hora es? What time is it?
¿A quién le importa? Who cares?
tener hambre to be hungry
tener sed to be thirsty
tener sueño to be sleepy

dar la gana de to feel like
preocuparse por to worry about
sin embargo and yet
quien no trabaja he who doesn't work

WORD REMINDER

aeroplano or avión m. airplane, plane
autobús m. bus
barco boat
buque m. ship
cerca de about, near
dentro de within
despertarse to wake up
dormitorio dormitory
entre between

esperar to wait (for)
gente f. people
hacia toward
momento moment
parque m. park
telégrafo telegraph
televisión f. television
tranvía m. trolley
en punto exactly, on the dot

CONVERSACIÓN

1. ¿Sabe Vd. qué hora es en este momento? 2. ¿A qué hora se desayuna
Vd. por la mañana? 3. ¿A qué hora come Vd. por la tarde? 4. ¿Qué
hace un muchacho cuando tiene sed? 5. ¿Cuándo se acuesta la gente,
por lo general? 6. ¿Cuántos días tiene este año? 7. ¿Qué hay alrededor
de muchos parques? 8. ¿Cuándo cantan más los pájaros, en el invierno
o en la primavera? 9. ¿Dentro de cuántas horas estará Vd. en su
dormitorio? 10. ¿Se despierta Vd. siempre a las siete en punto?
11. ¿Entre qué horas duerme Vd.? 12. ¿Prefiere Vd. escuchar la radio
o mirar la televisión?

EJERCICIOS

I. *Make up short sentences using the following hours. Remember that*
AM *is* de la mañana *and* PM *is* de la tarde *or* de la noche *when you are*
naming the hour.

11:05 AM	6:10 PM	5:00 AM	12:10 AM
7:32 PM	3:05 PM	10:25 PM	12:10 PM
3:27 AM	9:52 AM	4:30 PM	8:20 PM

II. Make up short sentences in Spanish using each of the following expressions containing prepositions:

1. ¿a qué hora?
2. a mí
3. con Vd.
4. con el amigo
5. dentro de
6. da la gana de
7. en un día
8. en el otoño
9. para nosotros
10. por lo general
11. para ella
12. preocuparse por

III. Ask questions using each of the following idiomatic expressions and be sure the one who replies also uses the idiom:

1. tener hambre. 2. tener sed. 3. tener sueño. 4. dar la gana. 5. no importa. 6. tener que. 7. hay que. 8. es la hora de.

IV. PRÁCTICA ORAL. Listen to each sentence as given by the instructor. Then on the cue supply the complete sentence with the new expressions:

1. Cuando me levanto, siempre tengo hambre (me despierto, trabajo, me paseo, juego). 2. Si Vd. tiene sueño, puede acostarse (hambre — comer; sed — beber; sueño — dormir; prisa — irse). 3. Nosotros no sabemos la hora del cine (él no sabe, Vd. no sabe, ellos no saben, yo no sé). 4. ¿Encuentra Vd. a muchos amigos en el parque? (en la casa, en el buque, en el autobús, en el café). 5. ¿Espera Vd. los programas de televisión? (mira Vd., escucha Vd., busca Vd.). 6. Si Vd. va a Europa, ¿quiere Vd. ir en barco? (en aeroplano, en auto, en tren, en tranvía). 7. ¿Le da a Vd. la gana de dormir cuando tiene sueño? (comer — tiene hambre; beber — tiene sed; descansar — está cansado).

V. Complete the following parts of sentences:

1. La tierra da una vuelta alrededor . . . 2. Cuando tenemos sed . . .
3. Para vivir bien hay que . . . 4. María y Pedro se pasean . . .
5. ¿No encuentra Vd. que la vida . . .? 6. En la primavera me gusta . . .
7. Quien no trabaja . . . 8. Cuando estamos cansados . . .

VI. Prepare at home and read fluently in Spanish:

1. It's a quarter past eleven and we are all sleepy. 2. Peter's brother is a lawyer, but his father is a doctor. 3. At half past five all the childen are looking at television in our house. 4. We never meet in the morning; we always meet in the afternoon. 5. He is expected to (*use* **deber**) arrive at seven o'clock and we are to meet him there. 6. At what time do you have lunch? At twelve on the dot? 7. If you are tired of walking, why don't you sit down? 8. Does your brother wake up at eight or at nine in the morning? 9. He can sleep at our house, if he wants to. 10. Who cares if the days are long in the summer and short in the winter?

Book stalls, Madrid, Spain

LECCIÓN 6

Planes para el verano

33. Interrogative Words

Interrogative words are adjectives, pronouns, or adverbs that are used to ask questions. The most common ones are:

¿cuándo? when?

¿dónde? or ¿a dónde (adónde)? where?

¿por qué? why?

¿qué? what? which?

¿quién? (¿quiénes?) who? whom?

¿cuál? (¿cuáles?) which one? (which ones?)

¿cuánto? (¿cuánta?) how much?

¿cuántos? (¿cuántas?) how many?

All interrogative words have a written accent to distinguish them from similar words which are not interrogative.

34. Future Tense

The future tense expresses an action which will take place at some time in the future. In Spanish it is expressed by attaching the proper ending to the infinitive of regular verbs.

	1ST CONJ.	2ND CONJ.	3RD CONJ.
yo	hablaré	aprenderé	viviré
tú	hablarás	aprenderás	vivirás
él, ella, Vd.	hablará	aprenderá	vivirá
nosotros, −as	hablaremos	aprenderemos	viviremos
vosotros, −as	hablaréis	aprenderéis	viviréis
ellos, ellas, Vds.	hablarán	aprenderán	vivirán

43

Signpost in Madrid, Spain

35. Future of Irregular Verbs

All irregular verbs follow the same pattern in the future. Once you learn the first person singular, just drop the –é and add the following endings for the rest of the conjugation: –ás, –á, –emos, –éis, –án.

Notice the first person singular of common irregular verbs:

caber to fit	cabré	querer to wish	querré
decir to say	diré	saber to know	sabré
haber to have	habré	salir to go out	saldré
hacer to do	haré	ser to be	seré
ir to go	iré	tener to have	tendré
poder to be able	podré	valer to be worth while	valdré
poner to put	pondré	venir to come	vendré

36. Numerals

Numbers above one hundred are as follows:

200	doscientos, –as	800	ochocientos, –as
300	trescientos, –as	900	novecientos, –as
400	cuatrocientos, –as	1000	mil
500	quinientos, –as	101	ciento (y) un
600	seiscientos, –as	1001	mil y un
700	setecientos, –as	2000	dos mil

Notice that while **ciento** becomes plural in the multiples of one hundred, **mil** does not change in form. The article **un** is not used before **ciento** or **mil,** but it is used before **millón.** The plural of **millón** is **millones.** The noun following **millón** is preceded by **de.**

Hay cuatrocientas personas.	There are four hundred people.
Tenemos tres mil dólares; somos ricos.	We have three thousand dollars; we are rich.
Caracas tiene más de un millón de habitantes.	Caracas has more than a million inhabitants.

Planes para el verano

Nuestro padre nos llevará a España el mes próximo; en realidad llevará a toda la familia. Saldremos de Nueva York en avión

y llegaremos a Madrid en siete horas, más o menos. Él tiene que
ir por negocios, y nosotros iremos de visita, para hacerle compañía. Viviremos en una pensión, donde estaremos como en 5
familia.

¿Cómo? ¿Vd. no sabe lo que es una pensión? Pues, es una
casa grande donde se alquilan habitaciones y se toman las comidas
también. La pensión es hotel, restaurante y casa particular al
mismo tiempo. Es más barata y más simpática que un hotel, 10
donde sólo se encuentran turistas.

¿Cuánto tiempo pasaremos en Madrid? Pues, mi padre se
quedará un año entero. Por lo contrario, mamá, mi hermana y
yo volveremos a nuestra casa a principios de septiembre, porque
tendremos que continuar los cursos en la universidad. Tengo 15
grandes ganas de ver a Madrid, porque me dicen que es ahora una
de las capitales más bellas de Europa. Tiene calles anchas y bonitas, con parques y avenidas de una hermosura incomparable. Hay
fuentes en las grandes plazas y flores multicolores en las aceras.
Las calles están limpias, más que en cualquiera otra gran ciudad. 20
Hay sucursales de las mayores empresas internacionales, sobre
todo de los Estados Unidos.

La ciudad ha crecido de una manera fantástica en los últimos
años, y los precios también. Sin embargo, yo no tendré que preocuparme por los precios, y podré gozar, sin cuidados, de la 25
belleza de esa ciudad.

USEFUL EXPRESSIONS

en realidad in fact
más o menos more or less
por negocios on business
ir de visita to go for a visit
para hacerle compañía to keep him
    company
por lo (el) contrario on the other
    hand

a principios de toward the beginning
    of
tener ganas de to have a desire to,
    feel strongly about
de una manera fantástica fantastically
en los últimos años in the last few
    years

WORD REMINDER

apenas hardly; as soon as
asunto matter, topic
debajo de under
encima de on top of
enviar to send
este *m.* east
explicar to explain
guerra war
habitación *f.* room
norte *m.* north
oeste *m.* west

permanecer to remain, stay
pueblo town
rato while, a bit of time
sitio place
Sudamérica South America
sur *m.* south
tarjeta postal postcard
con cuidado with care
sin cuidados without worry
en seguida immediately
la mayor parte de most of

CONVERSACIÓN

1. ¿Cuándo irá Vd. a España? 2. ¿Irá Vd. solo, o con toda la familia?
3. ¿Dónde pasarán Vds. la mayor parte del tiempo? 4. ¿Qué es una
pensión? 5. ¿Por qué va la gente a una pensión en vez de a un hotel?
6. ¿Va su padre a Madrid por negocios? 7. ¿Está Madrid al este o al
oeste de España? 8. ¿Enviará Vd. muchas tarjetas postales a sus
amigos? 9. ¿Tiene Vd. muchas ganas de ver a Madrid? 10. ¿Qué
hay en las grandes plazas de Madrid? 11. ¿Qué es una sucursal de una
empresa? 12. ¿Qué hacen los estudiantes a principios de septiembre?
13. ¿Cuánto tiempo piensa Vd. permanecer en España?

EJERCICIOS

I. Use the correct form of **ser** *or* **estar** *in the following sentences:*

1. ¿Dónde *is* Madrid? 2. ¿*Is* bueno el restaurante? 3. Las habitaciones
que se alquilan *are* grandes. 4. ¿Cuándo *will you be* en Sudamérica?
5. Los negocios *are* malos. 6. ¿Quién *is* aquí en vez de su hermano?
7. La casa *is* fría, me parece. 8. Las frutas *are* buenas cuando *they
are* maduras. 9. ¿Cómo *are* sus padres en estos días? 10. La mujer
nunca puede creer que *she is* vieja. 11. Las frutas *are* encima de la
mesa; *they are not* debajo de la mesa. 12. No podemos saber si él *will
be* contento en este sitio.

II. Change the verbs in italics in the following sentences to the future and read the sentences aloud:

1. ¡Qué ciudad tan bonita! Nos *quedamos* aquí un rato. 2. ¿Cuánto tiempo *pasa* su hermano en el oeste de los Estados Unidos? 3. Las sucursales *son* importantes para la empresa. 4. En nuestro viaje a España, *visitamos* a Barcelona. 5. Nuestra mamá nos *explica* el asunto con cuidado. 6. ¿*Puede* Vd. divertirse sin cuidados? 7. La mayor parte de la gente *vive* en los pueblos. 8. No *están* en la ciudad en el verano. 9. En una casa particular no se *alquilan* habitaciones a los extranjeros. 10. Por el contrario, en una pensión todos *son* extranjeros.

III. DIÁLOGO. Present the following dialogue in class:

— Señor profesor, ¿qué planes tiene Vd. para el verano?
— Pues, pienso ir a España con la familia.
— ¡Qué bueno! ¿Cuántos son de familia?
— Somos cuatro. Mi esposa, dos niños y yo.
— ¿Y les gustará a los niños hacer el viaje?
— Ya hace un año que van haciendo planes. No se habla de otra cosa en casa.
— ¿Y cuándo volverán Vds.?
— Volveremos el siete de septiembre. La escuela se abre el nueve.
— ¿Por qué no se quedan más? A los niños no les molestará.
— Claro que a ellos no les importa, pero a nosotros sí. Tienen que volver a la escuela.
— ¿Se quedarán Vds. en un hotel o en una pensión?
— En una pensión, porque resulta más barato. Los profesores tienen que hacer economías, sabe Vd.
— Sí, es verdad. Sin embargo, aun con economía me gustaría hacer un viaje por España.

IV. Prepare at home and read fluently in Spanish:

1. We shall be in Spain next month. 2. How many restaurants and how many hotels are there in this city? 3. Do they rent rooms in a boarding-house and does one take his meals there also? 4. Do you have a great desire to see Granada and Seville? 5. The streets are cleaner than in any other large city. 6. If we know Spanish we'll be able to travel through South America. 7. There are many small towns in Mexico and the people speak Spanish. 8. We live far from foreign countries, and yet it's important to know another language. 9. Where will you live if you go to South America? In what country? 10. Many cities have grown fantastically in the last few years.

Street in downtown Bogotá, Colombia

LECCIÓN 7

Una carta entre amigas

37. Direct Object Personal Pronouns

An object pronoun which cannot be used independently of the verb is called a conjunctive object pronoun. The following are the direct object pronouns:

SINGULAR			PLURAL		
1st person	**me**	me	**nos**	us	
2nd person	**te**	you (*fam.*)	**os**	you (*fam.*)	
3rd person	**le (lo)**	him, you (*pol.*)	**los**	them (*m.*), you (*pol. m.*)	
	lo	it (*m.*)	**las**	them (*f.*), you (*pol. f.*)	
	la	her, you, it (*f.*)			

In the third person singular **le** is used to refer to a masculine person, **lo** is used to refer to a masculine thing, and **la** refers to a feminine person or thing. However, in Spanish America **lo** is used for both a person and a thing.

Claro que le conoces muy bien.	Of course you know him very well.
Si no lo resuelvo . . .	If I do not solve it . . .

In the third person plural **los** refers to masculine persons or things and **las** refers to feminine persons or things.

¿Vio Vd. los nuevos edificios? — No los vi.	Did you see the new buildings? — I did not see them.
Mi hermano no llevó las cartas. Las dejó en la mesa.	My brother did not take the letters. He left them on the table.

The direct object form of **usted** is, therefore, **le** (*m.*) and **la** (*f.*); and the direct object form of **ustedes** is **los** (*m.*) and **las** (*f.*).

Sus esposas los buscan a Vds., señores.	Your wives are looking for you, gentlemen.

38. Position of Object Pronouns

All object pronouns come immediately before the verb, even though the sentence is in the negative or in the interrogative form, unless the verb is an affirmative imperative, an infinitive, or a participle used independently. (*Cf. Sections 40, 83*)

Me quiere mucho.	He loves me very much.
Tienes que aconsejarme.	You must advise me.

39. Command Forms

Commands in the polite (**usted**) form are expressed by the present subjunctive of these verbs used as an imperative. You will learn or review all of the present subjunctive very soon, but meanwhile the polite command forms for the regular conjugations are as follows:

I	*II*	*III*
hable Vd. speak	**aprenda Vd.** learn	**viva Vd.** live
hablen Vds. speak	**aprendan Vds.** learn	**vivan Vds.** live

In other words the polite command forms for the first conjugation end in –e in the singular and –en in the plural; for the second and third conjugation they end in –a in the singular and –an in the plural. The subject pronoun (**Vd.** or **Vds.**) comes after the verb and is used with the command form except where it would be repeated in the same sentence.

Escriba Vd. una carta larga.	Write a long letter.
Escriba Vd. y aconseje a su amigo.	Write and advise your friend.

The actual imperative forms in Spanish are familiar commands, used with **tú** and **vosotros**.

I	*II*	*III*
(tú) habla speak	**come** eat	**vive** live
(vosotros) hablad speak	**comed** eat	**vivid** live

A command given to a group of people including the speaker is in the first person plural form. It is expressed either by the first person plural of the present subjunctive or by the expression **vamos a** + the infinitive. It is translated by *let us* + a verb.

I	*II*
hablemos **vamos a hablar** } let us speak	**comamos** **vamos a comer** } let us eat

III

vivamos
vamos a vivir } let us live

40. Position of Object Pronouns with a Command Form

When a command form is in the affirmative, the object pronoun, whether direct or indirect, comes after the verb and is attached to it.[1] Moreover, a written accent is placed over the syllable originally stressed.

Aconséjame, por favor.   Advise me, please.

If the command form is in the negative, the object pronouns come before the verb, the same as with any verb form in the indicative.

No lo coma Vd. ahora.   Do not eat it now.

41. Present Indicative of *poner, hacer, decir*

poner to put	**pongo, pones, pone, ponemos, ponéis, ponen**
hacer to do	**hago, haces, hace, hacemos, hacéis, hacen**
decir to say	**digo, dices, dice, decimos, decís, dicen**

---

[1] When the reflexive pronoun **os** is added to the command form ending in –**d**, the –**d** is dropped, except in **idos**.

Una carta entre amigas

Bogotá, 8 de julio de 1971

Juana querida:

Tienes que ayudarme. Me encuentro con un problema que no
sé resolver, y me da tanto cuidado que si no lo resuelvo, no sé lo
5 que va a ser de mí. Sabes que eres mi mejor amiga y tú sola puedes
ayudarme. ¡Déjame entrar directamente en el asunto, sin más ni
más!

Conoces a nuestro amigo Fernando Caballero, ¿verdad? Claro
que le conoces, ya que fuimos juntas a varias fiestas familiares y
10 otras funciones de la universidad. Es el chico bajo y rubio, que
tiene dos hermanas, Anita y Silvia, y que estudia medicina. ¿Te
acuerdas además que en octubre pasado fuimos juntas con tu
amigo Pablo al juego de fútbol en Cambridge?

Bueno, él está aquí de visita en Bogotá, y nos hemos visto mucho
15 en las últimas semanas. Confieso que me encanta. Anoche se me
declaró, y quiere casarse pronto. ¿Qué es lo que debo hacer?
Le quiero mucho, pero ¿casarme en este momento? Es pobre, no
tiene empleo, está sólo en su segundo año universitario, quiere
estudiar medicina, todavía le quedan seis años de estudios. En
20 cuanto a mí, yo tengo veinte y cinco años, como bien sabes, y no
me voy poniendo más jóven. Pero ¡casarme con un chico de
veinte años, dejar mi empleo aquí y volver a Boston, buscar otro
empleo y acostumbrarme a la vida de casada, dejar a todos los
otros jóvenes que son tan simpáticos!

25 Por otro lado, los años pasan y los jóvenes mayores ya están
casados. Los que van al ejército quieren esperar a la vuelta antes
de casarse; de manera que la situación es algo difícil para las
chicas. ¡Dichosa tú que ya tienes arreglada la boda con Pablo!

¡Aconséjame, por favor, y sácame de este aprieto! ¡Escríbeme
30 una larga carta y envíala en seguida! Te lo agradeceré mucho.

Afectuosamente,

Ana

USEFUL EXPRESSIONS

Me da tanto cuidado. It worries me so much.

No sé lo que va a ser de mí. I don't know what is going to become of me.

Déjame entrar en el asunto. Let me get to the point.

sin más ni más without further ado

fiestas familiares parties

Se me declaró. He proposed to me.

¿Qué es lo que debo hacer? What am I going to do?

en cuanto a mí as for me

vida de casado (casada) married life

por otro lado on the other hand

esperar a la vuelta to wait until one's return

Sácame de este aprieto. Get me out of this fix.

WORD REMINDER

acerca (de) about

admiración admiration

admirar to admire

afecto affection

agradable agreeable

agradar to please, be agreeable

bailar to dance

broma jest, joke

cierto sure

contestación answer

noticia news

novia fiancée (*girl*)

novio fiancé (*boy*)

orden *f.* order

pensar to think

perdonar to forgive

pronto immediately, quickly

verdadero true

último last

estar de acuerdo to agree, be in agreement

no tener razón to be wrong

tener miedo to be afraid

CONVERSACIÓN

1. ¿Tiene Vd. muchos problemas que no puede resolver? 2. ¿Sabe cada estudiante lo que va a ser de él? 3. ¿Es buena idea para una muchacha consultar a su amiga sobre el asunto de su novio? 4. ¿Van las señoritas a muchas fiestas familiares? 5. ¿Hay buenos juegos de fútbol en su universidad? 6. Cuando un joven invita a una señorita a una función, ¿es que quiere casarse con ella? 7. ¿Tiene un novio siempre mucha admiración por su novia? 8. ¿Quién quiere estudiar medicina en esta clase? 9. En la carta de esta lección, ¿le gustaría a Ana dejar su empleo? 10. ¿Le gustaría casarse con el joven? 11. ¿Le gustan todavía las fiestas y los bailes? 12. Si Vd. tiene que ir al ejército, ¿piensa Vd. casarse antes de irse, o a la vuelta?

EJERCICIOS

I. PRÁCTICA ORAL. Cue-in-Drills.

MODELS	CUES	RESPONSES
Conoce bien al joven.	le	Le conoce bien.
¿Escribe Vd. a su hermana?	su abuelo	¿Escribe Vd. a su abuelo?

A. (*Pronouns*) 1. Recibo las noticias (la, las, no la). 2. Perdona a la muchacha (la, no la, no las). 3. Admira a su novia (no la, la, nos, no nos). 4. Enviamos la última carta (la, las, no las, no la). 5. Están de acuerdo con el señor (con él, con ellos, con nosotros, con Vds.). 6. Me gusta invitar a los muchachos (los, le, la, las). 7. ¿Por qué no consulta Vd. a un buen amigo? (le, unos buenos amigos, los, a su padre). 8. Ayuda a sus padres (los, no los, a sus amigas, no las). 9. Aconséjame, por favor (le, la, nos, los). 10. Acabo de recibir una carta (la, las, unas noticias, los).

B. (*Idioms*) 1. Me gustaría estudiar medicina (letras, arte, música). 2. Espero que puedas sacarme de este aprieto (sacarnos, sacarle, sacarla). 3. No tiene más que catorce años (diez y nueve, veinte y tres, doce). 4. No sé lo que va a ser de mí (no sabe, no sabéis, no saben). 5. Es posible que tenga miedo (tenga razón, no tenga razón, no tenga miedo).

II. Fill in the blanks with the proper object pronoun for the word in italics:

1. Tengo un problema y no puedo resolver —— *it*. 2. No —— conozco *him* bien pero me agrada mucho. 3. Los países extranjeros son bonitos, pero no —— visitamos *them* porque no tenemos dinero. 4. —— *It* agradezco pero no estoy de acuerdo con Vd. 5. Si Vd. —— dice *it* en broma es que Vd. no —— conoce *him* bien. 6. Si Vds. quieren escribir —— *it* (*f.*), escriban —— *it* (*f.*) en seguida. 7. Los jóvenes mayores —— *them* (*f.*) aconsejan. 8. Ella debe ayudar —— *them*. 9. Ana tiene veinte y cinco años, pero no —— *it* confiesa. 10. El cuento es verdadero, pero, ¿quién va a creer —— *it*?

III. Complete the following in any way which will form sensible sentences:

1. Aconseje a su amigo de . . . 2. Pasan los años y . . . 3. Yo le quiero mucho, pero . . . 4. Siempre me invita a fiestas familiares, pero . . .

5. Los jóvenes mayores están casados y . . . 6. Si Vd. no me saca de este aprieto . . . 7. Cuando hay un juego de fútbol . . . 8. Los jóvenes que van al ejército . . . 9. ¿En qué año universitario . . . ? 10. La recuerdo con mucho afecto, pero . . . .

IV. Prepare at home and read fluently in Spanish:

1. It worries me so much because I do not wish to get married now. 2. You are her best friend and you can help her. 3. He likes medicine, but he does not wish to study for six years. 4. Do you remember that he invited us many times? 5. There are many events in our university during the year. 6. Are all of you ready for married life? 7. Please write a long letter and send it to your brother. 8. Let her get to the point without further ado. 9. She wants to leave them because she is going to get married. 10. He is poor and he has no job, but he loves her.

Partial view of a medical center in Mexico City, Mexico

LECCIÓN 8

El primer viaje en avión

42. Possession

To express possession in Spanish observe the following formula:

the boy's mother = the mother of the boy = **la madre del muchacho**

The verb **ser** is used when expressing *possession* or *belonging*.

¿Es suyo este periódico?   Is this your newspaper?

43. Possessive Adjectives

Possessive adjectives come before the nouns they modify when they simply indicate the possessor. When there is any emphasis or stress on the possession, these adjectives come after the noun.

The forms which come before the noun are as follows:

mi, mis	my
tu, tus	your (*fam.*)
su, sus	his, her, its, your (*pol.*), their
nuestro, –a, –os, –as	our
vuestro, –a, –os, –as	your (*fam.*)

A possessive adjective agrees in gender and number with whatever is possessed and not with the possessor. In deciding the gender and number of the possessive adjective refer to the object possessed and not the owner. In the third person, if a distinction is necessary between *his, her, your,* or *their,* Spanish clarifies the possessive by using **de él, de ella, de Vd., de ellos, de ellas,** or **de Vds.** after the noun.

¿Va Vd. a visitar a su familia de él?   Are you going to visit his family?

Usually the possessive adjective is replaced by the definite article when the clarifying expression **de él, de ella,** etc., is used.

¿Va Vd. a visitar a la familia de él?   Are you going to visit his family?

After the noun the forms are:

mío, mía, míos, mías	my
tuyo, tuya, tuyos, tuyas	your (*fam.*)
suyo, suya, suyos, suyas	his, her, its their, your (*pol.*)
nuestro, –a, –os, –as	our
vuestro, –a, –os, –as	your (*fam.*)

El periódico mío está aquí.   My newspaper is right here.

44. Possessive Pronouns

When a word not only expresses possession but takes the place of a noun, it is a possessive pronoun. In Spanish they are as follows:

el mío, la mía, los míos, las mías	mine
el tuyo, la tuya, los tuyos, las tuyas	yours (*fam.*)
el suyo, la suya, los suyos, las suyas	his, hers, theirs yours (*pol.*)
el nuestro, la nuestra, los nuestros, las nuestras	ours
el vuestro, la vuestra, los vuestros, las vuestras	yours (*fam.*)

The possessive pronoun must agree in gender and number with the noun for which it stands. To avoid confusion or to give emphasis, the third person pronoun may be clarified by adding **de él, de ella, de usted, de ellos, de ellas,** or **de ustedes.**

With possessive pronouns the article is omitted after the verb **ser** if the sentence expresses only possession. In the third person, however, not only the article but the pronoun itself may be omitted, using instead **es de él, son de usted,** etc.

Este periódico es mío. ¿Dónde está el suyo?   This newspaper is mine. Where is yours?

Éstos son de Vd.   These are yours.

45. The Verb *gustar*

For ordinary purposes we may say that Spanish has no verb meaning *to like* in the same sense as in English. All sentences containing the verb *to like* can mentally be changed to the verb *to please* in English before being turned into Spanish. Observe the following formula:

I like Spanish. = Spanish pleases me. = **Me gusta el español.**
They like to travel. = To travel pleases them. = **Les gusta viajar.**

The verb is always in the third person. The person who is pleased becomes the indirect object and goes before the verb. If the person who is pleased is a noun it is introduced by **a,** while the personal pronoun object also must be used in Spanish, although it is not translated in English.

Anthony likes the trip. = The trip pleases Anthony. = **A Antonio le gusta el viaje.**

46. Present Indicative of *caer, saber, ver*

caer to fall	**caigo, caes, cae, caemos, caéis, caen**
saber to know	**sé, sabes, sabe, sabemos, sabéis, saben**
ver to see	**veo, ves, ve, vemos, veis, ven**

El primer viaje en avión

— ¡Dispense Vd., señorita! ¿Está ocupado este asiento?
— No, señor, creo que no. Por lo menos no he visto a nadie ahí.
— ¿Permite Vd. que me siente, entonces?
— ¿Por qué no? Está Vd. en su derecho.   5
Pasa un largo rato, mientras van entrando los otros pasajeros. La señorita mira por la ventanilla.
— ¡Dispense Vd., señorita! ¿Es suyo este periódico?
— No señor, no es mío. Es de la compañía aérea.

10   — ¿Le gustaría a Vd. leerlo?

— No, gracias. — *Y sigue mirando por la ventanilla.*

— ¿Viaja Vd. sola, señorita?

— Sí, señor; así lo creía.

— ¡Perdone Vd., señorita! No quería molestarla.

15   — ¡Ah no, señor! No es molestia. Es que tengo mucho miedo.

— ¿Miedo de qué, señorita? ¿Es éste su primer viaje en avión? ¡ Parece imposible!

— Sí, señor, es mi primer viaje. Tengo miedo a la subida. ¿Cuándo vamos a subir?

20   — Pierda Vd. cuidado, que no es nada. ¿Cómo se llama Vd.?

— Mi nombre es Julieta Davis, ¿y el suyo?

— Antonio Mesera, a sus órdenes. Y ¿a dónde va? ¿Tal vez a visitar a su familia?

— No, señor, sigo hasta la Ciudad de México. Voy a estudiar
25 el español en la universidad.

— ¡Pero si Vd. lo habla perfectamente!

— Es Vd. muy amable. Lo hablo un poco.

— ¿Dónde lo aprendió Vd.?

— Lo aprendí en la Universidad de Hunter. Nuestros pro-
30 fesores son muy buenos.

— De eso no cabe duda, y las alumnas también. Yo he vivido en Nueva York y conozco a varias señoritas de esa universidad.

— Le gusta a Vd. Nueva York?

— Me encanta, pero le tengo miedo. Para mí es la única ver-
35 dadera ciudad de los Estados Unidos, aun teniendo problemas enormes.

— Es que los problemas son multiplicados por la variedad. Hay gente de todos los niveles económicos y sociales. A Vd. le gusta sin duda porque hay muchos de habla española.

40   — Tiene Vd. razón. Se puede vivir sin dificultad hablando sólo español.

— Por eso me gusta a mí también. Pero me da tanto miedo la subida del avión. ¿Cree Vd. que va a ser difícil?

— ¡Pierda Vd. cuidado! Ya hace diez minutos que estamos en
45 el aire.

USEFUL EXPRESSIONS

creo que no I don't think so
por lo menos at least
en su derecho within your rights
así lo creía I thought so
tengo miedo (de or **a)** I am afraid (of)
pierda Vd. cuidado don't worry

a sus órdenes if you please, at your command
no cabe duda there is no doubt
me encanta I adore it, it's wonderful
de todos los niveles of all levels
de habla española Spanish-speaking
sin dificultad without difficulty

WORD REMINDER

acabar de to have just (*accomplished an action*)
acercarse a to draw near
asegurar to insure, assure
atreverse a to dare, venture
bajar to go down
caerse to fall down, drop
cerrar to close
correr to run
cuenta bill
débil weak

demás: los (las) —, the rest, remainder
echar to throw
económico economical
entender to understand
ferrocarril *m.* railroad
jamás ever
lejano distant, far away
suceder to happen
variedad *f.* variety
mal de estómago *m.* upset stomach
sin duda undoubtedly

CONVERSACIÓN

1. ¿Nunca ha viajado Vd. en avión? 2. Cuando un asiento no está ocupado, ¿está una persona en su derecho de tomarlo? 3. ¿Se atreve su abuelo a viajar en avión hasta Europa? 4. ¿Tiene Vd. miedo cuando baja el avión? 5. ¿Es una buena idea la de asegurarse cuando se hace un viaje en avión? 6. ¿Siente Vd. mal de estómago cuando viaja en ferrocarril? 7. ¿Suceden muchas cosas mientras se viaja? 8. ¿Se pueden echar cigarrillos por la ventanilla de un avión? 9. ¿Tiene miedo de caerse la señorita Davis? 10. ¿Qué idioma va a estudiar la señorita? 11. ¿Le parece que la Ciudad de México es una ciudad muy lejana? 12. Para Vd., ¿cuál es la única verdadera ciudad del mundo?

EJERCICIOS

I. Use a possessive adjective in place of the articles in parentheses in the following sentences:

1. Aquí está (la) casa; la puerta está cerrada. 2. A (la) madre le gusta ir de compras conmigo porque soy yo la que llevo (los) paquetes. 3. A veces no entendemos a (los) padres. 4. ¿En qué bolsillo tienes (la) pluma, Pedro? 5. Cuando (los) amigos viajan en avión, siempre llevan (las) maletas consigo. 6. Cuando ella toma (el) almuerzo ya tiene mucha hambre. 7. ¿Te gusta tomar (el) café en cama? 8. La pobrecita tiene que hacer todos (los) viajes con (la) mamá; tendrá que casarse también con (la) mamá. 9. Nosotros sabemos que (el) español no es bueno, pero nos gusta hablar este idioma. 10. He leído todo el periódico y todavía no comprendo (la) opinión sobre esta guerra.

II. PRÁCTICA ORAL. Directed Discourse.

1. Pregunte a una muchacha si (le gusta hacer un viaje; le gusta viajar sola; le gusta viajar en avión). 2. Pregunte a un muchacho si (le gusta leer novelas; le gusta leer periódicos; le gusta ir a la escuela). 3. Pregunte a un amigo (cuándo le gusta almorzar; quién tiene que pagar la cuenta; cuánto cuesta la comida). 4. Pregunte a una amiga quién es más viejo (mi hermano o el suyo; su padre o el nuestro; su profesor o el de Vd.). 5. Pida Vd. a un compañero de (darle unos cigarrillos; tomar asiento; cerrar la ventana). 6. Pida Vd. a una muchacha de (esperar un minuto; perder cuidado; almorzar con Vd.). 7. Pregunte al profesor si (sabe otras lenguas; sabe cantar; conoce a muchos hispanoamericanos; ha hecho muchos viajes en avión).

III. Make complete sentences containing the following expressions:

1. sin duda. 2. no cabe duda. 3. perder cuidado. 4. dar miedo. 5. tener miedo. 6. por lo menos. 7. en su derecho. 8. a sus órdenes. 9. ser amable. 10. acabar de. 11. sin dificultad. 12. me encanta.

IV. Prepare at home and read fluently in Spanish:

1. My first trip by plane is wonderful. I was so afraid! 2. Are these seats occupied? We want to sit and have lunch. 3. Do you like to read the newspaper on the plane? 4. She speaks Spanish perfectly

because she is from a Spanish-speaking family. 5. I do not wish to bother you, if you prefer to be alone. 6. Our parents and hers are continuing on to Mexico City. 7. Don't worry; it's nothing at all. 8. What is your name and where are you going? 9. She keeps on looking through the window and does not answer. 10. Our university is beautiful and yours is beautiful too.

LECCIÓN 9

En la tienda de abarrotes

47. Demonstrative Adjectives

A demonstrative adjective points out a person or an object. In English there are two demonstrative adjectives (*this* and *that*), but in Spanish there are three.

este, esta, estos, estas this, these	refers to that which is near the speaker
ese, esa, esos, esas that, those	refers to that which is near the person spoken to
aquel, aquella, aquellos, aquellas that, those	refers to that which is away from both the speaker and the person spoken to

The demonstrative adjective is generally repeated before each word to which it refers.

Estos pimientos y estos tomates.   These peppers and tomatoes.

The forms **ese, esa, esos, esas** are used only when the speaker wants to indicate something or someone near the person addressed, or applying primarily to that person.

Déme Vd. una docena de esos huevos grandes.   Give me a dozen of those large eggs (*right next to you*).

48. Demonstrative Pronouns

A demonstrative word which is not followed immediately by the noun to which it refers is a pronoun rather than an adjective. When the demonstratives are used as pronouns, they have a written accent on

65

Market place in Oaxaca, Mexico

the syllable that is stressed. Therefore the demonstrative pronouns are:

éste, ésta, éstos, éstas	this (one), these
ése, ésa, ésos, ésas	that (one), those
aquél, aquélla, aquéllos, aquéllas	that (one), those

¿ **Quiere Vd. éstos grandes o ésos pequeños?**	Do you want these large ones or those small ones?

In addition to these forms there are three demonstratives which refer to a vague object, an idea, or some previous statement.

esto	this (*what I say*)
eso	that (*that which you said*)
aquello	that (*some statement in the past*)

Eso es todo por hoy.	That is all for today.

49. Negative Words and Expressions

The following are the most common negative words:

nadie no one, nobody
nada nothing
ninguno (ningún), –a no, not any, none
nunca never
jamás never
ni . . . ni neither . . . nor

Nadie puede entenderlo.	No one can understand it.

These negative words are generally used after the verb, which must then be preceded by **no.** They may be used before the verb for greater emphasis, in which case the **no** is omitted.

No se olvida nunca de enviar la cuenta. **Nunca se olvida de enviar la cuenta.**	He never forgets to send the bill.

50. The Preposition *a*

Whenever a noun or a disjunctive pronoun is used as the indirect object of a verb it is introduced by the preposition **a.**

The preposition **a** is also required before a direct object when it denotes a definite person or a personified object. This use is referred to as the personal **a**. The personal **a** is not used before an indefinite person or persons, nor is it used generally after **tener**.

¿ Conoces a nuestro amigo Fernando?	Do you know our friend Fernando?
¿ Ha visto Vd. un muchacho por aquí?	Did you see a boy around here?

51. Indirect Object Personal Pronouns

The indirect object is the person *to whom* or *for whom* an action is done. The indirect object pronouns are as follows:

me	to me	**nos**	to us
te	to you (*fam.*)	**os**	to you (*fam.*)
le	to him, to her, to you (*pol.*), to it	**les**	to them, to you (*pol.*)

To emphasize or clarify the meaning of any of these pronouns Spanish uses **a mí, a ti, a él, a ella, a usted, a nosotros, a vosotros, a ellos, a ellas, a ustedes** after the verb. When using these forms after the verb Spanish still retains the personal object pronoun before the verb.

Las uvas les gustan a ellas.	They (*f.*) like grapes.

En la tienda de abarrotes (México)

— Dependiente, ¿a cuánto son los huevos hoy?

— ¿Quiere usted éstos grandes o ésos pequeños? Los pequeños son a seis pesos la docena y los grandes son a siete y cinco.

— Déme usted una docena de esos huevos grandes, por favor. Y las habichuelas verdes, ¿a cuánto?   5

— Vd. quiere decir los ejotes. Éstos de aquí, a tres pesos el kilo. Aquéllos de allí, a cuatro y ocho.

— Tomo dos kilos de aquéllos. Me parecen mucho mejores.
¿Hay guisantes?
10   — Sí, los hay, señora Moncado, pero no son para Vd. Mañana
llegarán otros mejores.
— Bueno, los tomaré mañana. ¿Qué verduras hay?
— Los pimientos y los tomates son excelentes, y son baratos
hoy.
15   — No necesito tomates, pero déme Vd. medio kilo de pimientos.
Déjeme escogerlos. Tome Vd. éste, éste de aquí y éstos. Ahora,
¿qué frutas tienen Vds.?
— Hay naranjas buenas y maduras. Esas peras son magníficas.
Las fresas también son buenas, pues ésta es la estación de las fresas.
20   — ¿No hay plátanos, o bananas, como dicen Vds.?
— Sí, las hay, pero son pequeñas y todavía no están maduras.
Creo que no le gustarán.
— Pues, déme Vd. una docena de naranjas y una cajita de
fresas. ¿Tienen Vds. uvas?
25   — Sí, las tenemos, y son muy buenas. ¿Quiere Vd. un kilo de
estas uvas? Mire, ¡qué buenas!
— Tomo dos kilos. Las uvas les gustan a todos. A ver, ¿qué
más necesito?
— ¿Café? ¿azúcar? ¿té? ¿limones?
30   — No, creo que ya es todo. Tenga la bondad de enviarlos
pronto, y no se olvide de enviarme la cuenta. Muy buenas tardes.
— Buenas tardes, señora Moncado. Muchas gracias.

USEFUL EXPRESSIONS

tienda de abarrotes grocery store
¿a cuánto son ... ? how much are?
a seis pesos la docena six pesos a dozen
a siete y cinco seven pesos and five
  centavos
habichuelas verdes f. pl. (in Mexico
  ejotes m. pl.) string beans

Mire, ¡qué buena! See how good it is!
a ver let's see
Creo que ya es todo. I think that is all.
Tenga la bondad de enviarlos. Please
  send them.

WORD REMINDER

aceite *m.* oil
amarillo yellow
arroz *m.* rice
carne *f.* meat
cocina kitchen, cooking
comedor *m.* dining room
entrar en to enter
esquina corner
hermoso beautiful

hacienda farm
huerta vegetable garden, orchard
leche *f.* milk
mantequilla butter
pan *m.* bread
pollo chicken
precio price
preferir to prefer
región *f.* region

CONVERSACIÓN

1. ¿Cuál es el precio de los huevos en una tienda de abarrotes?
2. ¿Comen mucho pan y mantequilla los niños? 3. ¿Hay verduras en
una huerta, o en un jardín? 4. ¿De qué color son las habichuelas?
¿los plátanos? 5. ¿Les gustan a todos las fresas y las uvas? 6. ¿Cuáles
prefiere Vd., los pimientos o los tomates? 7. ¿Cuántas libras hay en un
kilo? 8. ¿Hay muchas naranjas en las huertas de la Florida? 9. ¿Sabe
Vd. qué es arroz con pollo? ¿Le gusta? 10. En su casa, ¿comen Vds.
en la cocina o en el comedor? 11. ¿Compra Vd. leche en la tienda de la
esquina, o no hay tienda cerca de su casa? 12. ¿Le gusta a su mamá el
té con limón?

EJERCICIOS

*I. Supply suitable demonstrative adjectives or pronouns to complete the
following sentences:*

1. —— naranjas y —— fresas son mejores que ——. 2. —— huevos que
Vd. tiene parecen más grandes que —— que yo tengo. 3. —— habichuelas verdes son muy buenas en —— sopa. 4. —— es la estación de
las fresas. 5. —— peras que vemos en —— tienda son muy hermosas.
6. ¿Cuestan mucho —— bananas? ¿Cuestan más —— que ——?
7. Las uvas están muy buenas —— verano. ¿Compra Vd. un kilo

de ——? 8. —— mujer con —— niño van siempre a —— misma tienda.
9. —— tomates son baratos, pero no tan baratos como ——. 10. Tenga
la bondad de enviarme —— cajita de uvas.

II. PRÁCTICA ORAL.

A. Answer the question based on the statement:

1. Yo no hago nada. ¿Y Vd? 2. Nosotros no decimos nada. ¿Y Vds.?
3. Vd. nunca puede trabajar. ¿Y él? 4. Ellos no dicen nada a nadie.
¿Y nosotros? 5. Yo nunca compro tomates. ¿Y ella? 6. Ella me
envía una carta por semana. ¿Y tú? 7. Nosotros compramos limones.
¿Y vosotros?

B. When the instructor cues in the word in parentheses, supply the whole sentence, but make the necessary changes:

1. Yo quiero un kilo de uvas (Vd., nosotros, él, Vds.). 2. Vd. no
necesita tomates (yo, nosotros, él, Vds.). 3. Nosotros tomaremos una
cajita de fresas (yo, Vd., él, Vds.). 4. Él tiene una tienda (yo, Vd., nosotros, Vds.). 5. Vd. está en su casa (yo, nosotros, él, Vds.). 6. Vds.
irán a España (yo, Vd., nosotros, él). 7. Yo creo que tengo razón
(Vd., nosotros, él, Vds.). 8. Vd. vivirá aquí (yo, nosotros, él, Vds.).
9. Nosotros sabemos lo que él quiere (yo, Vds., él, Vd.).

C. Cue in a pronoun in place of the words in parentheses:

1. Él toma (los pimientos, las naranjas, las bananas). 2. Tenga la
bondad de enviar (las frutas, los limones, el periódico). 3. (A Juan, a
María, a nosotros) gustan los guisantes. 4. Vds. hablan perfectamente
(el francés, el español y el italiano, la lengua). 5. Deje Vd. pasar (a
Pedro, a María, a los alumnos).

III. Three students improvise a conversation in a grocery store.

For preparation imagine that you are first the shopkeeper, then a
customer, then the husband of a lady who is doing the shopping.

La Merced market, Mexico City, Mexico

Central Square, San José, Costa Rica

LECCIÓN 10

Una entrevista

52. Past Tenses

In English an action which takes place at some time in the past is expressed in the past tense. In Spanish such an action is expressed in the past tense too, but Spanish uses one of three past tenses, *viz.* the present perfect, imperfect, or preterite, which may correspond to only one past tense in English. They are not interchangeable; each one expresses a particular aspect of an action, which will be explained with the treatment of each tense.

53. Past Participles

The past participle is the form of a verb which expresses the result of an action without expressing the action in progress. In order for the past participle to express the action, it must be used together with the verb **haber** in compound tenses. The past participle is formed as follows:

	1ST CONJ.	2ND CONJ.	3RD CONJ.
	stem + **ado**	stem + **ido**	stem + **ido**
Examples:	**hablado**	**comido**	**vivido**

Some verbs have irregular past participles, as for example those listed below:

decir — dicho	**poner — puesto**	**hacer — hecho**
volver — vuelto	**escribir — escrito**	**abrir — abierto**

54. Present Tense of *haber*

The verb **haber** is used to form compound tenses; it is not used to mean *have* in the sense of *possessing*. Here is the present indicative:

yo	**he**	nosotros, –as	**hemos**
tú	**has**	vosotros, –as	**habéis**
él, ella, Vd.	**ha**	ellos, ellas, Vds.	**han**

55. Present Perfect Tense: Formation

The present perfect tense is formed with the present tense of **haber** + the past participle of the verb conjugated. The past participle remains unchanged.

	1ST CONJ.	2ND CONJ.	3RD CONJ.
yo	**he hablado**	**he comido**	**he vivido**
tú	**has hablado**	**has comido**	**has vivido**
él, ella, Vd.	**ha hablado**	**ha comido**	**ha vivido**
nosotros –as	**hemos hablado**	**hemos comido**	**hemos vivido**
vosotros, –as	**habéis hablado**	**habéis comido**	**habéis vivido**
ellos, ellas, Vds.	**han hablado**	**han comido**	**han vivido**

56. Present Perfect Tense: Uses

The present perfect tense expresses an action which took place recently or is mentally connected by the speaker with the present. It is generally used when an action has taken place on the same day or in the period of time which is going on while the speaker is speaking.

¿Ha trabajado Vd. mucho en una oficina?   Have you worked long in an office?

57. Relative Pronouns

A relative pronoun connects two clauses by referring to a person or a thing mentioned in the first clause. In Spanish the most common relative pronoun is **que,** which refers to persons or things and may be used as subject or object of a verb. When referring to things **que** may be used even after a preposition, but in such a position it cannot refer to persons. **Que** is rendered by *who, whom, which,* or *that,* according to the sense.

Hay dos señoritas que quieren hablarle.	There are two young ladies who wish to talk to you.
Le envío un libro que acabo de comprar.	I am sending you a book which I just bought.

When referring to a person, the relative pronoun after a preposition is **quien** when referring to one and **quienes** when referring to more than one.

La mecanógrafa con quien yo hablé.	The typist with whom I talked.

Una entrevista

— Señor Alonso, hay aquí dos señoritas que quieren hablarle. ¿Las mando entrar?

— Sí, que pasen. Buenos días, señoritas. ¡Siéntense, por favor!

— Buenos días, señor. Yo me llamo Lola Jiménez y ésta es mi prima, Isabel Costa.   5

— Mucho gusto en conocerlas. ¿Vds. quieren trabajar aquí?

— Yo no; soy estudiante. Pero mi prima sí que quiere trabajo. Es mecanógrafa.

— Bueno. Necesitamos una buena mecanógrafa en este momento. Dígame Vd. ¿ha trabajado mucho en una oficina?   10

— Sí, señor. He trabajado dos años.

— ¿Aquí en los Estados Unidos?

— No, señor, en San José. Yo soy de Costa Rica.

— ¿Costa Rica? Es un país de la América Central, ¿verdad?

— Sí, señor, Costa Rica es un país muy pequeñito, cerca de   15 Panamá.

— Ahora sí que me acuerdo. Y ¿desde cuándo está Vd. aquí en los Estados Unidos?

— Hace sólo un mes que estoy aquí.

— ¿Y ha estudiado Vd. el inglés?   20

— Sí, señor, lo he estudiado, pero lo hablo muy poco. En verdad, hablo sólo español.

— Para este trabajo Vd. no necesita el inglés. Lo que Vd.
necesita es el español.

25   — Me alegro mucho, señor. Es tan difícil encontrar una buena
colocación sin saber el inglés.

— Tiene Vd. mucha razón. Pero aquí nuestro trabajo es todo
en español. ¿Quiere Vd. escribir a máquina una copia de este
papel, por favor?

30   — Con mucho gusto. (*Después de diez minutos.*) ¡Aquí está!

— Vd. lo ha hecho muy bien. ¿Puede volver mañana por la
mañana para empezar el trabajo?

— Sí, señor, se lo agradezco mucho.

— El sueldo empieza con cien dólares a la semana y las horas
35 son desde las nueve hasta las cuatro y media. ¿Está bien?

— Sí, señor, está muy bien para empezar.

— Entonces, hasta mañana a las nueve.

— ¡Hasta mañana y muchas gracias!

USEFUL EXPRESSIONS

mandar entrar to show someone in
que pasen let them come in
mucho gusto en conocerlas very
  pleased to know you
sí que quiere does want
en este momento at this moment

ahora sí que now I do
¿desde cuándo + pres.? how long
  + pres. perf.?
en verdad in fact, the truth is
escribir a máquina to type

WORD REMINDER

abrir to open
aceptar to accept
amistad *f.* friendship
arreglar to arrange
ascender to advance (*in rank*)
aumentar to increase
compañero companion
conseguir to get
correo mail
despacho office
dictado dictation

enfermo ill
experiencia experience
ganar to earn
interesar to interest
máquina (para escribir) typewriter
número number
peligro danger
reloj *m.* watch, clock
secretaria secretary
silla chair
sueldo pay, salary

CONVERSACIÓN

1. Cuando Vd. va a una entrevista, señorita, ¿fuma Vd.? 2. Vd. es una buena mecanógrafa, pero, ¿lee Vd. bien el español? 3. ¿Se gana mucho dinero en Costa Rica, sabe Vd.? 4. ¿Ha conseguido Vd. un buen sueldo en su empleo? 5. ¿Cuál es el número de su teléfono? 6. ¿Tiene Vd. buenos compañeros en esta ciudad? 7. ¿Es buena la amistad en esta vida? 8. ¿Quién abre el correo en un despacho? 9. ¿Qué trabajo tiene que hacer una secretaria? 10. ¿Le gusta a Vd. una colocación en que no se puede ascender? 11. Cuando le aumentan el sueldo, ¿lo acepta Vd.? 12. ¿Le interesa a Vd. visitar los países de Sud América?

EJERCICIOS

I. Change the verbs in the following sentences to the present perfect tense:

1. La señorita arregla las cartas. 2. El muchacho la manda entrar. 3. Ella trabaja demasiado. 4. Ahora me acuerdo de todo. 5. ¿Quién lleva la máquina a la oficina? 6. ¿Qué dice su primo? 7. ¿Dónde pone Vd. las copias que Vd. hace? 8. Yo vivo en Panamá. 9. Nosotros no queremos ir con Vds. 10. ¿Cuándo volverá la secretaria? 11. Yo como carne y papas. 12. Tú haces bien el trabajo. 13. Ponemos las sillas en el despacho. 14. No tengo mucha experiencia.

II. Supply the necessary relative pronouns in the following sentences:

1. El país —— yo visitaré es muy interesante. 2. La oficina en —— ella trabaja es muy linda. 3. Los estudiantes con —— Vd. viaja son mexicanos. 4. El reloj —— tengo es de oro. 5. La máquina —— Vd. ha comprado es vieja. 6. La mecanógrafa —— necesitamos tiene que ser española. 7. El peligro de —— yo le hablé ha pasado. 8. La copia —— Vd. ha hecho no me gusta. 9. Las cartas —— ellos han escrito ya están en el correo. 10. Los compañeros con —— trabajamos en el verano son buenos amigos.

III. PRÁCTICA ORAL. Cue-in Exercise.

1. ¿Desde cuándo trabaja Vd. aquí? (espera Vd., estudia Vd., se pasea Vd.). 2. En este momento él está muy ocupado (ellos, ella, nosotros). 3. Mucho gusto en conocerla, señorita Costa (señor Moreno, señores, señoritas). 4. Empieza a trabajar mañana por la mañana (mañana por la tarde, el lunes, dentro de dos semanas). 5. Hace una hora que le esperamos (dos horas, hora y media, dos días). 6. ¿Ha tenido Vd. mucha experiencia? (han tenido Vds., ha tenido él, has tenido tú). 7. De vez en cuando me da la gana de leer (de cantar, de escribir a máquina, de trabajar mucho, de viajar en autobús). 8. Por favor, sáqueme de este aprieto (sáquele, sáquela, sáquenos). 9. ¿La mando entrar ahora mismo, o más tarde, señor profesor? (le mando, los mando, las mando). 10. ¿Le ha pedido al jefe un buen sueldo, señorita Jiménez? (mucho dinero, un nuevo reloj, una buena colocación).

IV. Prepare at home and read fluently in Spanish:

1. They have not returned from South America yet. 2. I have never lived in this country before, but I like it now. 3. Why have they not written to us? Have they not had time? 4. Her secretary has never had much experience, but she is a good stenographer. 5. The English which I know is very little. 6. When you go for an interview you cannot talk (very) much. 7. They do not need a good stenographer at this time. 8. After ten minutes she can begin her work in the office. 9. The position which she holds is very good for a young lady. 10. The students with whom you arrived are from Costa Rica.

Rural scene, Costa Rica

Colegiata Church
Santillana del Ma
(Santander), Spai

Children playing a
bullfighting in Spai

LECCIÓN 11

El imperfecto gramatical

58. The Imperfect Tense: Formation and Uses

The imperfect is formed by taking the stem of a verb and adding the appropriate endings, given below:

	I	II	III
yo	habl –aba	com –ía	viv –ía
tú	–abas	–ías	–ías
él, ella, Vd.	–aba	–ía	–ía
nosotros, –as	–ábamos	–íamos	–íamos
vosotros, –as	–abais	–íais	–íais
ellos, ellas, Vds.	–aban	–ían	–ían

You will notice that the second and third conjugations have similar endings. All the endings of the second and third conjugations have an accent on the **i**, whereas the first conjugation has only one accent, on the **a** of the first person plural.

The imperfect, or past descriptive, describes an action or a state of being which was in progress at the time under consideration in the past. When we say that a friend was coming down the street, or the sun was shining, at some time in the past, the action *was coming* or *was shining* would be rendered in the imperfect tense. If we are talking about a trip and we say that we used to stop driving at four o'clock every day, *stopped* would be in the imperfect tense. Therefore, we say that the imperfect or past descriptive expresses a continued, customary, or repeated action in the past.

De niño yo vivía en una pequeña aldea.   As a boy I lived in a small village.

Mi padre trabajaba en los campos.   My father used to work in the fields.

Los veíamos cada mañana.   We used to see them every morning.

59. Irregular Imperfects

The imperfect is the most regular of all tenses in Spanish. Only three
verbs are irregular and the forms are as follows:

ser to be	**era, eras, era, éramos, erais, eran**
ir to go	**iba, ibas, iba, íbamos, ibais, iban**
ver to see	**veía, veías, veía, veíamos, veíais, veían**

60. The Conditional

The conditional is quite regular, if you will keep in mind the future
form of a verb and the imperfect endings of the second or third conjugation. To form the conditional, take the first person singular of
the future of any verb, regular or irregular, drop the **-é** and add the
endings **-ía, -ías, -ía, -íamos, -íais, -ían.**

Example: INFINITIVE **salir**   FUTURE **saldré**

CONDITIONAL **saldría, saldrías, saldría, saldríamos, saldríais, saldrían**

61. Personal Pronouns after Prepositions

Personal pronouns used after prepositions are called disjunctive personal pronouns. The forms are as follows:

mí	me	**nosotros, –as**	us
ti	you (*fam.*)	**vosotros, –as**	you (*fam.*)
él	him	**ellos**	them (*m.*)
ella	her	**ellas**	them (*f.*)
usted	you	**ustedes**	you
sí	himself, herself	**sí**	themselves

Note: **con** + **mí** becomes **conmigo, con** + **ti** becomes **contigo,** and **con** + **sí**
becomes **consigo.**

62. Present Indicative of *conocer, oír, reír, salir, traer*

conocer to know, be acquainted with	**conozco, conoces, conoce, conocemos, conocéis, conocen**
oír to hear	**oigo, oyes, oye, oímos, oís, oyen**
reír to laugh	**río, ríes, ríe, reímos, reís, ríen**
salir to go out	**salgo, sales, sale, salimos, salís, salen**
traer to bring	**traigo, traes, trae, traemos, traéis, traen**

El imperfecto gramatical

De niño yo vivía en una pequeña aldea cerca de Santander.
Nuestra familia se componía de mi padre, mi madre, la abuela,
dos hermanos mayores y yo. Mi padre trabajaba en los campos.
Mi madre le ayudaba en el tiempo de la cosecha y tenía el cuidado
de la casa y de los niños. Mi abuela cuidaba de mí, que era el 5
más pequeño. Mis hermanos iban a la escuela. Y mi único cuidado
era inventar maneras de pasar el tiempo.

Por la mañana mi primer cuidado era el desayuno. La abuela
lo preparaba para todos, con la excepción de mi papá, que comía
temprano y salía para el trabajo. Yo empezaba el desayuno con 10
mis hermanos, pero ellos comían de prisa porque tenían que ir a la
escuela. Yo, en cambio, comía despacio, pensando en los juegos
que quería hacer durante el día. Después salía a la calle, donde me
encontraba con mis amiguitos. ¡Qué claro estaba el sol y qué
agradable el aire fresco en esos días! 15

Después del mediodía volvían mis hermanos y todos almorzábamos juntos. Nunca era preciso llamarme dos veces; los ejercicios y los juegos me daban una hambre de lobo y comía con gusto.
Por la tarde se repetían las mismas actividades que en la mañana.

Ahora ya ha cambiado todo. La familia vive en la ciudad y 20
todos estamos siempre ocupados. Mi padre es viejo y descansa.
Mi abuela hace ya mucho tiempo que pasó a mejor vida. Mis
hermanos tienen sus profesiones y sus cuidados, y viven en ciudades
tan lejanas que nunca los veo. Mi madre, ahora abuela, se ocupa
de mis niños. Y yo, por mi parte, pienso en aquellos días de 25
tiempo gramaticalmente imperfecto, pero perfectos en la realidad.

USEFUL EXPRESSIONS

de niño as a boy
se componía de consisted of
tiempo de la cosecha harvest time
cuidaba de mí took care of me
de prisa in a hurry
hambre de lobo hunger of a bear (*lit.* wolf)

hace mucho tiempo a long time ago
pasar a mejor vida to pass away, die
por mi parte on my part
pensar en to think of (*devote thought to*)

WORD REMINDER

extraño strange
felicidad *f.* happiness
habitación *f.* home, dwelling; room
imaginar to imagine
memoria memory
ocurrir to occur, happen
pasado past
pensamiento thought

primo cousin
quizá(s) perhaps
responder to answer
rico rich
sobrino nephew
todo el mundo everybody
triste sad
valer to be worth

CUESTIONARIO

Make up suitable questions for which the following statements are the answers:

1. Mi madre tenía el cuidado de los niños. 2. La abuela preparaba el desayuno para todo el mundo. 3. No éramos ricos, ni tampoco éramos pobres. 4. A todos les gusta más reír que estar tristes. 5. Mi pensamiento volvía siempre a los juegos de la calle. 6. Una aldea es más pequeña que una ciudad. 7. Claro que me gusta el recuerdo de la vida del campo. 8. Mis hermanos y mis primos comían siempre de prisa. 9. Después del mediodía siempre almorzábamos juntos. 10. Aquellos días eran perfectos en la realidad.

EJERCICIOS

I. PRÁCTICA ORAL

A. Substitute the words in parentheses when they are cued in:

1. Mi padre trabajaba y yo le ayudaba (mi hermano, mi madre, mis abuelos). 2. Nosotros siempre preparábamos la comida y la comíamos (yo, él, Vd., Vds.). 3. Ellos no siempre contestaban cuando los preguntaban (nosotros, tú, ella, Vds.). 4. Mi abuela descansaba cuando estaba cansada (mi abuelo, mis hermanos, el profesor). 5. Le veían cada día cuando salía (nos, los, la, me).

B. Complete the sentence every time a pronoun is cued in:

1. Preparaba el desayuno para (mí, Vd., él, ella). 2. El trabajo era demasiado para (nosotros, Vds., él, ti). 3. La abuela tenía el cuidado de (mí, él, nosotros, Vd.). 4. No quería vivir con (Vds., ellos, ellas, nosotros). 5. No pienso nunca en (ella, ellas, Vd., Vds.). 6. La habitación era demasiado pequeña para (ellos, nosotros, Vds., ellas). 7. La vida del campo no es extraña para (él, ti, nosotros, mí).

II. Make up original sentences using the following expressions:

1. de prisa. 2. de niños. 3. hambre de lobo. 4. con la excepción de. 5. pensar en. 6. al mediodía. 7. ocuparse de. 8. empezar a. 9. en cambio. 10. hace mucho tiempo.

III. Add an adjective or a descriptive phrase to each of the following words:

1. el pensamiento. 2. el abuelo. 3. un sobrino. 4. una habitación. 5. la felicidad. 6. una hambre. 7. la aldea. 8. el tiempo. 9. una calle. 10. el juego.

IV. Make up orally in Spanish a lengthy sentence based upon each of the following ideas:

1. Where I lived as a child. 2. The work that my father used to do. 3. My trip to school. 4. The games we used to play. 5. Exercise gave us a good appetite. 6. How we spent the afternoons. 7. How everything has changed now. 8. My brothers and sisters have professions. 9. The tasks assigned to my mother. 10. The good old days.

Floating gardens in Xochimilco, Mexico

LECCIÓN 12

Un viaje a Xochimilco

63. Reflexive Verbs

When a verb indicates an action which reverts to the subject, it is called reflexive. The action is made to revert to the subject by the use of reflexive pronouns, which are as follows:

me	myself	**nos**	ourselves
te	yourself (*fam.*)	**os**	yourselves (*fam.*)
se	himself, herself, itself, yourself	**se**	themselves, yourselves

The addition of reflexive pronouns does not change the original form of the verb, therefore all regular reflexive verbs will follow the model given here:

lavarse to wash (oneself)

	PRESENT	FUTURE	PRESENT PERFECT
yo	**me lavo**	**me lavaré**	**me he lavado**
tú	**te lavas**	**te lavarás**	**te has lavado**
él, ella, Vd.	**se lava**	**se lavará**	**se ha lavado**
nosotros, –as	**nos lavamos**	**nos lavaremos**	**nos hemos lavado**
vosotros, –as	**os laváis**	**os lavaréis**	**os habéis lavado**
ellos, ellas, Vds.	**se lavan**	**se lavarán**	**se han lavado**

64. Reflexive for the Passive

The third person of a verb can be used to express the general application of an action, with no one in particular as the subject. Such a statement takes the passive voice in English, or is expressed by a general subject such as *people, one, you*, etc. We have, for example, such general statements as *Spanish is spoken here* or *They sell flowers in that*

store, where the subject of the action can be anybody. Such statements are expressed in the reflexive form in Spanish. If the subject is
in the singular, the verb goes in the singular; if the subject is in the
plural, the verb goes in the plural. The first sentence would be **Aquí
se habla español,** with **habla** in the singular because **español** is in the
singular. The second sentence would be **Se venden flores en esa tienda,**
with **venden** in the plural because **flores** is really the subject in Spanish
and it is in the plural.

65. Preterite Tense: Formation and Uses

The preterite is another of the past tenses in Spanish. For regular verbs
it is formed by taking the stem and adding the endings given in this
table:

	hablar	**comer**	**vivir**
yo	**habl** –é	**com** –í	**viv** –í
tú	–aste	–iste	–iste
él, ella, Vd.	–ó	–ió	–ió
nosotros, –as	–amos	–imos	–imos
vosotros, –as	–asteis	–isteis	–isteis
ellos, ellas, Vds.	–aron	–ieron	–ieron

Notice that the second and third conjugations have the same endings.

The preterite is used to express a simple, completed action in past
time or an historical event. When we say: *He ate at the restaurant
around the corner,* the verb *ate* is in the preterite if we are referring to
a particular occasion, but it is in the imperfect if we mean that the
person ate there regularly. In Spanish the two tenses are not interchangeable; knowing which one to use in every case is an ability
acquired with observation.

Hicimos un viaje a Xochimilco.	We took a trip to Xochimilco (*that time*).
Vivíamos con una familia mexicana.	We lived with a Mexican family (*for a length of time*).

66. *Acabar de* + Infinitive

When an action has taken place a short while before the time mentioned
in the sentence, English uses the word *just* with the proper form of a

verb. In Spanish, if the sentence refers to present time, use the present of **acabar** + **de** + infinitive: **Acaban de llegar a esta ciudad,** *They have just arrived in this city.* If the sentence refers to some time in the past, use the imperfect of **acabar** + **de** + infinitive: **Acababan de llegar,** *They had just arrived.*

67. *Hacer* + Infinitive

When the subject of a sentence causes someone else to do an action, Spanish uses the verb **hacer** followed by an infinitive. Where we say *I'll have the boy bring the groceries*, we mean that someone else (*the boy*) is going to do the action (*bring the groceries*). Spanish says: **Haré traer los comestibles al muchacho.** The person who actually performs the action becomes the indirect object (notice **al muchacho).**

68. Some Common Verbs Irregular in the Preterite

hacer to do, make	**hice, hiciste, hizo, hicimos, hicisteis, hicieron**
ser to be *or* **ir** to go	**fui, fuiste, fue, fuimos, fuisteis, fueron**
estar to be	**estuve, estuviste, estuvo, estuvimos, estuvisteis, estuvieron**
decir to say	**dije, dijiste, dijo, dijimos, dijisteis, dijeron**

Un viaje a Xochimilco

En un día de verano mi esposa y yo hicimos un viaje a Xochimilco. Vivíamos aquel verano con una familia mexicana en un apartamento modernísimo en el Paseo de la Reforma, en la Ciudad de México. El viaje en automóvil nos llevó menos de una hora. Nuestra patrona nos había aconsejado ver este famoso 5 lugar, y fue tanto su entusiasmo que hicimos el viaje lo más pronto posible.

Xochimilco es sin duda una de las maravillas del mundo. La patrona nos dijo que antiguamente éste era un lago en que los
10 indios construyeron jardines en barcos, es decir jardines flotantes. Ahora los jardines no flotan más, y lo que se ve es la naturaleza en su forma más hermosa. Hay numerosos canales entre una vegetación tropical de árboles y flores. Hay barcas adornadas con flores que flotan silenciosamente sobre el espejo de las aguas, y de
15 vez en cuando las melodías de los remadores completan el encanto de la vista y la fragancia de este lugar. (Confieso que la fragancia es algo diferente a veces.)

Recuerdo que en uno de los canales más apartados de la muchedumbre de turistas, oímos una guitarra española, tocada divina-
20 mente. El canto de las más lindas melodías, el toque de los mejores nocturnos al piano, nada de lo que hay de más dulce puede compararse con las notas suaves y melodiosas de una guitarra que se oye de lejos sobre las tranquilas aguas de Xochimilco. (¡Me voy poniendo tan romántico!)

USEFUL EXPRESSIONS

hacer un viaje to take a trip
sin duda undoubtedly
algo diferente something else

lo que hay de más dulce the sweetest music
de lejos from afar, in the distance
me voy poniendo I am getting

WORD REMINDER

acostumbrarse to become accustomed
aprovechar to take advantage of
arriba up, above
asustarse to become frightened
costumbre *f.* custom
curiosidad *f.* curiosity
diapositiva lantern slide
distancia distance

dudar to doubt
durar to last
enamorarse de to fall in love with
figurarse to imagine
gozar to enjoy
interés *m.* interest
parar to stop
sombra shade

CONVERSACIÓN

1. Cuando Vd. vaya a México, ¿aprovechará la ocasión de visitar a Xochimilco? 2. ¿Qué distancia hay entre la Ciudad de México y Xochimilco si el viaje dura media hora? 3. ¿Qué construyeron allí los indios antiguamente? 4. ¿Tiene Vd. mucha curiosidad por conocer las costumbres de los indios? 5. ¿Puede uno acostumbrarse a vivir en las islas flotantes? 6. ¿Hay que levantarse temprano para gozar de la naturaleza? 7. Cuando Vd. piensa en Xochimilco, ¿se figura Vd. un lugar muy bonito? 8. Cuando Vd. viaja, ¿se enamora Vd. de los lugares que visita? 9. ¿Tiene Vd. mucho interés en oír una guitarra? 10. ¿Sabe Vd. si hay mucha fragancia en los canales de Xochimilco?

EJERCICIOS

I. DIÁLOGO. Present the following dialogue in class:

— ¿Estuvo Vd. alguna vez en México?
— Acabo de volver. Hice un viaje el mes pasado.
— ¿Fue Vd. en carro o en avión?
— Fui por[1] avión. El viaje en carro es maravilloso, pero toma demasiado tiempo.
— ¿Qué tal le pareció la Ciudad de México?
— Me pareció una de las ciudades más modernas de las Américas.
— ¿Hay edificios grandes como aquí en San Francisco?
— Hay edificios aun más grandes, más modernos, y más hermosos.
— ¿Hay parques y avenidas anchas? ¿Hay teatros y cines?
— Hay parques, avenidas bellas, teatros modernos, y cines elegantes.
— ¿Hay mucho tráfico, como aquí en los Estados Unidos?
— Hay muchos automóviles y gran tráfico. Hay de todo y se vive muy bien.
— Entonces tendré que hacer yo también un viaje.
— Hágalo pronto y Vd. se enamorará del lugar.

[1] In modern Spanish **por** is used as well as **en** with words like **avión, tren,** etc.

II. Repeat the following sentences, using the proper form and tense of
acabar (de):

1. Hemos visto este famoso lugar. 2. Nuestra patrona nos ha aconsejado. 3. Han llegado barcas adornadas con flores. 4. Los remadores
han cantado. 5. Ha llegado una muchedumbre de turistas. 6. Se
puso romántico. 7. Tocaba nocturnos al piano. 8. Los indios construyeron jardines en barcos. 9. La familia había hecho un viaje.
10. Habían oído una guitarra española.

III. Make up original sentences using both words in the same sentence:

1. verano, apartamento. 2. patrona, automóvil. 3. maravilla, jardín.
4. canal, flor. 5. muchedumbre, turista. 6. nota, guitarra. 7. nocturno, piano. 8. remador, encanto. 9. fragancia, vegetación. 10.
naturaleza, figurarse.

IV. Prepare at home and read fluently in Spanish:

1. He fell in love with the place when he saw it. 2. We stopped in the
shade for half an hour. 3. There are beautiful gardens above. 4. The
boats are decorated with flowers and they float through the canals.
5. They advised us to see Xochimilco. 6. A crowd of tourists visits
the place every summer. 7. He has just played some nocturnes on the
piano. 8. I remember the fragrance of the flowers. 9. Melodies are
heard in the distance. 10. Our landlady told us that Xochimilco is
one of the wonders of the world.

Columbus Circle, Mexico City, Mexico

LECCIÓN 13

Un viaje en automóvil

69. Radical-changing Verbs of the First Class

There are some verbs in which the vowel of the stem changes when it falls under the stress. You have observed already that the expression for *I want* is **quiero,** with **ie,** but the infinitive is **querer,** with **e.** You have noticed that *I meet* is **encuentro,** with **ue,** but the infinitive is **encontrar.** There is a group of verbs which has this type of irregularity, and we call this group radical-changing verbs.

If the vowel of the stem or radical vowel is **o** it becomes **ue** under the stress. If the radical vowel is **e** it becomes **ie.** Where the radical vowel does not fall under the stress, there is no change.

We are considering here only the verbs of the first and second conjugations. Of the tenses studied so far, the radical changes occur only in the first, second, third persons singular, and the third person plural of the present tense. The verbs that undergo these changes are indicated by **(ie)** and **(ue)** in the vocabulary.

	pensar (ie) to think		**entender (ie)** to understand
pienso	pensamos	**entiendo**	entendemos
piensas	pensáis	**entiendes**	entendéis
piensa	**piensan**	**entiende**	**entienden**

	contar (ue) to count		**volver (ue)** to return
cuento	contamos	**vuelvo**	volvemos
cuentas	contáis	**vuelves**	volvéis
cuenta	**cuentan**	**vuelve**	**vuelven**

95

There is one first conjugation verb in which the radical **u** changes
to **ue** under the stress:

jugar (ue) to play

juego	jugamos
juegas	jugáis
juega	**juegan**

Verbs of the third conjugation which undergo radical changes will
be treated in Section 118.

70. *Volver a* + Infinitive

When the subject repeats an action already performed, Spanish uses
the verb **volver a** + an infinitive.

Volvió a tocar la guitarra.   He played the guitar again.

71. Orthographic Changes in Verbs

A verb form in Spanish has a tendency to keep the same basic sounds
of the root regardless of changes in the ending. Since the consonant
letters **c** and **g** have two different sounds depending on the vowel
which follows, the spelling is changed in some forms. Changes made
in the writing of a word are called orthographic changes, and verbs
which undergo these changes are called orthographic-changing verbs.
A verb like **llegar,** for example, adds **u** after the **g** whenever the ending
begins with an **e.**

PRETERITE   **llegué,** llegaste, llegó, llegamos, llegasteis, llegaron

This change occurs also in the present subjunctive and in the imperative, as you will see later on.
    Likewise a verb ending in –**car** changes **c** to **qu** whenever the ending
begins with **e.** Take **buscar** *to seek, to look for:*

PRETERITE   **busqué,** buscaste, buscó, buscamos, buscasteis, buscaron

Verbs ending in –**zar** change the **z** to **c** before **e**. Take **empezar (ie)** *to begin:*

PRETERITE   **empecé,** empezaste, empezó, empezamos, empezasteis, empezaron

Verbs ending in –**ger** and –**gir** change the **g** to **j** when the ending begins with **a** or **o**. Take **coger** *to seize* or **dirigir** *to direct:*

PRES. IND.   **cojo,** coges, coge, cogemos, cogéis, cogen
PRES. IND.   **dirijo,** diriges, dirige, dirigimos, dirigís, dirigen

Un viaje en automóvil

El domingo hicimos un viaje en auto con algunos amigos. El padre de la familia con que pasamos el día es un amigo con quien trabajábamos en Nueva York hace dos años. Está aquí en México con su esposa y su hijo de nueve años. Vinieron a México el año pasado y van a quedarse aquí tres o cuatro años más. Él fue en- 5 viado por el gobierno de los Estados Unidos para estudiar los idiomas indios, de los que hay muchos en México.

La esposa preparó la merienda para la jira. Como parte princi- pal de la comida compró un pollo asado en una rotisería de las que hay aquí en México. El pollo era excelente. Además preparó una 10 ensalada de papas, pastas secas, jamón, ensalada de verduras, y muchas otras cosas. También llevó café caliente. Toda la comida era muy buena.

Nos habíamos dado cita para las once de la mañana en nuestro hotel. Pero hubo un larguísimo desfile en el Paseo de la Reforma, 15 y nuestro amigo tuvo que dar un gran rodeo antes de llegar a nuestro hotel, de manera que no llegó hasta las doce. Sin embargo nos quedó bastante tiempo para dar un buen paseo en auto.

Primero estuvimos en el Desierto de los Leones, que queda como a veinte y cinco kilómetros de la ciudad. Es éste un lugar 20

muy alto en las montañas, tan alto que el frío penetra en los huesos.
Si no me engaño, está el lugar a diez mil pies de altura. Allí se
encuentra uno de los más antiguos monasterios de este continente.
El gobierno mexicano lo cuida, y vale la pena visitarlo para
25 conocer bien la historia y las costumbres de este país.

Después del Desierto de los Leones, nos fuimos hasta Toluca,
atravesando un paisaje que es la octava maravilla del mundo. Las
altas montañas, con sus árboles verdes, sus piedras rojas y amari-
llas, sus arroyos de plata y sus nubes blancas en el azul cristalino
30 del cielo ofrecen a la vista una gama de maravillosos colores.

En el centro de este paisaje, bajo el sol caliente del mes de
noviembre, nos sentamos en el campo y tomamos la excelente
comida que la esposa de nuestro amigo nos había preparado. ¿Se
puede pasar un día más agradable?

USEFUL EXPRESSIONS

hace dos años two years ago
jira (campestre) picnic
ensalada de papas potato salad
pastas secas cookies
ensalada de verduras green salad
nos habíamos dado cita we had made
  an appointment
dar un rodeo to take a roundabout
  way

de manera que so that
dar un paseo en auto to go for a drive
**queda como a veinte y cinco kilóme-
  tros** is situated about twenty-five
  kilometers away
si no me engaño if I remember correctly (if I am not mistaken)
de altura in altitude

WORD REMINDER

chocolate *m.* chocolate
hoja leaf
nombrar to name
partir to leave
pintar to paint
planta plant
plato dish
plaza square

realidad *f.* reality
reconocer to recognize
rodear to surround
semejante similar
sencillo simple
vaso glass
vino wine
dar un paseo to take a walk

CONVERSACIÓN

1. ¿Le gusta a Vd. dar un paseo en auto los domingos? 2. ¿Con quiénes hicieron Vds. un viaje en auto por México? 3. ¿Cuándo vinieron a México los amigos? 4. ¿Está hermosa la naturaleza en un día claro? 5. ¿Le gusta a Vd. pintar plantas, árboles y algo semejante? 6. ¿Se usan muchos platos en una jira campestre? 7. ¿A qué hora partieron Vds. para la jira? 8. ¿Le gusta a Vd. tomar un vaso de vino con la comida? 9. ¿Puede Vd. nombrar algunas cosas que Vd. come en una jira campestre? 10. ¿Lleva Vd. un buen recuerdo del Desierto de los Leones? 11. ¿Cree Vd. que México sea un país encantador? 12. Cuando Vd. lee un libro sobre México, ¿reconoce Vd. todos los lugares que ha visto?

EJERCICIOS

I. Make up original sentences using both words in each one:

A. 1. jóvenes, juegan. 2. juega, tenis. 3. cierro, automóvil. 4. cierran, ventanas. 5. nos despertamos, nueve. 6. te despiertas, temprano. 7. empieza, desfile. 8. empiezan, paseo. 9. se recuerda, Xochimilco. 10. me recuerdo, jira.

B. 1. pagué, cuenta. 2. gocé, paseo. 3. empecé, viaje. 4. saqué, notas. 5. entregué, ejercicios. 6. busqué, jamón. 7. llegué, temprano. 8. cojo, tranvía. 9. dirijo, sinfonía. 10. llegaron, siete.

II. Ask questions containing the following expressions:

1. dar un paseo en auto. 2. darse cita. 3. ensalada de verduras. 4. ensalada de papas. 5. primero. 6. cinco mil pies de altura. 7. de manera que. 8. hace diez años. 9. jira campestre. 10. una gama de colores.

III. Use pronouns instead of the words in parentheses:

1. Compró (un pollo asado) en una rotisería. 2. Preparamos (la ensalada de papas) en pocos minutos. 3. Tomamos (la comida sencilla) y volvimos al auto. 4. Dijimos (a la esposa) que todo nos gustó.

5. Atraviesan (los campos). 6. Cuando oigo (una sinfonía) estoy muy contento. 7. Pinta (los arroyos) con muchos colores. 8. Encontramos (a nuestros amigos) en el Desierto de los Leones. 9. Veían (el cielo) de un color azul cristalino. 10. No vale la pena visitar (el monasterio).

IV. Describe briefly in Spanish the following subjects:

1. Unas montañas que Vd. ha visto. 2. Un paisaje cerca de su casa. 3. Una comida que su madre ha preparado. 4. Un paseo en auto. 5. Un día de invierno. 6. Una costumbre extraña. 7. Un cuadro pintoresco. 8. Una muchacha que Vd. conoce. 9. Su profesor de español. 10. Algunos trajes en la clase.

V. Translate at home and recite orally in class:

1. He crossed the country again in the summer. 2. The church is one of the oldest on the continent. 3. If I remember correctly, the place is not far from the city. 4. She is thinking of visiting Mexico, but she does not understand Spanish. 5. The young men play a great deal of tennis when they come out of school. 6. The stones were red, yellow, blue, and green. 7. I looked for ham, but I could not find it. 8. The cold penetrated the bones, but there were no clouds in the sky. 9. I am seizing the opportunity to write all my letters. 10. They meet at four every day and take chocolate.

MÉXICO,
LA AMÉRICA
CENTRAL Y
EL CARIBE

Océano Atlántico

San Juan
PUERTO RICO
HAITÍ REP. DOMINICANA
Santo
Domingo
Port au Prince
Kingston
JAMAICA
Mar Caribe
Santiago
★La Habana
CUBA
Canal de Panamá
Panamá
PANAMÁ
San José
COSTA RICA
NICARAGUA
Managua
HONDURAS
Tegucigalpa
HONDURAS BR.
Belice
Mérida
YUCATÁN
Sisal
Campeche
GUATEMALA
Guatemala
San Salvador
EL SALVADOR

Golfo de México

Veracruz
Puebla
Cuernavaca
Oaxaca
Orizaba
Tampico
Pachuca
Ixmiquilpan
Querétaro
México
Acapulco
San Luis Potosí
Durango
Guadalajara
Zacatecas
Saltillo
Monterrey
Nuevo Laredo
Laredo
SIERRA MADRE ORIENTAL

Chihuahua
SIERRA MADRE OCCIDENTAL
Ciudad Juárez
El Paso
Río Grande
Nogales
San Diego
La Paz
Golfo de California

Océano Pacífico

MÉXICO

Conversation in a Spanish café

LECCIÓN 14

El café

72. Present Subjunctive: Formation

The subjunctive expresses the relation of one action to another from the point of view of the mood implied, as for example doubt, uncertainty, or some other modification which the speaker wishes to express. The forms of the present subjunctive of regular verbs are as follows:

	I	*II*	*III*
yo	**hable**	**coma**	**viva**
tú	**hables**	**comas**	**vivas**
él, ella, Vd.	**hable**	**coma**	**viva**
nosotros, –as	**hablemos**	**comamos**	**vivamos**
vosotros, –as	**habléis**	**comáis**	**viváis**
ellos, ellas, Vds.	**hablen**	**coman**	**vivan**

Notice that the present subjunctive forms are similar for verbs of the second and third conjugations.

73. Uses of the Subjunctive

A. The present subjunctive is used in a main clause to express a command in the polite form **(Vd.).** The command forms for the regular verbs are:

hable Vd.	**coma Vd.**	**viva Vd.**
hablen Vds.	**coman Vds.**	**vivan Vds.**

Mencione el asunto.	Mention the subject.
Empiece (Vd.) la discusión.	Begin the discussion.

B. The subjunctive is used in dependent clauses after the following:

1. Expressions of wishing or desiring.

¿ Quiere Vd. que se discuta algo?   Do you want something to be discussed?

2. Verbs of requesting, urging, or commanding.

Dígale que ponga quince litros de gasolina.   Tell him to put in fifteen litres of gasoline.

3. Expressions of fear, doubt, or denial.

Dudo que sea cierto.   I doubt that it is certain.

4. Verbs of permitting or forbidding, approving or disapproving.

Nunca permitiré que él venga.   I shall never let him come.

5. After impersonal verbs or expressions.

Es necesario que le hable ahora mismo.   I must talk to him right now.

This is only a brief introduction to the uses of the subjunctive. The mood will be treated fully in Part II.

74. Present Subjunctive of *ser, tener, ir, venir*

Many verbs are irregular in the present subjunctive. Following are four of the most common ones:

ser	sea, seas, sea, seamos, seáis, sean
tener	tenga, tengas, tenga, tengamos, tengáis, tengan
ir	vaya, vayas, vaya, vayamos, vayáis, vayan
venir	venga, vengas, venga, vengamos, vengáis, vengan

75. Idiomatic Present and Idiomatic Past

An action begun in the past and continuing in the present is expressed by the present tense in Spanish. When we say *He has been here for two hours* we mean that the person came two hours ago and is still here. Spanish says **Hace dos horas que está aquí,** using the present

tense **está** for the English *has been*. To express this type of sentence
you use **hace** + the expression of time + the present tense of the verb.
In asking a question you use **¿desde cuándo?** + the present tense in
Spanish, corresponding to *how long* + the present perfect in English.
This is known as the idiomatic present.

When referring to the past, an action begun prior to the main action
and continued up to the time of the main action takes the imperfect
tense in Spanish. When we say *He had been watching the game for an
hour when the ball hit him*, we mean that the action of *watching* had
begun prior to the *hitting* and was still going on when the ball hit.
Spanish says: **Hacía una hora que miraba el juego cuando la pelota le
pegó,** using the imperfect **miraba** where English used the pluperfect
had been watching. In this type of sentence Spanish uses **hacía** + the
expression of time + the imperfect tense. This is known as the idiomatic past.

El café

El café es el centro de la vida social madrileña para los hombres,
como lo es en todo país mediterráneo. Los Estados Unidos no
tienen nada semejante porque la gente va con demasiada prisa.
Aquí los hombres no tienen ningún sitio donde puedan reunirse
y discutir los problemas de la vida. Si van a un «bar», cada dis- 5
cusión se hace confusa después de varios vasos de cerveza. En los
círculos o clubes sociales, la mayoría de los socios quieren que
todos callen, o por lo menos quieren que se olviden los problemas
del mundo mientras están en el círculo.

Por el contrario, en los cafés madrileños se reunen los letrados, 10
poetas, artistas, músicos, y diplomáticos de la capital. El café que
se consume en un mes no sería bastante para el comercio de un
solo día en una tienda americana. Pero las discusiones de un solo
día son más de lo que se discutiría en un mes en un bar americano.
En cada grupo hay generalmente uno o dos hombres distinguidos 15

que llevan la discusión. Los otros se agrupan alrededor de ellos,
apoyando sus opiniones o añadiendo algo por su parte. Así se
forman las escuelas de pintura, de crítica, de poesía, y todo lo que
hay de más intelectual o estético en la vida española.

20   Para entender la vida española hay que comprender la idea del
café. En un café todos son iguales, el rico y el pobre, el artista y el
barbero, el profesor y el alumno. Nadie tiene pretensiones sociales.
¿Quiere Vd. que se discuta el comunismo? Mencione el asunto en
un café. ¿Quiere Vd. discutir la bomba atómica? Pronta discusión.
25 ¿Quiere Vd. saber algo sobre el arte moderno? Empiece la discusión de algún cuadro. ¿Duda Vd. que el mundo sea redondo, a
pesar de los viajes lunares? Alguién en el café apoyará su opinión.

El café es, sin duda, el verdadero centro de la vida social de
España. ¡Lástima que por lo general los extranjeros no tomen
30 parte en las discusiones!

USEFUL EXPRESSIONS

nada semejante nothing like it
se hace muy confusa becomes very
  confused
llevan la discusión carry on the discussion

alrededor de around
por su parte on their part
tomar parte to take part
bomba atómica atomic bomb
viaje lunar moon trip

WORD REMINDER

(el) agua *f.* water
(el) alma *f.* soul
  asistir (a) to be present at
  caballero man, gentleman
  equivocarse to be mistaken
  hielo ice
  jerez *m.* sherry
  libertad *f.* liberty
  luz *f.* light

merecer to deserve
nacer to be born
pastel *m.* tart, pie
paz *f.* peace
sabroso tasty
sorpresa surprise
teatro theater
recibir to receive
voz *f.* voice

CONVERSACIÓN

1. ¿Qué sitio es el centro de la vida social madrileña? 2. ¿Hay algo semejante al café en los Estados Unidos? 3. ¿Hay muchos caballeros que se reunen en un café? 4. ¿Se puede discutir cualquier asunto, como por ejemplo la paz o la libertad? 5. Cuando Vd. entra en una discusión, ¿es posible que Vd. se equivoque? 6. En los círculos americanos, ¿se bebe mucho café? 7. ¿Sabe Vd. si están abiertos los cafés de noche después del teatro? 8. ¿En qué país va con demasiada prisa la gente? 9. ¿Se discute bien la política después de varios vasos de cerveza? 10. ¿Hay muchos letrados, artistas y diplomáticos en su ciudad? 11. ¿Qué importancia tiene el café en la vida española? 12. ¿Toman parte los extranjeros en la vida social del café?

EJERCICIOS

I. PRÁCTICA ORAL. Cue-in Exercise.

1. Dudo que él venga (ellos vengan, él comprenda, ella cante bien). 2. Queremos que Vd. vaya con él (ella vaya, tú vayas, ellos vayan). 3. Es preciso que Vd. comprenda (nosotros comprendamos, yo estudie mucho, él haga el viaje). 4. No permitiremos que Vd. mencione el asunto (ellos mencionen, vosotros mencionéis, ella mencione). 5. Es importante que él quede satisfecho (ella quede, yo quede, nosotros quedemos). 6. ¿Tiene Vd. miedo de que él hable demasiado? (ellos hablen, yo hable, nosotros hablemos). 7. Comience Vd. la discusión (empiece Vd., termine Vd., continúe Vd.). 8. Les enviaremos un recuerdo, pero nada más (les daremos, le enviaré, te dejaré). 9. Te escribiré una carta cuando viaje por España (le escribiré, les enviaré, te escribiremos). 10. El comercio no les gusta a las mujeres (nos gusta a nosotros, le gusta a Vd., me gusta a mí).

II. Make up sentences containing the following groups of words:

1. el barbero, el profesor, rico. 2. el artista, el músico, pobre. 3. el poeta, el diplomático, la discusión. 4. apoyar, añadir, los otros. 5. la mayoría, el socio, callar. 6. cerveza, vaso, beber. 7. redondo, el mundo, dudar. 8. semejante, parecido, decir. 9. el papel, tomar, distinguido. 10. la prisa, existir, el café.

III. Complete the following sentences in any meaningful way:

1. Hace tres días que . . .   2. Hace quince años que . . .   3. Hacía mucho tiempo que . . .   4. Hacía dos meses que . . .   5. ¿Cuánto tiempo hace que . . .?   6. Hacía varios años que . . .   7. ¿Quieren Vds. que . . .?   8. Por el contrario, yo creo que . . .   9. El centro de la vida social . . .   10. Las escuelas de crítica . . .

IV. Prepare at home and read fluently in Spanish:

1. In every Mediterranean country people sit at a café.   2. If you are too much in a hurry, why don't you come tomorrow?   3. I like to forget the problems of the world.   4. He will never permit his wife to go (that his wife should go) into a café.   5. Everything which is of interest comes from these discussions.   6. Who has more social ambitions, the husband or the wife?   7. If I am not mistaken, politics and beer do not mix well.   8. What a surprise she gave us when she arrived! 9. Are there many distinguished men in your social group?   10. The lunar trips leave no doubt that the world is round.

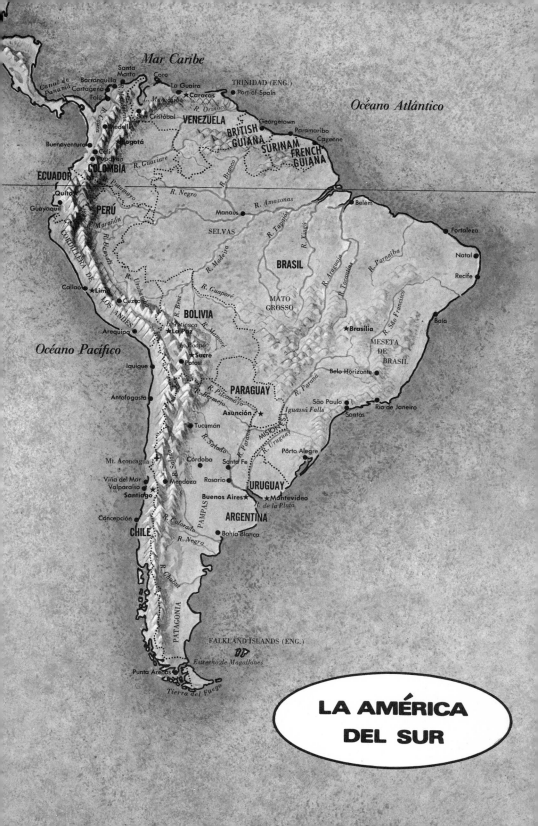

Avenida Libertador, Caracas, Venezuela

PART TWO

Inca ruins, Machu Picchu, Peru

LECCIÓN 15

Los incas del Perú

Review

*Articles, 2, 4. Gender of Nouns, 1. Plural of Nouns, 3.
Present Tense of the Indicative, 6.*

76. Gender of Nouns (Cont.)

Nouns ending in **–dad, –tad, –tud, –ción,** and **–ie** generally refer to abstract words and are feminine.

la verdad the truth   **la serie** the series   **la calvicie** the baldness

77. Plural of Indefinite Articles

The indefinite articles **un** and **una** have plural forms: **unos** and **unas,** meaning *some.* The words **algunos** and **algunas** also mean *some,* but **algunos** and **algunas** mean *some* in the sense of a *few,* whereas **unos** and **unas** simply denote an indefinite number.

Hay unos templos aztecas.   There are some Aztec temples.
Algunas civilizaciones son muy viejas. Some (A few) civilizations are very old.

78. Neuter Articles and Pronouns

Besides the articles **el** and **la** there is a neuter article **lo,** used only in the singular. **Lo** with a masculine adjective denotes the essence of a quality. **Lo bueno** means *that which is good*; **lo hermoso** means *that which is beautiful*.

Remember that the demonstratives have a neuter form to designate an indefinite object or idea. **Esto** refers to something near the speaker or that which the speaker is saying. **Eso** refers to something near the person addressed or what someone has just said. **Aquello** refers to some remote object or idea. Of these three demonstratives **eso** is the most common.

Eso nos han dejado los incas. That is what the Incas have left us.

79. Uses of *¿no es verdad?* and *¿verdad?*

When a question is raised over a statement, English uses such expressions as *aren't you? doesn't he?* etc. In Spanish such rhetorical questions are asked by the expression **¿no es verdad?** or simply **¿verdad?,** which consequently has many English equivalents.

Las ruinas de Machu-Picchu son majestuosas, ¿no es verdad? The ruins of Machu-Picchu are majestic, aren't they?

80. Uses of *por* and *para*

Por and **para** are frequently translated alike in English, thus making it difficult to tell which one to use in Spanish. Since **por** and **para** each have their definite uses and cannot be interchanged, it is important to know these uses.

para	*por*
1. is used before the person for whom something is intended. **Esta carta no es para mí.** This letter is not for me.	1. expresses *for whose sake* or *on whose account* an action is done. **Por el amor de Dios . . .** For the love of Heaven . . .
2. expresses the purpose for which an action is done. **para defender la cultura** in order to defend the culture.	2. expresses the agent by whom an action is performed. **producidos por estas civilizaciones** produced by these civilizations.

3. expresses the limit of time in the future by which an action is to be accomplished.

Lean el capítulo para mañana. Read the chapter for tomorrow.

4. With the verb **estar, para** expresses *to be about to* in the sense of being ready.

Estoy para salir. I'm about to leave.

5. **Para** expresses destination or limit of space.

Salgo para Boston. I am leaving for Boston.

3. expresses the extent of time during which an action is done.

Vd. ha leído por tres horas. You have read for three hours.

4. With the verb **estar, por** expresses the intention to perform an action.

Estaba por confesarlo, pero se calló. He was about (inclined) to admit it, but he kept quiet.

5. **Por** frequently expresses the means of transportation.

Le gusta viajar por avión. She likes to travel by plane.

6. **Por** is used to express the amount for which something is bought or sold.

Lo compraron por seis pesos. They bought it for six pesos.

7. **Por** is the only one of the two which means *through* or *per*.

Se distingue por su color. It is distinguished through its color.
El diez por ciento. Ten per cent.

Los incas del Perú

— Rosa, ¿ha visto Vd. la película sobre el Perú? Debe de ser muy interesante para Vd.

— Sí, Josefa, la encontré excelente. Para mí las viejas civilizaciones son tal vez más importantes que las presentes. Y el Perú ha

5 sido quizás la tierra americana donde se han desarrollado más culturas.

— Yo sabía algo de los incas, pero en la película se hablaba de culturas anteriores.

— Es que la cultura incaica florecía a la llegada de los españoles
10 a este continente, pero hay varias civilizaciones importantes anteriores a la incaica.

— ¿Cómo sabemos todo esto?

— Hoy se están llevando a cabo numerosas investigaciones para descifrar el misterio de las civilizaciones preincaicas. Estas
15 civilizaciones nos han dejado enormes monumentos de piedra; unos son templos, como el de la famosa puerta monolítica; otros son fortalezas construidas con enormes bloques de piedra, como la de Sacsahuaman, cerca de Cuzco.

— ¿Vd. aprendió todo esto en la película?

20   — No, Josefa; ya sabe Vd. que tengo gran interés por estas cosas. En la costa peruana florecieron ñumerosas culturas. Al norte floreció la de Chimú, que nos ha dejado las ruinas de Chanchán, y una muralla tan impresionante como la de la China. Esta muralla subía de la costa por las montañas de los Andes, para
25 defender la cultura de Chimú de los ataques de los pueblos del sur.

— Ahora comprendo lo que decía la película sobre la muralla. Y el tesoro de Paracas, ¿qué es eso?

— El tesoro de Paracas es algo tan importante como los mejores tesoros de Egipto. En la costa sur del Perú floreció la cultura de
30 los nazcas. Allá, en la península de Paracas, se ha encontrado una serie de momias de personajes de la realeza, con sus joyas y tejidos. ¡Imagínese la importancia de ese tesoro!

— ¿Se han descubierto otros objetos importantes?

— Tantos que en el Museo Antropológico de Lima se encuentra
35 una gran riqueza de objetos artísticos de la más alta calidad. Hay objetos de cerámica, tejidos, dibujos y esculturas maravillosas.

— Entonces, ¿cuál es la importancia de los incas?

— Los incas, más modernos que estas otras civilizaciones, heredaron su cultura, y con su genio político y militar construyeron
40 grandes obras públicas. Construyeron, por ejemplo, las dos grandes carreteras que cruzaban de un extremo a otro el imperio

incaico. Añadieron nuevas fortalezas, que se pueden ver todavía
en numerosas partes de lo que fue su gran imperio. Las majestuosas ruinas de Machu-Picchu son unos de los monumentos más
notables de la civilización incaica. En la agricultura, construyeron 45
los campos formados por terrazas escalonadas. Los incas dieron
una cierta unidad a las culturas anteriores y sobre ellas levantaron
su imperio, el más poderoso de América.

EXPRESIONES ÚTILES

debe de ser it must be
a la llegada upon the arrival
se están llevando a cabo there are
being carried on
bloques de piedra stone blocks
tan impresionante como as impressive
as

personajes de la realeza people of
royal blood
de la más alta calidad of the highest
quality
grandes obras públicas great public
works
terrazas escalonadas scaled terraces

RESUMEN PRÁCTICO

1. En el Perú se han desarrollado varias culturas anteriores a la de
los incas.
2. A la llegada de los españoles en el Perú florecía la cultura incaica.
3. Las investigaciones que se están llevando a cabo revelan el misterio
de esas culturas anteriores.
4. Entre los monumentos preincaicos hay una puerta monolítica y
una fortaleza de bloques de piedra.
5. La muralla y las ruinas de Chanchán pertenecen a la cultura de
Chimú.
6. La muralla servía para defender esta cultura de los ataques de los
pueblos del sur.
7. Las momias de los personajes de la realeza llevan joyas y tejidos
maravillosos.
8. Los incas, con su genio político y militar, construyeron grandes
obras públicas.

9. Los campos formados por terrazas escalonadas ayudaron mucho la agricultura.
10. Las ruinas de Machu-Picchu son un notable monumento de la cultura incaica.

EJERCICIOS

I. CONVERSACIÓN

1. ¿En qué país americano se han desarrollado quizás más culturas?
2. ¿Qué civilización florecía a la llegada de los españoles en el Perú?
3. ¿Qué revelan las investigaciones que se están llevando a cabo?
4. Mencione Vd. algunos de los monumentos que quedan. 5. ¿Qué monumentos nos ha dejado la cultura de Chimú? 6. ¿Para qué servía la muralla de Chanchán? 7. ¿Qué llevan las momias del tesoro de Paracas? 8. ¿Qué museo importante hay en Lima? 9. ¿Qué genio peculiar tenían los incas y qué hicieron con ese genio? 10. ¿Dónde se encuentran algunos de los monumentos más notables de la civilización incaica?

II. Ponga Vd. las oraciones siguientes en el plural:

1. Una civilización se considera más importante que la otra. 2. El poeta escribió un poema sobre el planeta. 3. Tome Vd. el tranvía para visitar el pueblo. 4. El guía me enseñó el tesoro que está en el museo. 5. Es un tejido que no se encuentra en otra ciudad. 6. La carretera moderna cruza el país. 7. El monumento más notable de aquella civilización es la muralla. 8. El campo cultivado se encuentra en la terraza escalonada.

III. Lea Vd. las siguientes oraciones con la forma debida, **por** o **para**:

1. Esa película no es (por, para) Vd. No le gustará. 2. (Por, Para) mi parte, no encuentro interesante este asunto. 3. Construyeron la muralla (por, para) defenderse. 4. Estaba (por, para) confesar y las palabras no le salían. 5. Estaban (por, para) salir en ese momento. 6. Le gusta viajar (por, para) avión más que (por, para) tren. 7. Las

fortalezas fueron construidas (por, para) los incas (por, para) defender su cultura. 8. Los monumentos producidos (por, para) esta civilización fueron enormes.

IV. Tradúzcanse[1] *oralmente las frases siguientes:*

1. It must be an interesting film. 2. Perhaps it is more important. 3. Something about the Incas. 4. Upon the arrival of the Spaniards. 5. Investigations are being carried on. 6. Enormous stone blocks. 7. As impressive as the one in China. 8. What has been discovered? 9. On the scaled terraces. 10. They can still be seen.

V. Complétense las oraciones siguientes:

1. Para mí las viejas civilizaciones ... 2. La cultura incaica florecía ... 3. Con los bloques de piedra se construyeron ... 4. Esta muralla subía de la costa ... 5. Los Andes son las montañas más ... 6. El tesoro de Paracas es ... 7. En el Museo Antropológico de Lima se encuentra ... 8. Las dos carreteras cruzaban ...

VI. Escríbase en español:

1. The interesting fact is that there were some important civilizations before the Incas. 2. It is difficult to know the age of these monuments. 3. It isn't easy to decipher the mystery of these cultures, is it? 4. There are some fortresses constructed with stone blocks, but they are not many. 5. Many objects of art belong to civilizations prior to the powerful Inca empire. 6. We are about to study the genius of the Incas; through this genius they became so important. 7. Some day we'll be able to visit all those ruins, won't we? 8. The wall is very impressive, but it is only one of the many monuments of that civilization.

---

[1] The reflexive form of the present subjunctive may be used to give general directions to a group in an impersonal way. (Cf. Section 125.)

LECCIÓN 16

El turismo en México

Review

Personal Pronouns, 17. Direct Object Pronouns, 37–40.
Indirect Object Pronouns, 51. Present of ser, 14; estar, 19.
Uses of ser and estar, 20.

81. Double Object Pronouns

When two object pronouns, one direct and one indirect, both depend on the same verb, the indirect comes before the direct, regardless of whether the pronouns are before or after the verb. If both pronouns are third person, the indirect object pronoun becomes **se,** whether it is singular or plural.

Me lo escribieron ayer.	They wrote it to me yesterday.
Se lo dejo todo a Vd.	I leave it all to you.

82. Table of Personal Pronouns

SUBJECT	DIRECT OBJECT	INDIRECT OBJECT	OBJECT OF PREPOSITION
yo	**me**	**me**	**mí**
tú	**te**	**te**	**ti**
él	**le, lo**	**le**	**él**
ella	**la**	**le**	**ella**
Vd.	**le, lo, la**	**le**	**Vd.**
nosotros, –as	**nos**	**nos**	**nosotros, –as**
vosotros, –as	**os**	**os**	**vosotros, –as**
ellos	**los**	**les**	**ellos**
ellas	**las**	**les**	**ellas**
Vds.	**los, las**	**les**	**Vds.**

Silversmiths at work in Taxco, Mexico

Plaza del Palacio de Gobierno, Veracruz, México

83. Position of Object Pronouns

We learned in Section 38 that personal object pronouns, whether direct, indirect, or reflexive, come before the verb, except with an infinitive, a command form in the affirmative, or a participle used independently. An object pronoun depending on a present participle used alone is attached to it and an accent is placed on the next to the last vowel of the original form of the participle.

> **olvidándose muchas veces**   forgetting frequently

If the participle is used with the verb **estar** in a progressive form, the object pronoun may come either before **estar,** or after the participle and attached to it.

> **Lo estamos estudiando** *or* **Estamos estudiándolo.**   We are studying it.

When an infinitive is complementary to another verb, the object pronouns may come either before both verbs or be attached to the infinitive.

No lo puedo comprender *or* **No puedo**   I cannot understand it.
comprenderlo.

When two pronouns are attached to an infinitive, the infinitive bears a written accent on the last vowel of the original form. When two pronouns are attached to a present participle, the participle bears a written accent on the next to the last vowel of the original form. In other words infinitives or participles do not change their stress when pronouns are attached.

¡Dime, María!   Tell me, Mary.
Quiere explicárselo a Vd.   He wants to explain it to you.
Explicándomelo, se olvidó de lo que   While explaining it to me, he forgot
decía.   what he was saying.

84. Negative Commands

When the command forms are in the negative, the present subjunctive is used instead of the imperative for the familiar forms. Polite command forms are in the subjunctive both for the affirmative and the negative.

I	*II*	*III*
habla — no hables	come — no comas	abre — no abras
hablad — no habléis	comed — no comáis	abrid — no abráis

With negative command forms, object pronouns are placed before the verb.

¡No me diga!   Don't tell me!

NOTE: Remember that when the reflexive pronoun **os** is attached to the affirmative second plural command form, the **-d** of the verb is dropped (except in **idos).**

¡ Callaos todos, niños!   All of you children be quiet!

85. ¿ Dónde? and ¿ A dónde (Adónde) ?

The English interrogative *where* may mean either *in what place* or *to what place.* When it means *in what place,* Spanish uses **dónde.** When it means *to what place,* Spanish uses **a dónde (adónde).**

¿A dónde vas, amigo mío?   Where are you going, my friend?

El turismo en México

PEDRO. ¡Dime, María! ¿Por qué prefieres viajar por México y no por otro país?

MARÍA. Porque a México se puede ir en cualquier mes, y con gran facilidad. No hay estación alguna preferida. En todas las estaciones el país es muy atractivo, por la bondad de su clima y el 5 encanto de la naturaleza. Se puede ir allá en auto, o tomar el avión y llegar en pocas horas.

JOSÉ. ¿No hace demasiado calor en el verano?

MARÍA. No, querido, no hace demasiado calor, y llueve regular- mente. El clima es templado y agradable, salvo en las tierras bajas 10 tropicales. En Oaxaca y Cuernavaca, no lejos de la capital misma, hay una eterna primavera, principalmente en esta última ciudad, donde van a pasar sus fines de semana numerosas familias mexi- canas.

15   PEDRO. Pero a mí me gusta el verano y el calor.

MARÍA. Pues, puedes ir muy bien en el verano. Uno de los encantos que tiene México es que allí la naturaleza es rica en contrastes. Para los aficionados a los deportes de mar, a la pesca o a la natación, están las soleadas costas de Acapulco, con sus playas

20 que superan en belleza natural a las más famosas del mundo. Y para los que prefieren el golf, no hay nada mejor.

JOSÉ. Las playas os las dejo a vosotros. Para mí sólo hay las montañas para pasar las vacaciones.

MARÍA. Bueno, si eres amante de las excursiones por las mon-

25 tañas, tienes a tu disposición una larga lista de ellas, desde las gigantescas de Popocatépetl e Ixtaccíhuatl, cerca de la capital, hasta la de Orizaba, que se alza solitaria y majestuosa entre Puebla y Veracruz.

PEDRO. Yo, en cambio, prefiero la vida urbana.

30 MARÍA. Para los que prefieren la vida urbana, el principal encanto del país reside exactamente en las ciudades: en las viejas coloniales como Puebla, Guadalajara, Taxco y Morelia; y en las más modernas, como Cuernavaca y gran parte de la misma capital de México, en donde se juntan armoniosamente lo antiguo

35 con lo moderno. La capital es ahora una de las ciudades más grandes y modernas del Nuevo Mundo, rivalizando con las mayores de los Estados Unidos en su carácter cosmopolita e internacional.

En estas encantadoras ciudades se conserva el tesoro más rico

40 del arte colonial español en América. No hay nación alguna de este continente que cuente con tantos y tan notables monumentos como México. Las grandes catedrales de México, como la de su capital, la de Taxco y la de Puebla, no tienen igual en América. En cualquiera de las viejas ciudades coloniales, por pequeña que

45 sea, hay una enorme riqueza artística. Su arte no es una simple copia del español o del europeo, sino que se distingue por su originalidad. En estos monumentos se notan las mismas ideas artísticas que animan los viejos monumentos mayas y aztecas, que son orgullo de la nación mexicana.

50   JOSÉ. María, ¿dónde aprendiste tantas cosas de México?

MARÍA. Primero aprendí el idioma español, como lo hacéis

vosotros. Después recibí una beca, que me permitió pasar dos años en la Universidad de México, que es una maravilla de modernidad. Tú sabes que en México hay muchos programas de estudio.

PEDRO. Si yo pido una beca, ¿me la darán?

MARÍA. Nadie puede garantírtela, pero claro que si no la pides, nadie te la presentará. ¡Pídela en seguida, y espera el resultado!

EXPRESIONES ÚTILES

no hay estación alguna preferida there is no favorite season
ir en auto to drive (to a place)
el fin de semana the weekend
los deportes de mar the sea sports
amante de lover of, fond of
gran parte de most of, a large part of

contar con to have, possess
por pequeña que sea no matter how small (it) is
se distingue por (it) is distinguished by
una maravilla de modernidad a paragon of modernity

RESUMEN PRÁCTICO

1. En México no hay estación alguna preferida; todas son casi iguales.
2. En los lugares altos hay una eterna primavera, y en los bajos hace mucho calor.
3. En México hay deportes de mar, pesca, natación, y excursiones por las montañas.
4. Las ciudades coloniales conservan el tesoro más rico del arte colonial español en América.
5. Entre las viejas ciudades coloniales son notables Puebla, Guadalajara, Taxco y Morelia.
6. Tal vez las catedrales más conocidas son la de Ciudad de México, la de Taxco, y la de Puebla.
7. En los monumentos modernos se notan las ideas artísticas que animan los viejos monumentos mayas y aztecas.
8. Por pequeña que sea una ciudad colonial mexicana, siempre tiene algo de interés artístico.

EJERCICIOS

I. CONVERSACIÓN

1. ¿Cuál es la estación preferida para los que van a México? 2. ¿Por qué es muy atractivo el país? 3. ¿Cree Vd. que hay mucho turismo en México? 4. ¿Qué ciudades tienen eterna primavera? 5. ¿Dónde pasan sus fines de semana numerosas familias mexicanas? 6. ¿Es Vd. aficionado a los deportes de montaña? 7. ¿Se puede nadar mucho cuando hay buenas playas? 8. ¿Le gustarían a Vd. las soleadas costas de Acapulco? 9. Mencione Vd. a lo menos tres altas montañas de México. 10. ¿En qué se distingue el arte de México del de España? 11. ¿Sabe Vd. dónde se pueden encontrar monumentos de arte mexicano? 12. ¿Es importante la capital de México como gran ciudad?

II. Pónganse las oraciones siguientes en forma negativa:

1. ¡Pasa tus vacaciones en Puerto Rico! 2. ¡Dígame Vd. la razón! 3. ¡Vayan Vds. a Europa! 4. ¡Déjame aconsejarte! 5. ¡Visite Vd. a Guadalajara! 6. ¡Mire Vd. los encantos! 7. ¡Míralo bien! 8. ¡Estudiad el arte mexicano! 9. ¡Estúdielo Vd. en México! 10. ¡Permítame Vd. acompañarle!

III. Tradúzcanse oralmente las frases siguientes:

1. They gave me a scholarship. 2. They gave it to me. 3. We tell her the story. 4. We tell it to her. 5. I look at the cathedrals. 6. I look at them. 7. They showed him the street. 8. They showed it to him. 9. Tell me what you know. 10. Don't tell me all.

IV. Complétese el párrafo siguiente con las palabras **por** o **para**:

—— comprender la cultura mexicana hay que viajar —— este país. Cuando se pasa —— aquellas calles viejas se comprende el encanto de la vida colonial, que floreció hace varios siglos y todavía sigue floreciendo. Todo allí se distingue —— su originalidad y —— el arte exquisito que representa. No siempre se puede viajar —— tren —— llegar a los lugares más pintorescos. —— pequeñas que sean las ciudades todavía siguen siendo muy interesantes. —— mí no hay nada más hermoso que un pueblecito en las montañas donde la vida sigue igual —— generaciones.

V. Prepárense oralmente una o dos oraciones sobre cada uno de los temas siguientes:

1. Lo antiguo y lo moderno en la Ciudad de México. 2. La riqueza artística de las ciudades coloniales. 3. El arte colonial mexicano. 4. Los viejos monumentos mayas y aztecas. 5. Cuernavaca como ciudad donde se pasan las vacaciones. 6. Las playas de Acapulco. 7. Las montañas gigantescas de Popocatépetl e Ixtaccíhuatl. 8. El clima de México.

VI. Escríbase en español:

1. Many people go to Europe, but it's easier to go to Mexico because one can drive. 2. All the seasons of the year are attractive on account of the mildness of the climate. 3. I like to spend the summer in any place except in the low, tropical lands. 4. Where do you go if you are fond of mountain excursions? 5. Those who prefer city life find these colonial cities enchanting. 6. No matter how small it is, each city has many artistic treasures. 7. I hope the university will give you a scholarship to study in Mexico. 8. Then you'll understand the charm which Mexico has for all those who visit the country.

Antonio Buero Vallejo, Spanish playwright

Teatro de la Zarzuela, Madrid, Spain

LECCIÓN 17

El teatro en España

Review

Present of Some Irregular Verbs, 26, 32.
Future Tense, 34. Conditional, 60.

86. Present Participle and Progressive Construction

The present participle of all verbs ends in **–ndo.** For regular verbs it is formed by taking the stem and adding **–ando** for the first conjugation and **–iendo** for the second and third.

> **hablar — hablando   comer — comiendo   vivir — viviendo**

For irregular verbs the present participle is formed frequently in the same way. Remember, however, that an unstressed **i** between two vowels becomes **y** and therefore the present participle will frequently end in **–yendo.**

> **leer — leyendo   creer — creyendo   construir — construyendo**

Moreover, for radical-changing verbs of the second and third class the stem vowel changes from **o** to **u** or from **e** to **i** in the present participle, as you will see in Section 118.

> **morir — muriendo   sentir — sintiendo**

The present participle is used with the verb **estar** to form progressive constructions, denoting that an action is or was actually in progress.

> **Estamos leyendo.**   We are reading (*right now*).
> **Estaba comiendo.**   He was eating (*right then*).

87. Present Participle Alone

The present participle in an independent construction may express *the means by which* an action is done.

Pensando se llega a una conclusión.   By thinking one comes to a conclusion.

88. Infinitive After Prepositions

After prepositions in Spanish the infinitive is the only form of the verb which is normally used.

Mucho gusto en verle.   Very pleased to see you.

After the preposition **en** the present participle is used by some authors for special effects, but this is rather rare.

89. Compound Prepositions

Some phrases are used as prepositions. Following is a list of the most common of these prepositional phrases or compound prepositions.

acerca de about	**fuera de** outside of
antes de before	**a fuerza de** through, by means of
al cabo de after, at the end of	**gracias a** thanks to
a causa de on account of	**junto a** next to
cerca de near	**al lado de** by the side of, beside
en cuanto a as for	**a lo largo de** alongside
debajo de under	**lejos de** far from
delante de in front of	**en lugar de** instead of
dentro de inside of, within	**en medio de** in the midst of
después de after	**por medio de** by means of
detrás de behind	**a pesar de** in spite of
(por) encima de on top of, above	**a propósito de** as regards
en frente de opposite	**a través de** across
frente a facing	**en vez de** instead of

90. *Hay que, tener que,* and *deber*

Obligation is expressed in three ways:

Hay que refers to a general obligation. **Hay que trabajar** means *There is work to be done.* The implication is: *One must work.*

Tener que refers to a definite personal obligation to do something in particular. **Tiene que escuchar al profesor** means *He has to listen to the professor.*

Deber refers to a personal obligation as a sense of duty. **Vd. no debe pensar así** means *You ought not to think that way.*

91. *Haber de* and *deber de*

Haber de followed by an infinitive denotes an action which is expected or supposed to take place.

> **Ha de llover mucho.**   It is going (expected) to rain a great deal.

Deber de followed by an infinitive denotes an assumption; it is usually translated by *must.*

> **Debe de ser mi primo.**   He must be my cousin.

El teatro en España

El teatro es uno de los grandes espectáculos nacionales de España, unido a su tradición, a su historia, religión y costumbres sociales. Como teatro nacional, espejo de su vida y cultura, el teatro español nació en Madrid, cuando en 1560 se trasladó a aquel lugar la capital de España; y con Madrid fue creciendo, 5 como si los dos fueran inseparables.

El creador del teatro nacional fue Lope de Vega (1562–1635), autor de más de mil comedias y autos religiosos. Lope de Vega llevó a su teatro la historia de España — principalmente la que quedó viva en la tradición de los romances o baladas que cantaba 10 el pueblo español. Sus comedias de capa y espada, donde la realidad se combina con la poesía y la ilusión, entusiasmaban a todas las clases sociales que llenaban los corrales, como entonces se

llamaban los primeros teatros. El teatro nacional, que con Lope
15 de Vega y Tirso de Molina (1584–1648) fue eminentemente popular por sus temas y espíritu, se hizo más cortesano y aristocrático,
más simbólico y poético, con don Pedro Calderón de la Barca
(1600–1681).

Entre las formas más bellas del teatro español del Siglo de Oro
20 figuran los autos sacramentales, composiciones dramáticas ale-
góricas, en una jornada, que, por referirse generalmente al misterio
de la comunión, se representaban el día de Corpus Christi en las
plazas públicas. En Madrid primero se representaban en la Plaza
de Oriente, delante de la familia real; luego en la del Consejo de
25 Castilla, que era entonces el gobierno de España; y más tarde en la
del Ayuntamiento de la villa, que es todavía hoy uno de los rincones
más atractivos del viejo Madrid. Para la representación de los
autos sacramentales se utilizaban los mismos carros que servían
para trasladarlos de un lugar a otro. Así podían verlos los vecinos
30 y sus invitados desde sus balcones, y la muchedumbre desde la
plaza.

Hoy como ayer, y como en el Siglo de Oro, el teatro sigue
siendo el espectáculo por excelencia de Madrid y una de las principales atracciones que tiene la ciudad para los miles de forasteros
35 que la visitan. El día del estreno de una obra dramática es uno de
los más importantes de la vida madrileña, desde el otoño hasta
fines de la primavera, que es la época de la temporada teatral. En
el verano las compañías más notables hacen un recorrido por
provincias, sobre todo por el norte, donde hace más fresco, para
40 presentar las últimas novedades del arte dramático.

El teatro español tiene un lugar tan importante en las letras de
España que dos de los tres premios Nobel recibidos por españoles
han correspondido a dos dramaturgos: José Echegaray (1832–
1916), autor de *El gran Galeoto*; y Jacinto Benavente (1866–1954),
45 conocido por *Los intereses creados* y *La malquerida*.

En el siglo XX hubo un renacimiento del teatro. Los principales dramaturgos, anteriores a la guerra civil, son Ramón María
del Valle-Inclán (1866–1936), creador del teatro expresionista de
los esperpentos, con *Los cuernos de Don Friolera*; Federico García
50 Lorca (1898–1936), autor de tensas tragedias, como *La casa de*

Bernarda Alba, estrenada, después de su muerte, en Buenos Aires; y Alejandro Casona (1903–1966), cuya obra más famosa, *La dama del alba*, fue compuesta en el exilio en la Argentina. El dramaturgo más notable de la postguerra civil es Antonio Buero Vallejo, autor de *Historia de una escalera*. 55

EXPRESIONES ÚTILES

unido a together with
fue creciendo kept on growing
comedia de capa y espada cloak and dagger drama
en una jornada (in) one act
por referirse because they referred
hoy como ayer today as in the past
por excelencia par excellence

el día del estreno the opening day
miles de forasteros thousands of outsiders
a fines de la primavera toward the end of spring
hacen un recorrido (they) make a tour
las letras de España the literature of Spain

RESUMEN PRÁCTICO

1. El teatro español nació en Madrid, cuando la capital de España se trasladó allí de Toledo.
2. Lope de Vega fue autor de más de mil autos religiosos y comedias.
3. En las comedias de capa y espada la realidad se combina con la ilusión.
4. Los tres grandes dramaturgos del Siglo de Oro fueron Lope de Vega, Tirso de Molina y Calderón de la Barca.
5. Hoy como ayer el teatro sigue siendo una de las principales atracciones de la capital.
6. En el verano las compañías teatrales hacen un recorrido por provincias para presentar las últimas novedades.
7. Los dos dramaturgos españoles que ganaron el premio Nobel fueron José Echegaray y Jacinto Benavente.
8. Otros famosos dramaturgos modernos son Ramón María del Valle-Inclán, Federico García Lorca, Alejandro Casona, y Antonio Buero Vallejo.

EJERCICIOS

I. CONVERSACIÓN

1. ¿En qué época nació el teatro nacional en España? 2. ¿En qué ciudad ha ido creciendo el teatro nacional? 3. ¿Nacieron muchos grandes dramaturgos en la capital de España? 4. ¿De dónde tomaba sus temas Lope de Vega? 5. ¿Cómo se llamaban los primeros teatros? 6. ¿Cuáles son los tres grandes dramaturgos del Siglo de Oro? 7. ¿A qué tema se refieren generalmente los autos sacramentales? 8. ¿Cómo se trasladaban de un lugar a otro los autos sacramentales? 9. ¿Es importante el día del estreno de una obra dramática? 10. ¿Cuánto tiempo dura la temporada teatral? 11. ¿A dónde van las compañías teatrales en el verano? 12. ¿Qué dramaturgos del siglo veinte conoce Vd.?

II. Empléense participios presentes en lugar de las formas inglesas:

1. By transferring la capital a Madrid, esta ciudad llegó a ser más y más importante. 2. By bringing a su teatro la historia de España, Lope de Vega creó el teatro nacional. 3. El imperio se extendía por todo el continente, enclosing en él muchos países. 4. By constructing una muralla, podían defender los pueblos. 5. By remaining en Madrid podrá Vd. ver muchos espectáculos. 6. By making un recorrido por provincias, pueden presentar las últimas novedades del arte dramático. 7. Estamos studying los grandes dramaturgos españoles.

III. Háganse oraciones completas con las frases siguientes:

A. 1. a causa de. 2. lejos de. 3. por medio de. 4. delante de. 5. por encima de. 6. a pesar de. 7. a propósito de. 8. en lugar de. 9. al cabo de. 10. gracias a.

B. 1. el creador del teatro en España. 2. la tradición de los romances. 3. los primeros teatros. 4. las plazas públicas. 5. la familia real. 6. de un lugar a otro. 7. los miles de forasteros. 8. las últimas novedades.

IV. Tradúzcase oralmente al español:

1. The capital kept on growing. 2. Author of a hundred comedies. 3. Everything combines with reality. 4. They are writing letters.

5. One must read in order to understand. 6. He has to visit the city.
7. Must you go? 8. The play (comedia) must be good. 9. They trans-
ferred from one place to another. 10. The most representative per-
sonalities.

*V. Prepárese oralmente una oración sobre cada uno de los temas
siguientes:*

1. El premio Nobel. 2. Federico García Lorca. 3. El día del estreno.
4. Las comedias de capa y espada. 5. Los autos sacramentales. 6.
Las atracciones de Madrid. 7. La plaza pública. 8. Los grandes
dramaturgos.

VI. Escríbase en español:

1. We are reading about the Spanish theater and its history. 2. The
capital has always been the home of the great dramatists. 3. Who is
the author of more than a thousand plays and religious autos? 4. They
are dramatic compositions in one act and refer to the mystery of
Communion. 5. We have to attend a performance tonight, but there
is a crowd in the square. 6. Do you think that the opening day is the
best one for a play? 7. By writing good plays he won the Nobel
prize in literature. 8. Today as in the past good plays can make all
social classes enthusiastic.

LECCIÓN 18

El paisaje de Chile

Review

Interrogative words, 33. Relative Pronouns, 57.
Past Tenses, 52–56.

92. Relative Adjectives, Pronouns, and Adverbs

The complete list of the common relative adjectives, pronouns, and adverbs is as follows:

que who, whom, which, that
quien, quienes (he) who, (they) who, whom (*when preceded by a preposition*)
el cual, la cual, los cuales, las cuales who, whom, which; **lo cual** which
el que, la que, los que, las que who, whom, which, (he, they, the one, the ones) who; **lo que** what, that which
cuanto, –a, –os, –as all that (those), as much (many) as
cuyo, –a, –os, –as whose
cuando (*relative adverb*) when
donde (*relative adverb*) where

The most common relative pronoun is **que,** which refers to both persons and things and may be used as the subject or the object of a verb. As object of a preposition **que** refers to things only.

El hombre que viaja aprende mucho.	The man who travels learns a great deal.
El país que visitamos es atractivo.	The country we are visiting is attractive.

137

After prepositions **que** may be used to refer to things only.

El gusto con que trabaja.   The pleasure with which he works.

The relative pronoun **quien,** with its plural form **quienes,** refers to persons only. It is used most commonly after prepositions. **Quien** is generally used when the clause is parenthetical and adds an extra rather than an essential meaning.

Roberto es un amigo del señor Rosas,   Robert is a friend of Mr. Rosas, who
quien vive en Córdoba.   lives in Córdoba.
BUT: **El señor que vive en Córdoba es**   The man who lives in Córdoba is a
un amigo de Roberto.   friend of Robert.

Quien is frequently used with the meaning of *he who.*

Quien no trabaja no come.   He who does not work does not eat.

El que in all its forms is also used with the meaning of *he who* or *the one who.*

Los que llegan temprano encuentran   Those who get there early find places.
sitios.

El cual in all its forms is used as the relative pronoun whenever there is a chance for confusion. It is commonly used after **por** and **sin.**

Pasé la tarde con el primo de mi es-   I spent the afternoon with my wife's
posa, el cual es pintor.   cousin, who is a painter.

Lo cual or **lo que** refers to an indefinite antecedent or to an idea. **Lo cual** generally refers to something more specific than **lo que.**

Chile está entre el mar y las montañas,   Chile is between the mountains and
por lo cual es muy estrecho.   the sea, for which reason it is very
                     narrow.
No nos gusta lo que hacen.   We don't like what (that which) they
                     are doing.

Cuanto in all its forms has the force of *all that (which), as much* (or *as many) as possible.* It may be used either as an adjective or as a pronoun.

Le gusta ver cuantas películas puede.   He likes to see as many films as
                     possible.

Cuyo in all its forms is a relative pronoun denoting possession. It comes directly before the noun it modifies and agrees with it in gender and number.

Hay regiones cuyas montañas son altísimas.	There are regions whose mountains are extremely high.

Donde or **cuando,** alone or preceded by a preposition, may be used as relative adverbs.

El lugar para donde ella se marcha es bonito.	The place where she is going is beautiful.

93. Interrogative Adjectives and Pronouns

In the use of interrogatives, we learned in Section 33 that the adjectives and pronouns are **qué, quién (quiénes), cuál (cuáles)** and **cuánto (cuánta, cuántos, cuántas).**

¿Quién? (¿Quiénes?) is a pronoun and refers only to persons.

¿Quién fue el creador del teatro nacional?	Who was the creator of the national theater?

¿Qué? is both a pronoun and an adjective. As a pronoun it refers to things and is invariable in form. It may be used either as the subject or the object of a verb or a preposition.

¿Qué le gusta a Vd.?	What do you like?
¿Qué ha preguntado?	What did he ask?
¿En qué piensa ella?	What is she thinking about?

¿Qué? with **ser** calls for an explanation or a definition.

¿Qué es una costa accidentada?	What is an indented coast?

¿Qué? as an adjective carries the meaning of *what one(s)* or *which one(s)*.

¿Qué papeles desea Vd.?	What papers do you want?

¿Cuál? (¿Cuáles?) distinguishes between several persons or objects already known and simply asks *which one(s)*.

¿Cuáles son los productos principales?	Which are the main products?
¿Cuáles quiere Vd.?	Which ones do you want?

¿**Cuánto** (–**a**, –**os**, –**as**)? may be used either as an adjective or as a pronoun. As an adjective it agrees with the word it modifies, which comes right after it. As a pronoun it agrees with the person or object referred to.

¿**Cuántos picos hay?**	How many peaks are there?
¿**Cuánto me cuesta?**	How much will it cost me?

The normal way to express *whose?* is by the expression ¿**de quién?** or ¿**de quiénes?** followed by the verb **ser.**

¿**De quién es esa tragedia?**	Whose is that tragedy?

El paisaje de Chile

La naturaleza americana supera a la europea en la magnitud de sus proporciones. En el continente americano, tan rico y variado en paisajes de gran belleza, Chile ocupa uno de los primeros lugares por los contrastes que presentan sus tierras. Si al norte de
5 Chile está el desierto de Atacama, donde apenas llueve, en el extremo sur de la tierra chilena hay regiones de incesante lluvia, y otras cuyas montañas están cubiertas eternamente de nieve. En el este de Chile se alzan majestuosos los Andes — que le sirven de frontera natural con la Argentina — cuyos picos más altos, el
10 Aconcagua y el Tupungato, son los mayores colosos naturales del continente americano. Mientras que en el occidente, frente a la larga costa chilena, se abre inmenso e infinito el Océano Pacífico.
Chile es una larga y estrecha faja de tierra emparedada entre el mar infinito y las montañas gigantescas de los Andes, entre el
15 desierto, donde el agua es un tesoro, y las regiones de las lluvias y nieves permanentes, donde la humedad es muy alta. Pocos países pueden compararse con Chile en la majestad de sus montañas, que, a pesar de su grandeza, son accesibles al hombre y atraen todos los años numerosos turistas que van a practicar en ellas los
20 deportes de invierno. Su costa accidentada está adornada con

miles de islas e islotes, que hacen de ella un paraíso para los pintores de marinas. La costa chilena, de más de dos mil kilómetros,
es como un mosaico de todas las costas de la tierra: unas veces
seca, otras húmeda, cubierta de vegetación hasta la misma orilla;
unas veces suave y otras terriblemente escarpada.   25

La zona central de Chile, donde está situada su capital, Santiago, es una de las regiones más agradables del continente. De
carácter muy semejante a los valles de Sacramento y San Joaquín
en California, es una tierra de tipo mediterráneo, donde crecen
la vid y el olivo y se cultivan las plantas más variadas. Esta 30
zona central chilena es una de las más ricas huertas de América,
cuyos productos — y de una manera señalada el vino y las frutas
— no sólo sirven para su propia población, sino que se exportan
a otras naciones de América y aun de Europa.

Por eso no es extraño que tierra tan preciada fuera tenazmente 35
defendida, más que ninguna otra de la América del Sur, por sus
pobladores primitivos, los indomables araucanos. La conquista de
Chile, comenzada por Almagro y Valdivia a mediados del siglo
XVI, no se terminó hasta el XIX, por los propios chilenos, después
de que el país se emancipó de España.   40

Los chilenos no se han dejado vencer jamás por las dificultades
de sus montañas, de sus desiertos, de los volcanes, o de las nieves
perpetuas; ni tampoco se han dormido en los laureles de los encantos de sus regiones centrales; sino que, enérgicos y emprende-
dores, allá en el extremo sur de América, han logrado formar, en 45
medio de esa naturaleza tan majestuosa, una de las civilizaciones
americanas más estimables.

EXPRESIONES ÚTILES

regiones de incesante lluvia regions of
  endless rains
los deportes de invierno winter sports
miles de islas e islotes thousands of
  islands and islets
de una manera señalada in a particular
  manner, in a special way

no se han dejado vencer they have not
  given in
no se han dormido en los laureles they
  have not rested on their laurels
sino que but rather
han logrado formar have succeeded
  in forming

RESUMEN PRÁCTICO

1. En Chile hay un extenso desierto al norte y tierras de incesante lluvia en el sur.
2. En las regiones de nieve permanente hay muchos deportes de invierno.
3. La costa accidentada de Chile tiene miles de islas e islotes grandes y pequeños.
4. Dos de los productos más famosos de Chile son el vino y las frutas.
5. La zona central de Chile es de carácter semejante a los valles de Sacramento y San Joaquín en California.
6. Los chilenos nunca se han dejado vencer por las dificultades de cualquier tipo.
7. Todos los pueblos del mundo pueden lograr formar una civilización estimable si se empeñan.

EJERCICIOS

I. CONVERSACIÓN

1. ¿Qué tipo de tierras se encuentra en Chile? 2. ¿Para qué le sirven los Andes a Chile? 3. ¿Cuáles son los mayores picos del continente americano? 4. ¿Son accesibles al hombre las montañas de Chile? 5. ¿Hay buena vegetación en toda la costa chilena? 6. ¿Qué es una costa escarpada? 7. ¿Es fértil la zona central de Chile? 8. ¿Tenemos valles semejantes en los Estados Unidos? 9. ¿Cuáles son los productos principales de las huertas de esta zona central? 10. ¿Cuáles fueron los pobladores primitivos de Chile? 11. ¿Cuándo empezó la conquista de Chile? 12. ¿Se han dejado vencer por alguna cosa los chilenos?

II. Llénense los espacios siguientes con un pronombre o adverbio relativo:

1. Hay regiones en — las montañas están siempre cubiertas de nieve. 2. Las montañas — picos son muy altos se llaman los Andes. 3. Chile es un país — costa accidentada está adornada con miles de islas e islotes. 4. Es una rica huerta — productos se exportan a otras naciones.

5. Los chilenos, de — hablamos, son un pueblo muy enérgico. 6. No sabemos las regiones — son más fértiles. 7. No comprendo — Vd. acaba de decirme. 8. El lugar — vivían los araucanos es una tierra muy preciada.

III. Dense los interrogativos necesarios en las oraciones siguientes:

1. ¿—— son los mayores colosos naturales del continente americano? 2. ¿—— pintores de marinas conoce Vd.? 3. ¿—— regiones prefiere Vd., las de lluvia o las regiones secas? 4. ¿—— fueron los pobladores primitivos de Chile? 5. ¿—— comenzaron la conquista de Chile? 6. ¿—— océano está frente a la costa chilena? 7. ¿ —— países pueden compararse con Chile? 8. ¿—— kilómetros tiene la costa chilena? 9. ¿—— está situada la capital de Chile? 10. ¿—— son los productos principales de Chile?

IV. Tradúzcase oralmente al español:

1. The magnitude of its proportions. 2. One of the foremost places. 3. In the extreme south. 4. It is eternally covered. 5. Opposite the coast. 6. A long and narrow strip. 7. The snowy regions. 8. Thousands of islets. 9. A painter of seascapes. 10. The vine and the olive tree grow. 11. For that reason. 12. The perpetual snows.

V. Háganse oraciones completas con las frases siguientes:

1. el país que. 2. los pintores de quienes. 3. el mar por el cual. 4. las tierras en las cuales. 5. quien mucho habla. 6. cuanto puedo. 7. las regiones cuyas montañas. 8. la costa cuya orilla. 9. lo que me gusta. 10. el que menos piensa.

VI. Para escribir en español:

1. It is a continent which is rich and varied in its landscape. 2. The desert is a place where it never rains. 3. The majestic peaks of the Andes are the biggest colossi of the American continents. 4. The immense and infinite ocean is to the west of the long, narrow strip of land. 5. There are thousands of islands and the coast is like a mosaic. 6. Is the region very pleasant where the capital is situated? 7. There are many plants whose fruits are exported to other nations. 8. The difficulties of the mountains, deserts, and volcanoes have never been too great for the Chileans.

Gardens in Aranjuez, Spain

LECCIÓN 19

Los jardines de España

Review

Possession, 42. Possessive Adjectives, 43.
*Possessive Pronouns, 44. The Verb **gustar**, 45.*

94. Possessives

Remember that in Spanish the possessive agrees with the thing possessed and not with the possessor. In order to know which form of the possessive pronoun to use, think back to the person or object referred to by the pronoun and use the same gender and number.

Vd. tiene sus guantes, pero ¿dónde están los míos?　You have your gloves, but where are mine?

　　When the possessive adjective comes after the noun for the sake of emphasis, the form is the same as that of the pronoun, but without the article.

Son amigos suyos, me parece.　They are friends of his, it seems to me.

　　When the possessive pronoun is used as a predicate nominative after the verb **ser,** the definite article is omitted.

La falta es tuya.　The mistake is yours.

　　With the verb **ser** the article is used with the possessive if the speaker wishes to distinguish between various objects of the same group.

No sé cuál es el suyo, pero éste es el mío.　I don't know which one is yours, but this one is mine.

145

The article without the possessive pronoun is used to show possession in the third person if the speaker wants to be clear about the possessor and if another possessive has just been mentioned.

La familia nuestra y la de Vds.	Our family and yours (*pl.*).
La casa nuestra y la de nuestro abuelo.	Our house and that of our grandfather.

95. Verbs Reflexive in Spanish but Not in English

Frequently there are verbs which are reflexive in form in one language but not in another. Just about every verb which is reflexive in English is also reflexive in Spanish, but not the other way around. Following is a list of common verbs which are reflexive in Spanish, but not in English.

acercarse (a) to draw near
acostarse to go to bed
acostumbrarse (a) to become accustomed
alegrarse (de) to be glad
apoderarse (de) to take possession of
arrepentirse (de) to repent
asustarse (de) to get frightened
atreverse (a) to dare
bañarse to take a bath
burlarse (de) to make fun of
caerse to fall down
callarse to be quiet
cansarse (de) to get tired of
casarse to get married
convencerse (de) to become convinced (about)
despedirse (de) to say good-bye to, take leave of
despertarse to wake up
detenerse to stop
divertirse to have a good time
dormirse to fall asleep

enamorarse (de) to fall in love with
encontrarse (con) to meet
enterarse (de) to find out
equivocarse to be mistaken
hacerse to become
irse to go away
levantarse to get up
ocuparse (de) to attend to
olvidarse (de) to forget
pararse to stop
pasearse to take a walk
ponerse to become, put on
preocuparse (por) to worry (about)
quedarse to remain
quejarse (de) to complain (about)
quitarse to take off
reírse (de) to laugh (at)
retirarse to withdraw
sentarse to sit down
sentirse to feel
vestirse to get dressed
volverse to become

96. Reciprocal Verbs

A reflexive may be used in a reciprocal sense, that is, the action is exchanged between various members of the subject. Such a use of a reflexive verb is translated by the expression *each other*.

Se quieren mucho.	They love each other a great deal.

Los jardines de España

No hay en Europa país alguno que tenga un suelo y un clima tan variado como el de España: la costa atlántica húmeda y templada; la meseta castellana alta y fría; las montañas majestuosas en el norte, centro y sur; y la costa mediterránea seca y agradable. En estas tierras crecen las más bellas flores, que sirven para ador- ₅ nar los patios, las ventanas y las terrazas de sus casas, y aun el tocado de sus mujeres, prestándoles singular gracia y encanto.

En país de suelo y clima tan variados se han desarrollado diferentes tipos de jardines a lo largo de la historia. El más antiguo de ellos se formó en Andalucía, cultivado por los árabes. El jardín ₁₀ andaluz más famoso fue el de Medina Azahara, levantado en el siglo X por los califas cordobeses en la Sierra de Córdoba, en donde se pueden ver aún hoy sus ruinas. Del jardín andaluz nos quedan el Generalife y los cármenes de Granada, el Alcázar y algunos patios de Sevilla. En África, por donde se extendió, se conserva ₁₅ uno de gran belleza en el Cairo. En nuestro siglo, con motivo de la Exposición de Sevilla, se construyó en esta ciudad andaluza el Parque de María Luisa, que es la versión moderna de este tipo de jardín.

Un tanto más moderno es el jardín del Levante español, de ₂₀ Baleares, Valencia y Cataluña, formado bajo la influencia de Italia, en el Renacimiento. En él los árboles, principalmente los frutales, se combinan con las flores en una mayor proporción que en el andaluz.

Un poco más tarde se crearon en el centro de España los jardines ₂₅ reales, que representaban el refinamiento de la vida cortesana española. El más viejo es el de Aranjuez, al sur de la capital de España. Madrid se fue rodeando de una serie de palacios con hermosos parques y jardines: el Escorial, el Pardo, la Zarzuela, la Granja y Montefrío. Y en el propio Madrid, además de su palacio, ₃₀ se levantaron el Palacete de la Moncloa y el jardín del Buen Retiro, hoy parque municipal de la capital española. El jardin real, más frío y serio que el andaluz y el levantino, es una síntesis de las varias culturas de España.

El último jardín español es el de los pazos gallegos, que tiene ₃₅

algo del carácter exuberante de la vegetación de la tierra. El jardín gallego es, en realidad, más parque que jardín; y recuerda en España los jardines ingleses que se pusieron de moda en Europa con el romanticismo hacia la mitad del siglo XIX. En el valle del
40 Río Ulla, que separa las provincias de La Coruña y Pontevedra, se pueden ver los maravillosos pazos de Oca y Santa Cruz de Ribadulla, joyas de los jardines gallegos.

EXPRESIONES ÚTILES

a lo largo de la historia in the course of history
con motivo de for the purpose of
un tanto más moderno somewhat more modern
se fue rodeando de became encircled with

además de besides
algo del carácter something of the character
se pusieron de moda became fashionable

RESUMEN PRÁCTICO

1. No hay país alguno en Europa que tenga un clima y un suelo tan variado como el de España.
2. A lo largo de la historia se han desarrollado varios tipos de jardines en España.
3. Entre los jardines más famosos figuran el jardín andaluz, el de Levante, el real, y el de los pazos gallegos.
4. Algunos jardines se desarrollaron con motivo de una exposición u[1] otro acontecimiento histórico.
5. En los jardines españoles se combinan los árboles frutales con las flores.
6. El jardín real representa una síntesis de las varias culturas de España.
7. Madrid se fue rodeando de una serie de palacios con jardines que son todavía hermosísimos.

[1] Before a word beginning with an **o**, the Spanish word **o** meaning *or* becomes **u**.

EJERCICIOS

I. CONVERSACIÓN

1. Mencione Vd. algunos de los varios climas de España. 2. ¿Cómo son sus costas? 3. ¿Para qué sirven sus flores? 4. ¿Se han desarrollado muchos tipos de jardines en ese clima tan variado? 5. Mencione Vd. algunos de los jardines andaluces que nos quedan. 6. ¿Qué es el Parque de María Luisa? 7. ¿En qué época se formó el jardín del Levante español? 8. En este tipo de jardín, ¿qué árboles se combinan con las flores? 9. ¿Qué parques cerca de Madrid tienen jardines famosos? 10. ¿Cómo se llama el parque municipal de la capital española? 11. ¿Qué representa el jardín real? 12. ¿Qué carácter tiene el jardín de los pazos gallegos?

II. Tradúzcase oralmente al español:

1. Their climate and ours. 2. Its coast and ours. 3. My flowers and yours. 4. Your terraces and theirs. 5. Her garden and his. 6. Its ruins. 7. In our century. 8. Our city and his. 9. Their beautiful palaces. 11. Your beauty and hers. 12. The garden whose origin. 13. The ladies whose hairdo. 14. The country whose culture.

III. Háganse oraciones que tengan las tres palabras en cada una:

1. dormirse, cuando, leer. 2. olvidarse, origen, país. 3. mujer, casarse, gustar. 4. irse, país, otro. 5. acostumbrarse, vida, española. 6. equivocarse, hablar, historia. 7. árabes, apoderarse, ciudad. 8. bañarse, gustar, océano. 9. despedirse, amigos, salir. 10. encontrarse, hablar, enamorarse.

IV. Complétense oralmente las oraciones siguientes:

1. Me gustan las casas cuyas terrazas . . . 2. Es un país cuyas costas son . . . 3. Éste es un jardín andaluz . . . 4. El Parque de María Luisa es la versión moderna . . . 5. Los jardines reales representaban . . . 6. El jardín gallego es en realidad . . . 7. España se enorgullece de que pocos jardines . . . 8. No se olvide Vd. de describir . . . 9. Nunca me canso de oír . . . 10. Para nosotros no sería difícil acostumbrarnos . . .

V. Háganse preguntas a otros estudiantes usando las palabras siguientes:

1. una península. 2. el jardín inglés. 3. el romanticismo. 4. de moda. 5. una síntesis. 6. el refinamiento. 7. los árabes. 8. la costa mediterránea. 9. con motivo de. 10. a lo largo de la historia. 11. un hermoso tocado. 12. la exposición. 13. los árboles frutales.

VI. Escríbase en español:

1. There is no country in America that has gardens like those of Spain. 2. The Atlantic coast, the Castilian plateau, the mountains and the Mediterranean coast all form part of the Iberian peninsula. 3. Flowers in the hairdo lend grace and charm to the Spanish women. 4. One Andalusian garden can still be seen in ruins in the Córdoba mountain range. 5. The patios and the terraces are somewhat more modern than those of Granada. 6. I like its parks because there are fruit trees and flowers. 7. Where can the Spaniards find palaces and gardens that are equal to their own? 8. Spanish culture is a synthesis of Arabic and European elements.

Gardens of the Royal Palace, La Granja de San Idelfonso (Segovia), Spain

Some of the 6000 oil well derricks in Lake Maracaibo, Venezuela

LECCIÓN 20

El petróleo y Venezuela

Review

*Adjectives, 11–13. Present Indicative of Some
Irregular Verbs, 41, 46.*

97. Position of Adjectives

Descriptive adjectives normally follow the noun in Spanish. Other
adjectives which normally follow the noun are adjectives of nationality,
adjectives modified by adverbs, and past participles used as adjectives.

Alberto es un artista francés.	Albert is a French artist.
Encontramos la ventana abierta.	We found the window open.
motores movidos a petróleo	motors run by gasoline (gasoline engines)

Adjectives denoting an inherent quality, or adjectives used figura-
tively precede the noun.

la blanca nieve	the white snow
las altas sierras	the high sierras
el insigne emancipador	the distinguished emancipator

Numerals and possessive, demonstrative, indefinite, and interrogative
adjectives normally precede the noun.

algunos compañeros	some companions
numerosos emigrantes europeos	numerous European emigrants
¿Qué productos vienen de Chile?	What products come from Chile?

153

Some adjectives may be used either before or after the noun. When used before the noun they express inherent qualities or are used in a figurative sense. When used after the noun they have a literal meaning.

el tremendo desarrollo	the tremendous (very great) development
Hubo un ruido tremendo.	There was a tremendous (frightening) noise.
la pobre nación	the poor (unfortunate) nation
una nación pobre	a poor (poverty-stricken) nation

98. Formation of Adverbs

In English adverbs are generally formed by adding –*ly* to the adjective. In Spanish they are formed by adding –**mente** to the feminine of the adjective. When the feminine of the adjective has a written accent, it is retained when forming the adverb.

tranquilo, tranquilamente   **fácil, fácilmente**

When two or more adverbs ending in –**mente** are used consecutively, the ending –**mente** is used only on the last one. The others remain in the form of the feminine of the adjective.

Habló fácil y claramente.   He spoke easily and clearly.

99. Common Words Used as Adjectives and Adverbs

There are some words which may be used either as adjectives or as adverbs. As adjectives they vary in gender and number; as adverbs they are invariable. Some of the common ones are: **mucho, tanto, demasiado, poco.**

Algunos creen que hay demasiada gente.	Some think there are too many people.
Come demasiado.	He eats too much.

100. Comparison of Adjectives

In order to form the comparative of an adjective, **más** is placed before the word.

moderno   **más moderno**

To form the superlative, the definite article is used before the word **más** or before the noun which is followed by **más.**

hermoso	**más hermoso**	**el más hermoso (la más hermosa)**

Venezuela es el país más próspero de la América del Sur.   Venezuela is the most prosperous country in South America.

The comparative of an adjective may be of a lesser rather than a greater degree. In this case the word **menos** is used instead of **más.**

costoso	**menos costoso**	**el menos costoso (la menos costosa)**

Compré el menos costoso de los coches.   I bought the least expensive of the cars.

101. Comparison of Adverbs

The comparative of an adverb is formed like the comparative of an adjective, by placing **más** before the adverb. The superlative is formed by **más** before the adverb, which is preceded by the article **lo** and may be followed by **posible** or an equivalent.

pronto	**más pronto**	**lo más pronto posible**

Salieron lo más pronto posible.   They left as soon as possible.
Salieron lo más pronto que pudieron.   They left as soon as they could.

102. Irregular Comparison of Adjectives and Adverbs

Following are the common adjectives with irregular comparison:

bueno good	**mejor** better	**el (la) mejor** the best
grande large	**mayor** larger	**el (la) mayor** the largest
malo bad	**peor** worse	**el (la) peor** the worst
pequeño small	**menor** smaller	**el (la) menor** the smallest

Encontró mejor colocación.   He found a better position.

Some common adverbs likewise have an irregular comparison:

bien well	**mejor** better	**(lo) mejor (posible)** best
mal bad	**peor** worse	**(lo) peor (posible)** worst
poco little	**menos** less	**(lo) menos (posible)** least
mucho much	**más** more	**(lo) más (posible)** most

The words **mayor** and **menor** indicate relative importance or refer to age (older and younger); when referring to size, Spanish uses **más grande** and **más pequeño.**

Su hermano mayor es más pequeño que él.	His older brother is smaller than he is.

103. Comparison of Equality

When a comparison shows equality, Spanish uses **tanto** or **tan** (adjective or adverb) followed by **como,** meaning *as . . . as.*

En esta calle hay tantos perros como gatos.	On this street there are as many dogs as cats.
Es una ciudad tan grande como Bogotá.	It is a city as large as Bogotá.

104. Absolute Superlative

When an adjective expresses the highest quality without relation to anything else, Spanish uses a form ending in **–ísimo,** which is equivalent to *very* or *extremely.* This form is made by dropping the final vowel of the adjective and adding **–ísimo.**

hermoso — hermosísimo   fácil — facilísimo

Hubo que construir larguísimas con- ducciones.	It was necessary to build very long pipelines.

Some adjectives have an irregular as well as a regular form in the absolute superlative. The most common ones are the following:

bueno	bonísimo	óptimo
grande	grandísimo	máximo
pequeño	pequeñísimo	mínimo

105. Translation of "than" in Comparisons

In a comparison the word *than* is translated by **que** except before numerals, where **de** is used. Even before numerals, when the statement is negative either **de** or **que** may be used.

Luisa es menos bonita que su hermana.	Louise is less pretty than her sister.
¡Lástima!	Too bad!
No tiene más de medio millón de habitantes	It has no more than a half million inhabitants.

When *than* introduces a clause, it is rendered by **de lo que.**

Habla más de lo que piensa.	He talks more than he thinks.

106 "In" after a Superlative

After a superlative the word *in* is translated by **de** if a comparison is intended. If *in* refers to actual location it is translated by **en.**

Es el país más próspero de la América del Sur.	It is the most prosperous country in South America.
Puede ser la más guapa en su país, pero aquí no lo es.	She may be the prettiest one in her country, but here she is not.

El petróleo y Venezuela

Venezuela, patria del insigne emancipador Simón Bolívar, es en nuestros días uno de los países más prósperos de la América del Sur. Pocos pueblos hispanoamericanos presentan hoy mejor situación económica que la de Venezuela, que no tiene deuda pública y cuyos ciudadanos no pagan tantos impuestos come los 5 de otros países americanos. Caracas, la capital de Venezuela, se ha convertido en estos últimos años en una de las ciudades más modernas del continente americano, con hermosas avenidas adornadas con majestuosos edificios. La prosperidad venezolana ha atraído al país numerosos emigrantes europeos. 10

Esta prosperidad de Venezuela se debe al petróleo, que es hoy la riqueza máxima de la nación. Venezuela figura a la cabeza de los

países exportadores de petróleo, y como productor es el segundo de América, después de los Estados Unidos. Los principales pozos
15 petrolíferos venezolanos se encuentran en la zona del Lago Maracaibo, que se comunica con el mar. El transporte resulta más fácil, y menos costoso, sobre todo si se compara con el de los países árabes, donde hubo que construir larguísimas conducciones por el desierto para llevar el petróleo a los puertos del Medite-
20 rráneo y del Golfo Pérsico.

La industria petrolera venezolana no es tan vieja como la de otros países americanos. Se fundó en 1917, poco antes de terminarse la primera guerra mundial. El tremendo desarrollo del automo-vilismo, de la aviación, y de los motores a petróleo dio un gran
25 impulso a la nueva industria venezolana. En los últimos años se han descubierto nuevos yacimientos petrolíferos en la región de Maracaibo y en otras partes de Venezuela, y se han aumentado considerablemente las reservas de petróleo.

La modernización de Venezuela va tomando de día en día un
30 ritmo más rápido. Una de las obras más importantes fue la cons-trucción de la nueva autopista que une a Caracas con el puerto de La Guaira, en el Mar Caribe. En lugar de la vieja carretera, que contaba con más curvas que días tiene un año, hay ahora una amplísima de varias vías en cada dirección. En la propia Caracas
35 se ha construido la Avenida Bolívar, modelo de la urbanización más avanzada, que divide la ciudad en dos partes, en norte y sur. Entre los numerosos edificios modernos de la ciudad figura en lugar preferente, por su arquitectura novísima y la grandeza de sus proporciones, la universidad.
40 No sólo en Caracas se siente el bienestar social que goza Venezuela, sino que éste llega a los más apartados rincones del país. En las ciudades venezolanas más modestas se ven nuevos hoteles, instalados con toda clase de comodidades, restaurantes, comercios y bancos, que sirven las crecientes necesidades de la
45 población de un país que mira con optimismo el futuro. En los últimos años el bienestar económico del país ha permitido el desarrollo de numerosas pequeñas industrias (conservas, tejidos, plásticos, etc.) en las que tienen una importante participación la técnica y el capital norteamericano.

EXPRESIONES ÚTILES

en nuestros días nowadays
a pesar de no ser in spite of not being
en estos últimos años in these last few
  years
se debe a is due to
pozo petrolífero oil well
se comunica con leads into, connects
  with

motores (movidos) a petróleo gasoline engines
más curvas que días tiene un año more
  curves than a year has days
varias vías various lanes
en lugar preferente in a prominent
  place
el bienestar social social welfare

RESUMEN PRÁCTICO

1. En nuestros días uno de los países más prósperos de la América española sigue siendo Venezuela.
2. A pesar de no ser la más grande capital del continente, Caracas tiene una actividad enorme.
3. Los pozos petrolíferos constituyen la riqueza principal de Venezuela.
4. Los motores movidos a petróleo son indispensables para la comunicación moderna.
5. En los últimos años se han organizado numerosas pequeñas industrias.
6. La universidad de Caracas figura en lugar preferente entre los edificios de la ciudad.
7. El bienestar social se siente en todos los rincones de este país.

EJERCICIOS

I. CONVERSACIÓN

1. ¿Cuál es uno de los países más prósperos de la América del Sur?
2. ¿Pagan muchos impuestos los ciudadanos de Venezuela? 3. ¿Tiene mucha actividad la capital de Venezuela? 4. ¿Hay muchos emigrantes europeos en Caracas? 5. ¿A qué se debe la prosperidad de Venezuela? 6. ¿Hay muchos países que superan a Venezuela como exportadores de petróleo? 7. ¿Dónde se encuentran los principales pozos petrolíferos

venezolanos? 8. ¿Resulta más fácil el transporte en Venezuela que en los países árabes? 9. ¿Cuándo se fundó la industria petrolera venezolana? 10. ¿Va progresando la modernización de Venezuela? 11. ¿Hay muchas comodidades en las ciudades venezolanas? 12. ¿Le parece a Vd. que Venezuela tenga un gran futuro?

II. Añádase un adjetivo apropiado a cada una de las siguientes palabras y después háganse oraciones completas:

1. deuda. 2. impuestos. 3. ciudadano. 4. continente. 5. avenida. 6. emigrante. 7. riqueza. 8. pozo. 9. conducciones. 10. industria. 11. guerra. 12. yacimiento. 13. ritmo. 14. carretera. 15. puerto. 16. urbanización. 17. edificio. 18. bienestar.

III. Dése la forma comparativa de cada uno de los adjetivos siguientes y después fórmense oraciones completas con el comparativo:

1. numeroso. 2. importante. 3. viejo. 4. nuevo. 5. rápido. 6. grande. 7. largo. 8. fácil. 9. costoso. 10. espacioso. 11. majestuoso. 12. moderno. 13. hermoso. 14. bueno. 15. próspero. 16. apartado.

IV. Tradúzcase oralmente al español:

1. A six-lane highway. 2. In spite of what you say. 3. One does not see that nowadays. 4. He has to pay from day to day. 5. The situation is better in the last few years. 6. Gasoline engines are common. 7. Instead of pipelines they use ships. 8. This city has more than two million inhabitants. 9. The lake connects with the sea. 10. We are studying the social welfare of the city. 11. The university figures in a prominent place. 12. They live in Caracas itself. 13. The avenue divides the city in two parts.

V. DIÁLOGO

Dos estudiantes, (A) y (B), discuten en español la importancia industrial de Venezuela.

A dice que la gente de Venezuela es tan próspera como cualquiera de las Américas.

B dice que Caracas es una de las más ricas y modernas de las ciudades.

A dice que la riqueza de Venezuela se debe al petróleo y habla de los pozos petrolíferos.

B dice que la industria petrolera de Venezuela no es muy vieja.

A habla de la modernización de las ciudades y las carreteras de Venezuela.

B cuenta algo de la universidad de Caracas.

VI. Escríbase en español:

1. The distinguished emancipator Bolívar was born in Venezuela, which is now an important industrial country. 2. Caracas does not have as many inhabitants as other extremely large cities, but it is one of the most active. 3. The transportation turned out to be less costly because they did not have to build long pipelines. 4. The principal oil wells are found on the lake, which seems very curious to me. 5. The tremendous development of gasoline engines has made the country extremely wealthy. 6. The new auto highway was finished several years ago and the capital connects with the port. 7. A few years ago we did not have eight-lane highways, but now there are even wider ones. 8. I should like to visit Venezuela, but they say the prices there are extremely high.

LECCIÓN 21

El norte de España

Review

Present Subjunctive, 72–74. Uses of the Subjunctive, 73.
Syllabication, 23, 24.

107. Imperfect Subjunctive

There are two common forms of the imperfect subjunctive, the –se
and the –ra forms. In order to form the imperfect subjunctive take the
third person plural of the preterite of any verb, regular or irregular,
drop the –ron and add –se, –ses, –se, ⸍semos, –seis, –sen for the –se
forms and –ra, –ras, –ra, ⸍ramos, –rais, –ran for the –ra forms. Notice
that in the first person plural there is an accent on the vowel preceding
the –semos or –ramos.

There is no difference in meaning between the –se and –ra forms.
The –se form is perhaps more literary, or at least the –ra form is more
common in conversational Spanish. The –ra form, however, has a
special use as a modified wish, in which case the –se form cannot be
used. (*Cf. Section 126.*)

108. Uses of the Subjunctive (Cont.)

The subjunctive indicates the manner in which the subject of an action
is affected by that action. There are certain types of clauses which
invariably go in the subjunctive. There are other clauses where the
speaker can intimate how he feels about a situation by the mood he
uses. The subjunctive is actually an instrument for expressing delicate
shades of meaning.

163

Romería del Rocío, Huelva, Spain

In Section 73 we outlined the general types of dependent clauses which are expressed in the subjunctive. They are dependent clauses used after the following:

1. Expressions of wishing or desiring.
2. Verbs of requesting, urging, or commanding.
3. Expressions of fear, doubt, or denial.
4. Verbs of permitting or forbidding, approving or disapproving.
5. Impersonal verbs or expressions.

Notice that in the first four classifications the dependent clause explains a feeling or mood on the part of the subject. In the last classification the subject is the clause itself.

109. The Subjunctive in Adjective Clauses

The subjunctive is used in an adjective clause whenever uncertainty or indefiniteness is expressed or implied. Adjective clauses are relative clauses; they may have either a simple antecedent or a compound antecedent. Compound antecedents are such words as **quienquiera** *whoever*, **dondequiera** *wherever*, **cualquiera** *whatever*, *any one*, etc. These compound antecedents express indefiniteness and therefore take the subjunctive.

Relative clauses go in the subjunctive whenever the antecedent is uncertain, indefinite, non-existent, or a superlative or its equivalent. In a sentence such as **Busco un alumno que sepa escribir poemas,** the relative clause is in the subjunctive because no such pupil has been found at the time of speaking. In a sentence such as **No veo ninguna señorita que sea fea,** the girl described is non-existent at the time of speaking. Common words which are the equivalent of a superlative are: **primero, último, único,** etc.

Caracas es la única ciudad que quisiera   Caracas is the only city I would like
conocer.   to know.

110. The Subjunctive in Adverbial Clauses

The subjunctive is used in:

(1) Clauses which express indefinite future time, after the following conjunctions:

cuando when	**mientras que** while, as long as
antes (de) que before	**así que** as soon as
hasta que until	**siempre que** whenever
luego que as soon as	

Cuando volvamos a España, visitaremos a Galicia.	When we go back to Spain, we shall visit Galicia.

Notice that these conjunctions take the indicative if the clause refers to past or present time.

Luego que volvió a probar los mariscos, le gustaron más.	As soon as he tried the shellfish again, he liked them better.

(2) Purpose clauses, after expressions such as:

> **para que** ⎫
> **a fin de que** ⎬ in order that, so that
>
> **de manera que** ⎫
> **de modo que** ⎬ so that, in such a manner that

Nos invitaron para que gozáramos de la vida española.	They invited us so that we might enjoy Spanish life.

Here again if the clause does not express purpose but result, the indicative is used.

Había muchas curvas, de manera que algunos pasajeros se marearon.	There were many curves, so that some passengers became nauseated.

(3) Clauses of concession or restriction, after such expressions as:

aunque although	**en caso (de) que** in case
a pesar de que in spite of the fact that	**con tal que** provided that
por bueno (malo) que however good (bad)	**a menos que (no)** unless
dado que since	**sin que** without

A pesar de que sea una de las más viejas . . .	Although it is one of the oldest . . .

When there is a pure admission of fact, the indicative is used even though the clause expresses concession.

Asturias se parece a Galicia, aunque es más montañosa que ella.	Asturias resembles Galicia, even though it is more mountainous.

El norte de España

Santander, 15 de junio, 1972

Querido Luis:

Son tantas las cosas que quisiera contarte de España que no sé
por donde empezar. Cuando primero volvimos a España, hicimos
5 el viaje en barco de Nueva York a La Coruña. La travesía duró
ocho días, y era como si hiciéramos un crucero por el Mediterráneo. Pero esta vez tomamos el avión de Nueva York a Madrid,
y allí otro de Madrid a La Coruña. En vez de ocho días, sólo
tardamos ocho horas en el viaje.

10 La Coruña siempre me produce una excelente impresión porque
pasé allí mi primera juventud. Sus casas tienen galerías pintadas de
blanco, con muchísimos cristales; y hay parques pintorescos a lo
largo de la orilla del puerto. Dicen que llueve mucho en el norte,
sobre todo en Galicia; pero tuvimos la suerte de que luciera el sol a
15 nuestra llegada y hasta ahora no ha llovido. Fuimos de La Coruña
a Santiago en un autovía, que es un tren muy rápido de un solo
coche.

Santiago de Compostela, donde está el sepulcro del Apóstol
Santiago, todavía conserva muchos monumentos de la época en
20 que fue el centro de las peregrinaciones de Europa. Pocas plazas
hay en España que sean tan monumentales como la de Santiago,
con su preciosa catedral, el Ayuntamiento, el hospital, y la
Escuela Normal. El ambiente de la ciudad hace transportar al
forastero a las épocas pasadas.

25 De Santiago fuimos a Villagarcía para visitar la familia de
Manuel Prado, que fue nuestro compañero en la escuela de verano
de Middlebury. Sus abuelos viven en una pequeña aldea próxima
al mar. Nos invitaron a una romería, para que gozáramos de la
vida española y para que oyéramos otra vez la famosa gaita gallega.

30 Volvimos a La Coruña para tomar el autobús de Oviedo, en
Asturias. El norte de España es muy agradable en verano. El
viaje de La Coruña a Oviedo es muy entretenido y variado, al
principio con el paisaje amable de la costa gallega y más tarde con

las montañas del interior. Nos detuvimos a comer en Ribadeo, y volvimos a probar los mariscos gallegos, que son tan estimados en 35 toda España.

Asturias se parece a Galicia, aunque es más montañosa que ella. Como la carretera tenía muchas curvas, algunos pasajeros del autobús se marearon. En las laderas de las montañas pacían vacas y terneras en los prados. Hay muchas industrias en Asturias. 40 Oviedo, con su universidad y su catedral, es una ciudad muy alegre y atractiva. En Oviedo alquilamos un taxi para ir a Gijón, en donde hay una de las mejores playas del norte de España. Allí probamos la sidra asturiana, que es la bebida predilecta del país. 45

De Gijón a Santander el paisaje es montañoso e impresionante. Si no fuera por el mar, que se ve de vez en cuando, uno se creería en Suiza. Como las clases del curso de verano no empiezan hasta el lunes próximo, me quedan varios días para recorrer a mi gusto esta provincia y visitar las Cuevas de Altamira y Santillana del 50 Mar. La Universidad de verano, que ocupa el antiguo palacio real, está situada en uno de los lugares más encantadores de Santander.

Todo me ha agradado y me hace esperar que voy a pasar un verano estupendo. 55

Saludos de mis hermanas y míos para ti y tu familia. Un abrazo de tu buen amigo.

Julio Valdés

EXPRESIONES ÚTILES

pintadas de blanco painted in white
a lo largo de all along
tuvimos la suerte de que we were fortunate because
tren de un solo coche a single coach train, beeliner

escuela de verano summer school
bebida predilecta favorite drink
si no fuera por were it not for
a mi gusto to my heart's desire
saludos de mis hermanas y míos best regards from my sisters and me

RESUMEN PRÁCTICO

1. Las casas y las galerías pintadas de blanco de La Coruña producen una excelente impresión.
2. Muchas ciudades españolas e hispanoamericanas tienen parques a lo largo de la orilla del mar.
3. Entre algunas ciudades de España se viaja en un autovía, que es un tren de un solo coche.
4. Santiago de Compostela tiene una catedral famosa donde está el sepulcro del Apóstol Santiago.
5. En el norte de España se encuentran playas muy atractivas y el verano es precioso.
6. El paisaje del norte de España se parece algo al paisaje montañoso e impresionante de Suiza.
7. Las Cuevas de Altamira tienen algunas de las pinturas más antiguas del mundo.

EJERCICIOS

I. CONVERSACIÓN

1. ¿Cuánto tarda el viaje en avión de Nueva York a La Coruña? 2. ¿Qué impresión produce La Coruña cuando uno la ve por primera vez? 3. ¿Llueve mucho en el norte de España? 4. ¿Qué es un autovía? 5. ¿Por qué es famoso Santiago de Compostela? 6. ¿Hace mucho calor en el norte de la península ibérica? 7. ¿Hay muchas industrias en Asturias? 8. ¿Qué ciudades se pueden visitar en Asturias y qué hay en ellas? 9. ¿Cuál es la bebida predilecta de Vd.? 10. ¿Cómo es el paisaje de Gijón a Santander? 11. ¿En qué ciudad hay cursos de verano? 12. ¿Sabe Vd. por qué son importantes las Cuevas 'de Altamira?

II. Dé Vd. la forma apropiada de cada verbo entre paréntesis:

1. Lo dijimos para que ellos lo (hacer, comprender, conocer, estudiar).
2. Buscamos un alumno que (querer, poder, saber, conseguir) hacerlo.
3. No conocía a nadie que le (comprender, gustar, invitar, apreciar).
4. Dondequiera que él (estar, viajar, llegar, vivir), no consiguió estar contento. 5. Me invitaron a visitarles para que (ver, gozar, apreciar, querer) el país.

III. Complete Vd. las oraciones siguientes con una frase en el imperfecto de subjuntivo:

1. Son muchas las cosas que yo (querer) . . . 2. Mi amigo quería que nosotros (conocer) . . . 3. Tuvo Vd. la suerte de que (lucir) . . . 4. Antes de viajar por Asturias dudábamos de que esta región (ser) . . . 5. Me parece que Vd. (deber) . . . 6. Volvimos a La Coruña antes de que ellos (llegar) . . . 7. No quisimos quedarnos aunque el país (gustar) . . . 8. No podíamos salir hasta que no (ver) . . . 9. No era posible que ellos no (conocer) . . . 10. En el viaje no vieron nada que no (ser) . . .

IV. Dése la forma apropiada del verbo en las oraciones siguientes:

1. Es probable que no (tener) tiempo para visitar todas las industrias. 2. No pudimos permitir que ellas (visitar) el país solas. 3. Tiene miedo de que no (llover) mucho durante el viaje. 4. Aunque la ciudad nos (producir) una excelente impresión, tuvimos que partir al día siguiente. 5. La ciudad fue el centro de las peregrinaciones de Europa, aunque en nuestros días pocos la (visitar). 6. Cuando (estar) en Santiago de Compostela, veremos el sepulcro del Apóstol Santiago. 7. No conozco ninguna plaza que (ser) tan monumental. 8. Dondequiera que uno (viajar) en España, el paisaje es impresionante. 9. La playa de Gijón es la mejor playa que yo (conocer). 10. No quiso pararse hasta que no (estar) cansado. 11. Dudan que (llover) mucho en el sur. 12. No vimos ninguna casa que (tener) galerías pintadas de blanco.

V. Tradúzcase oralmente, usando el imperfecto de subjuntivo:

1. In order that they might learn. 2. So that it could not be any better. 3. Until he arrived at the airport. 4. Although it had many curves. 5. In spite of the fact that it was attractive. 6. Without his knowing it. 7. He would like to tell you. 8. I did not know who he could be. 9. He was looking for someone who might live with him. 10. Before they visited the family. 11. You ought not to leave. 12. The best summer that he spent.

VI. Escríbase en español:

New York, September 24, 1972

1. Dear Ramón:

I want to tell you how I spent my last week in Spain before coming back to Boston. 2. First we went to Santander, where I saw some friends who were studying at the summer school. 3. From Santander we went to Gijón, where there is the best beach that I have seen. 4. From Gijón we took a taxi to go to Oviedo, because the distance is not great. 5. Although Oviedo is one of the oldest cities in Spain, it is one of the most lively. 6. On the trip we saw cows which were grazing on the mountain sides and sheep in the fields.

7. From Oviedo we went to La Coruña in a bus, and to Santander in a beeliner. 8. I did not see anyone on the trip who knew Boston, but many who had been to the United States. 9. Don't you think that Santiago de Compostela is one of the most interesting cities that you have seen?

10. From Santiago we took a plane to Madrid and from there to New York.

11. I shall write to you again next week, when I have more time. 12. Best regards to you and your family.

Your friend,

George

A view of the Magdalena, Santandar, Spain

Semana Santa (Holy Week), Seville, Spain

LECCIÓN 22

Las fallas de Valencia y la Semana Santa en Sevilla

Review

Past Participles, 53. Present Perfect, 55, 56.
Imperfect Indicative, 58, 59.

III. Compound Tenses of the Indicative

The present, imperfect, preterite, future, or conditional of the verb **haber,** followed by the past participle of a verb, forms the compound tenses of that verb.

Simple tenses of **haber** + past participle = compound tense.

ha	gustado	ha gustado	PRESENT PERFECT
habían	comenzado	habían comenzado	PLUPERFECT
hubo	oído	hubo oído	PRETERITE PERFECT
habrá	quemado	habrá quemado	FUTURE PERFECT
habríamos	cargado	habríamos cargado	CONDITIONAL PERFECT

112. Compound Tenses of the Subjunctive

The present or the imperfect subjunctive of **haber,** followed by the past participle of a verb, forms the compound tense of the subjunctive of that verb.

Simple tenses of **haber** + past participle = compound tense.

haya	alcanzado	haya alcanzado	PRESENT PERFECT SUBJVE.
hubiese hubiera	llegado	hubiese hubiera llegado	PLUPERFECT SUBJVE.

113. Uses of the Compound Tenses

The compound tenses are used practically the same way in Spanish as in English. There are only two major differences.

(1) When speaking of probability in past time, Spanish uses the future perfect for the immediate past and the conditional perfect for the more remote past. (The use of tenses to express probability is explained more fully in Section 127.)

Habrá hablado, pero yo no le oí.   He must have spoken, but I did not hear him. (*Recently*)

Habrían sido las cuatro cuando se marchó.   It might have been four o'clock when he went away. (*Some time ago*)

(2) The preterite perfect tense is used only after conjunctions such as **cuando, apenas (que), después (de) que, luego que, así que.** Otherwise use the pluperfect. In ordinary conversation the simple preterite is used in these cases.

Apenas hubo cantado, desapareció.   As soon as he had sung, he disappeared.

Apenas cantó, desapareció.   As soon as he sang, he disappeared.

114. Sequence of Tenses

The sequence of tenses applies only to sentences which require the subjunctive. When the verb in the independent clause is in the present, imperative, or future, the verb in the dependent clause is in the present or present perfect subjunctive. After the present indicative, however, the imperfect subjunctive may be used if the action refers clearly to past time.

No creo que el asunto sea tan importante.   I do not think the matter is so important.

Ella sentirá que Vd. no se haya quedado.   She'll be sorry you did not stay.

Dudo que lo supiera.   I doubt that he knew about it.

When the main verb is in the present perfect indicative, the dependent verb may be in the present, present perfect, or imperfect subjunctive.

No ha querido que se molestaran.   He did not want them to bother.

Han quedado muy contentos de que Vd. esté con nosotros.   They were very happy that you are with us.

When the main verb is in any of the other past tenses or in the conditional, the dependent verb will be in the imperfect or pluperfect subjunctive, depending on the sense.

Era imposible que no conociera la capital.   It was impossible that he did not know the capital.

Me alegré de que él lo hubiese encontrado.   I was glad he had found it.

Las fallas de Valencia y la Semana Santa en Sevilla

DIEGO. Conque, amigo Emilio, acaba de pasar Vd. una temporada en el este de España. Se dice que ésta es una de las regiones más pintorescas. ¡Cuéntenos algo! ¿Qué le ha gustado más?

EMILIO. Pues, me ha gustado todo. Las tierras de Levante y Andalucía son muy pintorescas, y además son muy templadas. El 5 mismo invierno se parece en ellas a la primavera de otras regiones. Es un encanto recorrer, en enero o en febrero, los campos de Valencia con sus miles y miles de naranjos cargados de flores. Después de haber dejado las frías tierras de la Mancha, nos parecieron hermosas las costas de Alicante y Málaga donde, a 10 fines de febrero, habían comenzado a florecer los almendros y cerezos.

JAIME. Conque ¿la primavera empieza muy temprano allí?

EMILIO. Sí, es verdad. La inauguración oficial de la primavera española tiene lugar en Valencia el 18 de marzo, la víspera de San 15 José, con las famosas fallas valencianas. Las fallas son monumentos alegóricos y satíricos construidos por los distintos barrios de la capital valenciana, en los que se representa alguna cosa de actualidad. Hay un concurso entre las fallas y se le da un premio a la de mayor arte y gusto. Al final de las fiestas se queman las fallas 20 en medio de gran alegría pública. Con estas fiestas coincide la

inauguración de la temporada de toros, pues las primeras corridas
se celebran esos días en la plaza de Valencia.

25   JAIME. He oído hablar mucho de las fallas valencianas, pero aun
más de la Semana Santa. ¿Se celebra ésta en Valencia?

   EMILIO. No, no, la Semana Santa se celebra en Sevilla, y tiene
lugar generalmente a principios de abril. La Semana Santa se
celebra con gran solemnidad en muchas ciudades españolas, pero
en Sevilla alcanza su máximo atractivo e interés.

30   DIEGO. ¿Cómo se celebra esa gran fiesta?

   EMILIO. El Domingo de Ramos, y el miércoles, jueves y viernes
de la Semana Santa, recorren las calles de Sevilla las procesiones
más impresionantes de España. La de la Macarena y la del Señor
del Gran Poder son las más conocidas. Los sevillanos que van en
35 estas procesiones están organizados en una serie de cofradías,
como la del Silencio, así llamada porque sus miembros se comprometen a no hablar durante todo este tiempo.

   DIEGO. Es ésta una fiesta algo triste, me parece.

   EMILIO. Sí, en verdad, hay en las procesiones algo triste. En las
40 que vimos, al paso de las procesiones se oía cantar en las calles la
triste y dolorosa saeta. Alguien generalmente la cantaba a la
imagen de la Virgen o del Salvador, para pedirle su ayuda. Al
comenzar el canto de la saeta la procesión se paraba y todo el
mundo guardaba silencio.

45   JAIME. ¿Había mucha gente en esta fiesta?

   EMILIO. Por supuesto, mucha. Miles de forasteros animaban
las calles de Sevilla los días de Semana Santa.

   DIEGO. ¿Hay otra fiesta más alegre en Sevilla? Siempre me he
imaginado la ciudad como centro de música y alegría. La ciudad
50 ha inspirado grandes compositores, como Albéniz, y Granados.

   EMILIO. Tiene Vd. razón; en Sevilla hay también mucha alegría.
Poco después de la Semana Santa se celebró la famosa feria de
Sevilla. En el extenso campo de la feria las familias sevillanas más
distinguidas habían instalado sus propias casetas con sus lonas
55 blancas para recibir a sus amistades. Día y noche corría la manzanilla generosamente, mientras el anfitrión atendía a sus amigos.
Se oía la bella música y el emocionado canto de Andalucía,
mientras había un continuo desfile de adornados carruajes, en los
que se veían las muchachas más bellas del país.

EXPRESIONES ÚTILES

recorrer los campos to go through the fields

fallas valencianas Valencian bonfires burnt on March 18

alguna cosa de actualidad a contemporary or current event

se comprometen a no hablar (they) vow not to talk

al paso de las procesiones during the processions

guardar silencio to keep silent

RESUMEN PRÁCTICO

1. Las tierras de Levante y Andalucía son pintorescas y muy templadas en el invierno.
2. En las costas de Alicante y Málaga florecen los almendros y los cerezos a fines de febrero.
3. Las fallas valencianas tienen lugar en la víspera de San José, es decir el 18 de marzo.
4. Las fallas son monumentos alegóricos y satíricos que representan alguna cosa de actualidad.
5. La Semana Santa que se celebra en Sevilla tiene lugar a fines de marzo o a principios de abril.
6. Los sevillanos que van en las procesiones están organizados en una serie de cofradías.
7. Las fiestas de Sevilla han servido de inspiración a muchos compositores famosos, como Albéniz, y Granados.

EJERCICIOS

I. CONVERSACIÓN

A. (*Basada en el texto.*) 1. ¿Dónde ha pasado una temporada Emilio? 2. ¿Son templadas las tierras de Levante y Andalucía? 3. ¿Qué se ve en los campos de Valencia? 4. ¿Qué florecía en las costas de Alicante y Málaga? 5. ¿Dónde y cuándo tiene lugar la inauguración oficial de la primavera española? 6. ¿Qué son las fallas y quién las construye? 7. ¿Dónde se celebra con más festividad la Semana Santa?

8. ¿Qué procesiones hay en Sevilla? 9. ¿Qué se oye al paso de las procesiones? 10. Describa un poco la famosa feria de Sevilla.

B. (*Basada en la experiencia personal.*) 1. ¿Cree Vd. que son bellas las muchachas de Andalucía? 2. ¿Ha asistido Vd. alguna vez a una corrida de toros? 3. ¿Recibe Vd. a menudo a sus amistades en su casa? 4. ¿Canta Vd. alguna vez? 5. ¿Le parecen a Vd. tristes las procesiones de la Semana Santa? 6. ¿Le gustaría visitar a Sevilla en la primavera? 7. ¿Conoce Vd. la música de Granados? 8. ¿Prefiere Vd. la primavera de su estado, o la de las tierras de Levante? 9. ¿Cuánto cuesta un viaje en avión de Nueva York hasta España? 10. ¿Hay buenas rebajas para grupos de estudiantes?

II. Ponga Vd. los infinitivos en la forma apropiada de uno de los tiempos compuestos y añada a cada oración otra frase para hacerla más larga:

1. ¿Qué le (gustar) más? 2. Nosotros (dejar) las frías tierras. 3. Los cerezos (comenzar) a florecer. 4. (Quemarse) las fallas. 5. Las corridas (celebrarse) en estos días. 6. Yo (oír) hablar de la Semana Santa. 7. (Alcanzar) su máximo atractivo. 8. Las procesiones (tener) un aspecto triste. 9. Alguien (cantar) en la calle. 10. Todo el mundo (guardar) silencio. 11. (Venir) mucha gente. 12. Los forasteros (animar) las calles. 13. Ellos (instalar) sus proprias casetas. 14. (Verse) las muchachas más bellas.

III. Ponga Vd. los verbos entre paréntesis en el tiempo del subjuntivo indicado:

1. (*Imperfect*) Quería que Vd. (pasar, contar, empezar, notar). 2. (*Present*) Me alegro que él (venir, empezar, hacer, ir). 3. (*Present perfect*) Están tristes de que Vds. (salir, caer, volver, ver). 4. (*Pluperfect*) No era posible que ella (cantar, dejar, oír, asistir).

IV. Tradúzcase oralmente al español:

1. We like to go through the fields. 2. Some contemporary event. 3. When do the festivities take place? 4. The men had vowed not to talk. 5. It is better to keep silent during the processions. 6. In any case we can see the city. 7. Toward the end of February they come to the capital. 8. The one who reveals the greatest art and taste. 9. The orange trees are laden with blossoms. 10. Why is there a contest between the floats?

V. Formúlense preguntas sobre cada uno de los temas siguientes y contéstese a las preguntas en la clase:

1. El Domingo de Ramos. 2. La Semana Santa. 3. Las cofradías. 4. La saeta. 5. Los forasteros. 6. La feria de Sevilla. 7. Las lonas blancas. 8. El canto de Andalucía. 9. Un desfile de carruajes. 10. El mayor gusto. 11. Los monumentos alegóricos. 12. Las frías tierras de la Mancha.

VI. Escríbase en español:

1. He had just spent a period of time in the lands of the East (of Spain) when we met him. 2. I do not know what must have pleased (*future perfect*) him most, but I do know that he wants to go back. 3. Had the festivities begun toward the end of March when you arrived? 4. The inauguration of spring will take place in Valencia on the eve of Saint Joseph's day. 5. Why do they give a prize to the **falla** which reveals the greatest art? 6. The celebration has a religious character, because Holy Week is really a religious time of the year **(temporada).** 7. I wish that you had seen the famous Seville fair, so that you could understand my enthusiasm. 8. The girls of Andalusia were the most beautiful that we had seen.

LECCIÓN 23

La aviación en Colombia

Review

Preterite Tense, 65. Reflexive Verbs, 63, 64.
Personal Pronouns after Prepositions, 61.

115. Augmentatives and Diminutives

Spanish is rich in suffixes which give a different shade of meaning to words, mostly nouns and adjectives, and even a few adverbs. These suffixes are of two types: augmentatives, which originally implied an increase in size, and diminutives, which implied a decrease in size. From this original idea there developed all types of shades of meaning, which are frequently difficult or even impossible to render into English.

The most common augmentative suffixes are **–ón, –azo, –ote,** and **–acho,** which imply large size, ugliness or awkwardness.

un hombre a man	**un hombrón** a great big man
una mujer a woman	**una mujerona** a great big woman
un señor a gentleman	**un señorón** an important gentleman
mucho much	**muchazo** quite a bit
pobre poor	**pobretón** quite poor

Sometimes augmentative suffixes take on a diminutive meaning:

una isla an island	**un islote** an islet
una cámara a hall	**un camarote** a cabin *or* stateroom
una calle a street	**un callejón** a narrow street

Sometimes an augmentative either adds a moral value or takes away from the value of something.

181

vianca plane

ogotá, Colombia

un padre a father	**un padrazo** a very indulgent father
un libro a book	**un libraco** a horrid book

Sometimes an augmentative is made on the basis of another augmentative.

pueblo town	**poblacho** shabby old town
poblachón big shabby old town	

The diminutive suffixes are much more common than the augmentative ones, and they are very important in understanding the correct shades of meaning implied. The most common ones are **–ito, –cito, –ecito; –illo, –cillo, –ecillo; –uelo–; –uco; and –ucho.** The endings **–ito, –illo** and their longer forms, and **–uelo,** denote smallness of size, endearment, and affection. They are used with nouns and adjectives.

casa house	**casita** (pretty) little house
pájaro bird	**pajarillo** or **pajarito** tiny little bird
jardín garden	**jardincito** tiny little garden
pueblo town	**pueblecito** little town, village
solo alone	**solito** all alone
pobre poor (man)	**pobrecito** poor little fellow, poor old fellow
viejo old (man)	**viejecito** little old man
plaza square	**plazuela** little square

These endings also change the meaning of adverbs, as in the following:

temprano early	**tempranito** quite early
en seguida at once	**en seguidita** right away, this moment
ahora now	**ahorita** in a moment, right now

The diminutives **–uelo, –uco,** and **–ucho** sometimes add a derogatory note, a sense of belittling.

mujer woman	**mujeruca** wench
casa house	**casucha** run-down hut

116. Indefinite Adjectives

Algún (alguna) means *some* when used before a noun. It may be used in a negative sense by placing it after the noun.

Oyeron algún ruido.	They heard some noise.
No oyeron ruido alguno.	They did not hear any noise.

Ningún (ninguna) is always negative, whether used before or after the noun.

Ningún abogado se atreve a contestarle.	No lawyer dares to answer him.

Todo (toda), when used in the singular, means *all* or *the whole* and sometimes *each* or *every*. When used in the plural it means *every*, in the sense of *all taken together*. (When used as a substantive, it means *everything*.)

Todo hombre es mórtal.	Every man is mortal.
Hágalo con todo cuidado.	Do it with complete care.
Le hablamos todos los días.	We speak to him every day.
Le gusta todo.	He likes everything.

Cualquier (cualquiera) denotes a very indefinite object or person, in fact anyone whatever. Before the noun either the form **cualquier** or **cualquiera** may be used; after the noun only **cualquiera** may be used. The plural form is **cualesquiera**.

Dígame Vd. cualquier cosa, pero no eso.	Tell me anything, but not that.

117. Indefinite Pronouns

Algo means *something*, *anything*, and **alguien** means *somebody*, *anybody*. They are both invariable and indicate something or somebody not previously mentioned.

¿Hay alguien que sepa la población de Colombia?	Is there anyone who knows the population of Colombia?
Hay algo de nuevo.	There is something new.

Alguno (–a, –os, –as), *some*, *any*, *a few* indicates someone, some people, some thing or some things from a group.

Algunos conocen la situación del país.	Some people know the situation in the country.
De dificultades, conozco algunas.	As for difficulties, I know a few of them.

Nadie, *no one*, **ninguno (–a),** *no one, not any*, and **nada,** *nothing*, are used whenever there is a negative meaning implied in the sentence.

Llegó sin que nadie lo supiese.   He arrived without anyone's knowing
                                             it.

Ese hombre no sabe nada de nada.   That man knows nothing at all.

La aviación en Colombia

La cordillera de los Andes se va abriendo en abanico a medida
que avanza por Colombia. Primero se divide en dos grandes
ramales: el de la izquierda se dirige hacia el istmo de Panamá;
mientras el de la derecha se vuelve a dividir en otros dos: uno, el
5 central, que forma la espina dorsal de las montañas colombianas;
y otro, el oriental, que va hacia Venezuela. En este complicado
sistema montañoso nacen numerosos ríos, algunos de ellos navegables, que van al Mar Caribe, al Océano Pacífico, al Orinoco y al
Amazonas.

10 El complejo sistema montañoso de Colombia dificultó sus
comunicaciones terrestres; en cambio, la extensa red de ríos
navegables favoreció el transporte fluvial, al que debe en gran parte
Colombia su desarrollo económico. Todavía hoy en día, para ir
desde el Atlántico a Bogotá o a los pueblecitos del interior de la
15 República hay que tomar un barco en Barranquilla y subir varios
días por el Río Magdalena hasta llegar a Girardot; allí espera el
tren que lleva al viajero al centro de Colombia o al Pacífico. El
Magdalena es y ha sido una de las principales arterias del país.

La dificultad de las comunicaciones terrestres no ha impedido el
20 desarrollo económico del país. Los valles colombianos son tierras
de gran fertilidad, excelentes para toda clase de cultivo. En ellos
se produce un café de primera calidad. La población de Colombia
— que pasa hoy de los veinte millones — ha crecido notablemente
en los últimos años. Sin embargo su crecimiento no se debe a la
25 llegada de emigrantes de otros países, como en Venezuela, sino a
su evolución interior. La economía colombiana es una de las más
equilibradas de los países hispanoamericanos, pues no está
dominada por un solo producto. Hay café, tabaco, algodón y

arroz en la agricultura; petróleo, hierro, cobre y esmeraldas en la
minería. El café, que es lo más importante, no llega a constituir la   30
tercera parte de la producción del país.

Los obstáculos que la naturaleza pone en Colombia al desarrollo
de las comunicaciones terrestres han servido de estímulo para que
el país organizara todo un amplio sistema de comunicaciones
aéreas. Colombia ocupa un puesto muy destacado en este tipo de   35
comunicación. A poco de terminar la primera guerra mundial, en
1919, se organizó en Colombia la primera compañía de esta clase,
que fue la Sociedad Colombiana-Alemana de Transportes
Aéreos (Scadta) que, durante la segunda guerra mundial, se trans-
formó en la Avianca. En la actualidad, existen en Colombia   40
alrededor de una docena de empresas de aviación comercial que
atienden al servicio de transporte de pasajeros y mercancías entre
la capital de la República y los centros más importantes del país.
Algunas de ellas extienden sus servicios hasta otros países de la
América del Sur, los Estados Unidos y Europa. La situación   45
especial de Colombia en el continente americano hace que algunos
de sus aeropuertos, como el de Barranquilla, en la entrada del
Magdalena, y el de Cali, en el interior del país, desempeñen un
papel muy activo en el sistema de las comunicaciones intercontinentales americanas. Puede afirmarse que uno de los principales   50
factores que ha impulsado el notable progreso económico de
Colombia en los últimos años ha sido el sorprendente desarrollo de
la aviación comercial.

EXPRESIONES ÚTILES

en abanico like a fan
a medida que as, in pace with
espina dorsal backbone, spinal column
desarrollo económico economic development
toda clase de cultivo all types of
   cultivation
no llega a constituir does not quite
   constitute

un puesto muy destacado a very
   prominent place
a poco de terminar shortly after the
   end of
en la actualidad at the present time
empresas de aviación comercial commercial airlines
hace que brings about the result that
desempeñar un papel to play a role

RESUMEN PRÁCTICO

1. En Colombia la cordillera de los Andes se divide en dos ramales, uno que va hacia el istmo de Panamá y otro hacia Venezuela.
2. La extensa red de ríos navegables ha favorecido el transporte fluvial en Colombia.
3. Los valles colombianos son tierras de gran fertilidad, que favorecen toda clase de cultivos.
4. La economía colombiana es muy equilibrada: café, tabaco, petróleo, hierro, cobre y esmeraldas.
5. Los obstáculos de la naturaleza han estimulado el desarrollo de un amplio sistema de comunicaciones aéreas.
6. Existen en la actualidad una docena de empresas de aviación comercial y transporte de pasajeros.
7. La aviación de Colombia desempeña un papel muy activo en las comunicaciones intercontinentales americanas.

EJERCICIOS

I. CONVERSACIÓN

1. ¿Cómo se desarrolla la cordillera de los Andes al llegar hacia el norte de la América del Sur? 2. ¿Qué produce el complicado sistema montañoso? 3. ¿De qué manera se han desarrollado las comunicaciones de Colombia? 4. ¿Cómo se llega al interior de Colombia? 5. ¿Qué puede Vd. contarnos del desarrollo económico del país? 6. ¿Qué diferencia hay entre la población de Colombia y la de Venezuela? 7. ¿Qué productos hay en Colombia? 8. ¿Qué condiciones han causado el desarrollo de las comunicaciones aéreas? 9. ¿Sabe Vd. algo de la historia de la Avianca? 10. ¿Qué influencia tiene la aviación comercial en el desarrollo económico del país?

II. Give the correct meaning of the following augmentatives and diminutives and use each one in an original sentence:

1. pueblecito. 2. mujeraza. 3. hijito. 4. florecita. 5. madrecita. 6. lugarcillo. 7. caballote. 8. vientecillo. 9. chiquito. 10. jardincito. 11. pollito. 12. Juanito. 13. Isabelita. 14. hijita.

III. Give an augmentative or diminutive as the equivalent for each of the following expressions:

1. in-a-moment.   2. the poor-little-fellow.   3. a pretty-little-house.
4. a tiny-little-garden.   5. the dear-little-child.   6. the large-chair
(armchair).   7. quite-early.   8. the tiny-little-bird.   9. the great-big-man.
10. a shabby-old-town.   11. a small-square.   12. all-alone.   13. a run-
down-hut.   14. a little-valley.

IV. DIÁLOGO

Dos estudiantes, (A) un colombiano y (B) un newyorkino, discuten la aviación.

A dice que Colombia fue uno de los primeros países del mundo en desarrollar la aviación comercial.

B está de acuerdo, pero añade que todos los países tienen ahora una enorme aviación comercial.

A cuenta el origen de la Avianca.

B habla de la enormidad del transporte en los grandes aeropuertos de Nueva York.

A habla de la importancia de la aviación para Colombia.

B habla de las muchas comunicaciones entre la América del Norte y la América del Sur.

A habla del futuro de la transportación aérea mundial.

Y la conversación sigue de esta manera lo más posible.

V. Escríbase en español:

1. There are many tiny-little-towns which can be reached only by air because the country is too mountainous.   2. The extensive network of navigable rivers has been very important for the development of the country.   3. The Andes form the spinal column of the Colombian mountains, but they extend as far as the Tierra del Fuego.   4. The lands are excellent for all types of cultivation, particularly coffee, tobacco, and rice.   5. The mountain range opens like a fan when it reaches Colombia and Venezuela.   6. Before the country organized a system of aerial communications there was no way of getting from one place to another.   7. At the present time the passenger transport service is just as important as the freight transport service.   8. The notable progress of Colombia is as great as the economic progress of Venezuela.

Carreta monument, Uruguay

LECCIÓN 24

La cultura en el Uruguay

Review

*Radical-changing Verbs, 69. Orthographic Changes in Verbs, 71.
Demonstratives, 47, 48.*

118. Summary of Radical-changing Verbs

In Section 69 we reviewed the radical-changing verbs of the first class,
which comprise verbs of the first and second conjugations. Verbs of
the third conjugation which have radical changes fall under two
groups, which we call second and third class for convenience. The
radical-changing verbs of the second class are –**ir** verbs which have the
same radical changes as those of the first class, but in addition they
have changes in the unstressed vowel preceding the stressed vowel in
the present and past subjunctive, in the present participle, and in the
third singular and plural of the preterite. Notice the changes as outlined in the following summary, comparing verbs of the first class and
the second class.

First Class	*Second Class*
–**ar** and –**er** verbs	–**ir** verbs only
First and second conjugations	Third conjugation
Stem vowel **o** > **ue** and **e** > **ie** when stressed	Stem vowel **o** > **ue** and **e** > **ie** when stressed
	o > **u** and **e** > **i** when unstressed in the subjunctive, present participle, and third person of the preterite

189

First Class		*Second Class*	
PRESENT –**ar** VERB		PRESENT –**ir** VERB	
encontrar to meet		**dormir** to sleep	
IND.	SUBJVE.	IND.	SUBJVE.
encuentro	encuentre	duermo	duerma
encuentras	encuentres	duermes	duermas
encuentra	encuentre	duerme	duerma
encontramos	encontremos	dormimos	durmamos
encontráis	encontréis	dormís	durmáis
encuentran	encuentren	duermen	duerman

IMPERATIVE	IMPERATIVE
encuentra	**duerme**
encontrad	dormid

PRESENT –**er** VERB		PRESENT –**ir** VERB	
mover to move		**sentir** to feel	
IND.	SUBJVE.	IND.	SUBJVE.
muevo	mueva	siento	sienta
mueves	muevas	sientes	sientas
mueve	mueva	siente	sienta
movemos	movamos	sentimos	sintamos
movéis	mováis	sentís	sintáis
mueven	muevan	sienten	sientan

IMPERATIVE	IMPERATIVE
mueve	**siente**
moved	sentid

PRET.	PAST SUBJVE. (–se, –ra)	
dormí	durmiese	durmiera
dormiste	durmieses	durmieras
durmió	durmiese	durmiera
dormimos	durmiésemos	durmiéramos
dormisteis	durmieseis	durmierais
durmieron	durmiesen	durmieran

Second Class

PRET.	PAST SUBJVE. (–se, –ra)	
sentí	sintiese	sintiera
sentiste	sintieses	sintieras
sintió	sintiese	sintiera
sentimos	sintiésemos	sintiéramos
sentisteis	sintieseis	sintierais
sintieron	sintiesen	sintieran

PRESENT PARTICIPLE

durmiendo   **sintiendo**

Radical-changing verbs of the third class are those –**ir** verbs which change only the **e** to **i,** but they do so in all of the forms where verbs of the second class have any changes. Notice the summary which follows.

Third Class

–**ir** verbs only. Third conjugation

The stem vowel **e > i** when stressed, and also when unstressed in the subjunctive (present or imperfect), the third person of the preterite, and the present participle.

servir to serve

PRESENT PARTICIPLE, **sirviendo**

PRES. IND.	PRES. SUBJVE.	IMPVE.	PRET.	IMPERF. SUBJVE. (–se,–ra)	
sirvo	**sirva**		serví	sirviese	sirviera
sirves	**sirvas**	**sirve**	serviste	sirvieses	sirvieras
sirve	**sirva**		**sirvió**	sirviese	sirviera
servimos	**sirvamos**		servimos	sirviésemos	sirviéramos
servís	**sirváis**	servid	servisteis	sirvieseis	sirvierais
sirven	**sirvan**		**sirvieron**	sirviesen	sirvieran

TABLE OF RADICAL CHANGES

CLASS I	EXAMPLE	CHANGE	TENSES INVOLVED
–ar, –er	**cerrar, contar**	**e > ie** **o > ue**	1st, 2nd, and 3rd pers. sing. and 3rd pers. pl. of pres. ind. and pres. subjve., and impve. sing.
CLASS II			
–ir	**sentir, dormir**	**e > ie** **o > ue** } stressed	Same as class I
		e > i **o > u** } unstressed	3rd pers. sing. and pl. pret.; 1st and 2nd pers. pl. pres. subjve.; all past subjve.; pres. part.
CLASS III			
–ir	**servir**	**e > i** stressed and unstressed	All the changes of class II, both stressed and unstressed.

119. Summary of Orthographic Changes in Verbs

Some verbs change their spelling to preserve the sound of the consonant preceding the ending. This change takes place with consonants which have a different sound before different vowels.

TABLE OF ORTHOGRAPHIC CHANGES

VERBS ENDING IN	CHANGE	BEFORE	EXAMPLES
–car	c > qu	e	**sacar** to take out
–gar	g > gu	e	**llegar** to arrive
–zar	z > c	e	**empezar** to begin
–guar	gu > gü	e	**averiguar** to verify
–cer, –cir (preceded by consonant)	c > z	a, o	**vencer** to conquer
–cer, –cir (preceded by vowel)	c > zc	a, o	**conocer** to know; **conducir** to lead
–ger, –gir	g > j	a, o	**dirigir** to direct
–guir	gu > g	a, o	**seguir** to follow

AUTOMATIC VOWEL CHANGES IN VERBS

1. An unaccented **i** between two vowels changes to **y**.

     concluir to conclude   **concluyo**, etc.

2. A stressed **i** or **u** coming as the last letter of a verb stem takes a written accent when followed by another vowel.

     enviar to send   **envíe**, etc.   **actuar** to perform   **actúo**, etc.

3. An unstressed **i** before an **e** is dropped when the verb stem ends in **ll, ñ** or **j**.

     bullir to boil   **bullendo**   **reñir** to quarrel   **riñendo**
          traer to bring   **trajeron**

120. Impersonal Expressions

When the subject of a verb is not known, or it is an action, or a whole clause, it is considered impersonal. In English such a subject is expressed by the words *one* or *it*.

Hay que llegar temprano.	One has to get there early.
Es preciso salir en seguida.	It is necessary to leave immediately.
Es posible que Vd. lo encuentre.	It is possible that you will meet him.

An impersonal expression denoting an action is followed by the infinitive if the subject of the action is not expressed.

Es posible aprender un idioma.	It is possible to learn a language.

An impersonal expression is followed by the subjunctive unless it expresses a truth or certainty.

Es preciso que Vd. le hable mañana.	It is necessary that you speak to him tomorrow.
BUT: **Es verdad que ella no canta bien.**	It is true that she does not sing well.

La cultura en el Uruguay

El Uruguay, que por su extensión es el país más pequeño de la América del Sur, ha tenido, sin embargo, una gran influencia en la vida cultural de los pueblos hispanoamericanos, entre los cuales ha ocupado un lugar destacado por la excelencia de sus institu-
5 ciones políticas, sociales y educativas. La propia tierra del Uruguay, que no presenta los grandes obstáculos naturales de los otros países de la América del Sur, ha favorecido el progreso de su pueblo y la rápida integración de todos sus elementos en la unidad nacional. No tiene el Uruguay grandes montañas ni impenetrables
10 selvas tropicales; y su clima templado es propicio para el desarrollo de la ganadería y la agricultura.

La colonización del Uruguay fue la última llevada a cabo por España en el continente americano. No tuvo lugar hasta fines del siglo XVIII, cuando el gobierno español, temeroso de que el Brasil se extendiera hasta la orilla oriental del Mar del Plata, estableció en estas tierras numerosas familias de campesinos llevados de las islas Canarias. Son éstos los que constituyen la base del pueblo uruguayo, cuya democracia, hasta los últimos años una de las más firmes y estables de la América española, descansa sobre la sólida columna de los agricultores que poblaron sus campos. Esta democracia tiene como símbolo a José Artigas, que, con sus gauchos uruguayos, fue el caudillo de la independencia de la República Oriental del Uruguay; fue él quien supo defenderla tenazmente contra sus vecinos poderosos, el Brasil y la Argentina, que aspiraban a dominar la pequeña y joven república platense. El Uruguay, después de los primeros años difíciles de su independencia, comenzó a disfrutar, en la segunda parte del siglo XIX, de una próspera paz política, desarrollando sus instituciones sociales y culturales en un grado no superado por ningún otro país de la América española. En los últimos años ha ido atravesando una crisis, como muchos otros países.

Montevideo, la capital del Uruguay, con su millón de habitantes y su activo puerto que guarda la entrada del Mar del Plata, es una de las ciudades más atractivas del continente americano. Pero el interés del país no se limita a su capital sino que se extiende a toda la República, cuyo nivel de vida y de cultura ha sido uno de los más elevados de los países hispanoamericanos. La legislación social del Uruguay puede servir de modelo por los avances sociales que en ella se han recogido. Las instituciones culturales uruguayas, tanto las de la enseñanza superior como de la elemental, figuran entre las mejores de América. Y su sistema de organización constitucional, con un gobierno colegiado, semejante al de Suiza en Europa, ha sido un testimonio vivo de la fuerza y de la eficiencia de la democracia en el Uruguay.

El Uruguay, y sobre todo su capital Montevideo, fue el seguro refugio donde buscaron asilo los emigrados políticos argentinos de

todos los tiempos. En Montevideo vivieron y se formaron muchos de los grandes argentinos de la llamada generación romántica (Echeverría, Mármol, Mitre, Sarmiento, etc.) que escribieron parte
50 de sus obras en el exilio en el Uruguay.

El Uruguay ha producido muchos hombres de letras y de ciencias. Entre los primeros figuran, por no citar más que los destacados, José Enrique Rodó, prosista, maestro de la generación modernista y uno de los mejores ensayistas de la literatura hispano-
55 americana; Florencio Sánchez, el dramaturgo más notable de la América española; y Horacio Quiroga, primer cuentista de las letras hispanoamericanas. Estos dos últimos escritores muestran la íntima compenetración que existe entre las letras uruguayas y las argentinas; pues Florencio Sánchez y Horacio Quiroga, aunque
60 uruguayos, vivieron, actuaron y escribieron en la Argentina.

EXPRESIONES ÚTILES

un lugar destacado an outstanding position
es propicio para is favorable to
fue llevada a cabo was accomplished
temeroso de que fearful lest
descansa sobre rests upon
disfrutar de enjoy
no superado por unsurpassed by
nivel de vida standard of living

puede servir de modelo can serve as a model
avances sociales social improvements
la enseñanza superior higher education
un gobierno colegiado government by council
testimonio vivo living testimony
primer cuentista foremost storyteller

RESUMEN PRÁCTICO

1. El Uruguay ha ocupado un lugar destacado por la excelencia de sus instituciones políticas, sociales y educativas.
2. El clima templado del Uruguay es propicio para el desarrollo de la ganadería y la agricultura.
3. El gobierno español estableció en estas tierras numerosas familias de campesinos llevados de las islas Canarias.
4. La democracia del pueblo uruguayo ha sido una de las más firmes y estables de la América española.

5. El sistema de organización constitucional consta de un gobierno colegiado, semejante al de Suiza.
6. En el Uruguay buscaron asilo los emigrados políticos argentinos de todos los tiempos.
7. Los más destacados hombres de letras del Uruguay fueron José Enrique Rodó, Florencio Sánchez, y Horacio Quiroga.

EJERCICIOS

I. CONVERSACIÓN. Expliquen Vds. en forma completa las siguientes ideas delante de la clase:

1. ¿Qué lugar ocupa el Uruguay entre los países hispanoamericanos?
2. ¿Qué influencia ha tenido la propia tierra en el desarrollo de la vida en el Uruguay? 3. ¿Cuándo y por qué razón tuvo lugar la colonización del Uruguay? 4. ¿Cuál es la base de la democracia uruguaya? 5. Explique Vd. la función de José Artigas en la independencia de la República. 6. ¿Qué papel desempeña Montevideo en la vida del país? 7. ¿Cómo son las instituciones sociales y culturales del Uruguay? 8. Describa Vd. brevemente el sistema político del Uruguay. 9. ¿De qué manera ha ayudado el Uruguay al desarrollo de los grandes hombres de la América del Sur? 10. ¿Ha producido el Uruguay mismo algunas figuras de primer orden?

II. Los verbos siguientes aparecen en este ejercicio:

extenderse (ie) to extend; **servir (i)** to serve; **contar (ue)** to relate, tell, count; **mostrar (ue)** to show; **sentirse (ie)** to feel; **dormir (ue)** to sleep; **cerrar (ie)** to close; **pensar (ie)** to think; **pedir (i)** to ask; **volver (ue)** to return. *Tradúzcase al español:*

1. They extend. 2. He served. 3. That he may tell (*pres. subjve.*).
4. That they may show. 5. Feeling. 6. They slept. 7. You (*fam.*) close. 8. We think. 9. Do you (*fam. pl.*) ask? 10. She returns. 11. That they may return. 12. That he might ask (*past subjve.*). 13. Think! 14. Close! 15. Is she sleeping? 16. That we might feel. 17. I show. 18. Tell us! 19. Serving. 20. It does not extend.

*III. Los verbos siguientes aparecen en la parte gramatical de la lección.
Tradúzcase al español:*

1. I took out. 2. That he may arrive (*pres. subjve.*). 3. That she may
begin. 4. That they may verify. 5. I conquer. 6. That they may know.
7. Do I lead? 8. He directed. 9. That I may follow. 10. He con-
cludes. 11. Concluding. 12. Let's send. 13. He performs. 14. It is
boiling. 15. They quarrelled. 16. That you (*fam. sing.*) might bring
(*past subjve.*). 17. That you may take out. 18. I arrived. 19. Begin!
20. Lead!

*IV. Hagan Vds. oraciones completas juntando las dos partes que damos
aquí y cambiando la forma del verbo cuando sea necesario:*

1. Es preciso. Él trabaja demasiado. 2. Es necesario. Ellos com-
prenden la vida cultural. 3. Es posible. A Vd. le gusta la poesía.
4. Es probable. Ellas llegan mañana. 5. Es verdad. Montevideo está
en el Uruguay. 6. Es preciso. Ellos leen nuestra literatura. 7. Es probable. Hay emigrantes políticos. 8. No es posible. El nivel de vida
está tan alto. 9. Es verdad. Hay muchos italianos en el Uruguay.
10. No es necesario. El profesor lo sabe.

*V. Formúlense preguntas completas con cada una de las frases siguientes
y contéstese a las preguntas en la clase:*

1. las instituciones políticas. 2. grandes obstáculos naturales. 3. el
clima templado. 4. numerosas familias. 5. los gauchos uruguayos.
6. el nivel de vida. 7. la enseñanza superior. 8. hombres de letras.
9. un gobierno colegiado. 10. la generación romántica.

VI. Escríbase en español:

1. I do not know why Uruguay occupies such a prominent place among
the Spanish American nations. 2. Is it because it has a great influence
on their cultural life? 3. The land itself has favored the rapid integration of all its elements, which has resulted in national unity. 4. Grazing
and agriculture have been important in the development of various
Latin American countries. 5. The government was fearful lest Brazil
should become too powerful. 6. The numerous families of farmers
which arrived now constitute the basis of the population. 7. Would
you know how to defend your country against powerful neighbors?

8. The social and cultural institutions have developed to an unsurpassed degree. 9. What kind of government does Switzerland have and why is it called a government by council? 10. Have you read many of the works of Latin American authors?

Dancers in Granada, Spain

LECCIÓN 25

Los bailes españoles

Review

Rule of Accent, 25. Present Indicative of Some Irregular Verbs, 62. Preterite of Some Irregular Verbs, 68.

121. Conditions

A. Simple conditions are those in which a direct result is expected from a direct statement: if something happens, something else happens also. When the *if*-clause is in the present, the result clause may be in the present, future, or imperative.

Si llueve { **necesito el paraguas.**	If it rains { I need an umbrella.
me quedaré en casa.	I shall stay home.
¡tome Vd. el tranvía!	take the trolley.

When the *if*-clause is in the past indicative, the result clause is in whatever tense of the indicative is required by the sense.

Si me veía me llevaba en su auto. If he saw me he used to take me in his car.

Si te ha escrito es que te quiere mucho. If he wrote to you it is because he likes you very much.

B. *Should-would* conditions are those in which the *if*-clause makes a hypothetical statement and the result clause follows up with the hypothetical result. It is all a supposition. In this type of condition the *if*-clause takes either the –se or –ra form of the imperfect subjunctive, but the result clause takes the conditional or occasionally the –ra form of the imperfect subjunctive. (The –se form is not used in the result clause.)

Si me llamase por teléfono, se lo diría (dijera) clara y francamente.	If he were to call me on the telephone, I would tell him clearly and frankly.

C. Contrary-to-fact conditions are those in which the *if*-clause makes an assumption which is recognized as not true at the time in order to indicate what the result of that assumption would have been.

In this type of sentence the *if*-clause goes in the imperfect or pluperfect subjunctive and the result clause goes in the conditional perfect or occasionally the pluperfect subjunctive (–ra form only).

Si yo fuera su jefe, Vd. no me habría (hubiera) hablado así.	If I were your boss, you would not have talked to me that way.

122. *Aun* and *aún*

The more common form of **aun** is without the accent; it has a written accent only when it can be substituted by **todavía.**

Aun los americanos bailan el flamenco.	Even Americans dance the flamenco.
Los dos jóvenes bailan aún.	The two young people are still dancing.

123. *Acá* and *allá*

Acá corresponds to **aquí,** but the general direction is more vague; it may carry the connotation of motion toward this place.

Ven acá, chico.	Come here, child.

Allá corresponds to **allí,** but it indicates a more general place or direction than **allí.**

Allá vamos.	There we go.

Los bailes españoles

Roberto Hubbard, estudiante norteamericano, se encuentra, en una terraza de un café de Madrid, con Fernando Mendoza, un joven español que es su compañero de estudios en la Universidad madrileña.

FERNANDO. Amigo Hubbard, ¿qué es de su vida? No le hemos visto por aquí en toda la semana de vacaciones y todos le hemos echado de menos.

HUBBARD. He aprovechado las vacaciones para dar una vuelta por Andalucía. Tomé el Talgo con aire acondicionado y me fui para Granada. Me encanta el sur de España. Sólo siento que las vacaciones hayan sido tan cortas. Si tuviera más tiempo hubiera visto mucho más en las ciudades andaluzas.

FERNANDO. ¿Qué le gustó más de Andalucía?

HUBBARD. Es difícil contestarle, porque hay tantas y tan distintas cosas que me gustaron, desde la naturaleza hasta la amabilidad de los habitantes. Todo allí es tan pintoresco. Sólo el clima es demasiado caliente para mí.

FERNANDO. ¿Le gusta a Vd. el baile andaluz, el baile flamenco?

HUBBARD. Muchísimo. Uno de los recuerdos más agradables que conservo es el de la noche que pasé en una cueva del Sacromonte de Granada, viendo bailar flamenco a las gitanas. Para mí el flamenco es el baile español más original e interesante.

FERNANDO. Lo es sin duda, aunque no sea un tipo de baile común a toda España. Es un baile propio de Andalucía.

HUBBARD. Al ver bailar flamenco a los gitanos y las gitanas, con su gracia, su ritmo y su animación, me parecía un baile típicamente gitano.

FERNANDO. No, el flamenco no es un baile gitano, aunque los gitanos figuren entre sus mejores intérpretes. En el flamenco hay toda una larga variedad de bailes, representativos de las varias formas de cultura que se desarrollaron en España, y de una manera principal en Andalucía.

HUBBARD. Sin embargo fueron los gitanos los que aportaron su espíritu artístico al baile flamenco.

FERNANDO. Claro. Los gitanos que llegaron a Andalucía a fines del siglo XV — por la época en que los Reyes Católicos conquistaban el reino de Granada — encontraron en España una serie de bailes populares, que ellos interpretaron de una manera excelente.

HUBBARD. Entonces, amigo Fernando, si no es el flamenco, ¿cuál es el baile que pudiera calificarse de nacional de España?

FERNANDO. Ese título le corresponde a la jota. Mire que el flamenco se baila hoy casi exclusivamente por profesionales del baile. En cambio la jota se baila por todo el mundo, por grandes y por chicos, en las fiestas populares de los pueblos y ciudades de
45 España. Aragón es la patria de la jota, que también es el baile representativo de Navarra y Valencia. Pero en toda España, desde Galicia hasta Cataluña, se baila la jota en las fiestas populares tanto del campo como de la ciudad. En muchos pueblos del norte de España las fiestas se terminan con una jota, que es la
50 señal de despedida.

HUBBARD. ¿Hay otros bailes populares, además de la jota, en España?

FERNANDO. Muchos más. En Galicia el baile popular es la muiñeira, que rivaliza con la jota; en Cataluña la sardana, y en el
55 País Vasco hay una enorme variedad de bailes típicos. Todos ellos son muy distintos entre sí. Los ritmos del baile se notan de una manera especial en la música de los compositores famosos, como Granados, Albéniz, De Falla, Ravel, Rimsky-Korsakov, etc. Los grandes guitarristas incluyen bailes en sus programas. Quizás
60 otro día podamos hablar un poco más de este tema tan interesante.

EXPRESIONES ÚTILES

compañero de estudios fellow student
no le hemos visto por aquí we haven't seen you around
le hemos echado de menos we have missed you
dar una vuelta take a trip (tour) through
Talgo con aire acondicionado air-conditioned Talgo train
una larga variedad a wide variety

de una manera principal principally
por la época en que at the time when
pudiera calificarse de might be classified as
profesionales del baile professional dancers
la señal de despedida the signal to go home (to leave)
rivaliza con vies with
distintos entre sí different from each other

RESUMEN PRÁCTICO

1. A los turistas lo que les gusta más en Andalucía es la cultura, la naturaleza, y la amabilidad de los habitantes.
2. Los turistas van en grupos a las cuevas del Sacromonte en Granada para ver bailar flamenco a los gitanos.
3. En el flamenco hay bailes representativos de las varias formas de cultura que se desarrollaron en España.
4. El baile que pudiera calificarse de nacional sería más bien la jota que el flamenco.
5. La jota se baila en las fiestas populares de los pueblos y ciudades de España.
6. Otros bailes que rivalizan en popularidad son la muiñeira en Galicia y la sardana en Cataluña.
7. Los ritmos del baile español han inspirado a muchos compositores de España y de otros países de Europa.

EJERCICIOS

I. CONVERSACIÓN. Que un alumno haga una oración sobre cada uno de los siguientes temas y que los otros le hagan preguntas:

1. Las regiones del sur de España. 2. Las cuevas del Sacromonte en Granada. 3. El baile flamenco y la cultura de España. 4. La llegada de los gitanos a España. 5. Los bailes populares de España. 6. Los grandes compositores españoles. 7. Los famosos guitarristas del mundo.

II. Completen Vds. las condiciones siguientes con oraciones originales:

1. Si le encuentro en un café de Madrid . . . 2. Si no la vemos por aquí . . . 3. Si tenemos vacaciones . . . 4. Si las vacaciones no fueran tan cortas . . . 5. Si el clima fuera mejor . . . 6. Si viajaran por España . . . 7. Si el baile fuera típicamente gitano . . . 8. Si Vd. pudiera encontrar mejores intérpretes del baile . . . 9. Si se baila por todo el mundo . . . 10. Si Vd. viera las fiestas populares . . .

III. Completen Vds. las condiciones siguientes con oraciones de su expereincia personal:

1. Si llueve . . . 2. Si hay sol . . . 3. Si hace frío . . . 4. Si hace calor . . . 5. Si no me gusta el baile . . . 6. Si no estuviera casado . . . 7. Si ella me llama por teléfono . . . 8. Si pudiéramos hablar español mejor . . . 9. Si estudiase más . . . 10. Si llegan mañana . . . 11. Si tuvieran más dinero . . . 12. Si no tuviera tanto trabajo . . .

IV. Tradúzcase oralmente al español:

1. We are fellow students in this university. 2. Have you seen her around? 3. How much we have missed them! 4. I want to take a tour through Aragon. 5. Is it characteristic of Galicia? 6. These dances are among the best in the world. 7. Principally in Andalucia. 8. At the time when there were Moors. 9. Are your friends professional dancers? 10. Which dance is the signal to go home? 11. The dances are different from each other. 12. It is an air-conditioned Talgo train.

V. Formúlense preguntas para las siguientes contestaciones:

1. Fernando Mendoza es su compañero de estudios. 2. Hemos aprovechado las vacaciones para dar una vuelta por el sur. 3. Quería ver sobre todo las ciudades andaluzas. 4. Me gusta todo, pero el clima es demasiado caliente. 5. Sí, he visto bailar flamenco a los gitanos. 6. No me parece que sea un tipo de baile común a toda España. 7. Los gitanos bailan con mucha gracia, ritmo y animación. 8. Lo que han aportado los gitanos al baile flamenco es su espíritu artístico. 9. Era la época de los Reyes Católicos. 10. Sí, la jota se baila en todas las fiestas populares. 11. Hay muchos otros bailes populares. 12. Sí, me gustan mucho los bailes españoles.

VI. Escríbase en español:

1. If I had the money, I would spend a couple of months taking a tour through the south of Spain. 2. If I were traveling through there, I would visit many Andalusian cities. 3. Aren't you sorry that the vacation has been so short? 4. I like everything, even the climate, although it is very warm in the summer. 5. On hearing some of the

jotas of Granados, the girls began to dance gracefully and with animation. 6. These are the forms of culture which developed in Spain during the last four centuries. 7. If I were to classify one as the national dance of Spain, it would be the jota, which is the most popular. 8. The popular feasts of towns and cities were the most picturesque moments of our trip.

Plaza del Congreso, Buenos Aires, Argentina

LECCIÓN 26

Buenos Aires, la metrópoli comercial de Hispanoamérica

Review

Present Subjunctive, Formation and Uses, 72, 73. Imperfect Subjunctive, Formation and Uses, 107–110.

124. *Ojalá* or *tal vez* with the Subjunctive

Ojalá expresses a strong wish that is not likely to come true. It is generally followed by the imperfect subjunctive.

¡Ojalá que pudiera visitar la luna algún día!	I wish I could visit the moon some day.

    Tal vez is followed by the subjunctive only when it is used in the sense of **quizá** and doubt is implied.

Tal vez venga a vernos, pero no es probable.	Perhaps he'll come to see us, but it is not probable.

125. The Independent Subjunctive

The present subjunctive is used in independent clauses to express a wish or an indirect command.

¡Vaya con Dios!	Go with God. (God bless you.)
¡Que vengan a verme!	Let them come to see me.

209

The present subjunctive is used to give general directions to a group in an impersonal way; in this case the reflexive form of the verb is used.

Complétense las oraciones siguientes.   Complete the following sentences.

126. Subjunctive in Modified Assertions

The **–ra** form of the imperfect subjunctive of **querer, poder,** and **deber** may be used to express a modified assertion instead of a direct assertion, or to express a modified wish.

DIRECT ASSERTION: **Vd. no debe hacer eso.**   You must not do that.

MODIFIED ASSERTION: **Vd. no debiera hacer eso.**   You ought not to do that.

MODIFIED WISH: **¿Pudiera Vd. ayudarme?**   Could you help me?

127. Probability

In Spanish the future tense or the future perfect may express an action which is only probable or is assumed to be so. The future refers to a present probability and the future perfect to a past probability.

Estará en casa en este momento.   He must be at home at this moment.
Nos habrán visto esta mañana.   They must have seen us this morning.

The conditional or the conditional perfect may likewise be used to express probability, but only referring to what may have happened in the past.

¿Qué horas serían cuando llegaron?   What time could it have been when they arrived?

Habrían sido las cinco.   It must have been five o'clock.

128. *Sino* and *sino que*

Sino (or **sino que**) is used to mean *but* after a negative statement where there is a contradiction. **Sino** is used when no clause follows and **sino que** when a clause follows.

No es un mar sino un estuario.   It is not a sea but an estuary.
No pido que Vd. me siga, sino que me escuche.   I don't ask that you follow me, but that you listen to me.

129. *(For Reference Only)* **Future Subjunctive**

Literary Spanish has a hypothetical subjunctive which is referred to as the future subjunctive. It denotes an indefinite condition or hypothesis, referring either to present or future time. The future subjunctive is formed by dropping the –**ron** of the third person plural of the preterite and adding –**re,** –**res,** –**re,** –**remos,** –**reis,** –**ren.** The future subjunctive is a literary tense; it is found in old Spanish, in literary works, and in legal terminology, but never in conversation.

Buenos Aires, la metrópoli comercial de Hispanoamérica

Si Nueva York es la metrópoli de la América del Norte y el centro más importante de las comunicaciones marítimas y terrestres de los Estados Unidos, Buenos Aires ocupa la misma posición en el sur del continente americano. La capital argentina, centro de las comunicaciones fluviales y del comercio de la América del Sur, 5 está situada en la orilla derecha del Río de la Plata, que es un ancho estuario de más de cincuenta kilómetros en su parte más estrecha. En él desembocan los ríos Paraná y Uruguay; y la orilla izquierda pertenece a la República Oriental del Uruguay, cuya capital, Montevideo, está casi a la entrada de este estuario. El Río 10 de la Plata es el punto de partida de una extensa red de comunicaciones fluviales, formada por varios grandes ríos de la América del Sur, como el Paraná, el Paraguay, el Uruguay, el Pilcomayo y el Salado. En las orillas de estos ríos se encuentran muchas de las ciudades más importantes de la Argentina (Rosario, Santa Fe y 15 Corrientes), del Paraguay (su capital Asunción) y otras del Uruguay y del Brasil.

Buenos Aires, desde su fundación en el siglo XVI, ocupó un

lugar muy importante en el sistema de las comunicaciones y el
20 comercio de la América del Sur. En sus orígenes dependió del
Perú, porque era el puerto en el Atlántico de este país, y estaba
unido a él por una larga carretera de varios miles de millas, que
unía a Lima con Buenos Aires y pasaba por las principales
ciudades argentinas, como Córdoba y Tucumán. Creció tanto la
25 vida y el comercio de Buenos Aires que, a fines del siglo XVIII, el
gobierno español estableció en ella la capital del nuevo virreinato
de la Plata. Buenos Aires fue la primera ciudad del continente que
se separó de España, proclamando su independencia el 25 de mayo
de 1810, que es hoy el día de la fiesta nacional de la Argentina.
30 Desde entonces la capital argentina ha ido creciendo a pasos
agigantados hasta convertirse en una ciudad de unos cuatro
millones de habitantes y de una enorme extensión urbana, la mayor
de toda la América latina.

Buenos Aires es no sólo muy grande, sino que es una de las
35 ciudades más bellas del mundo. No hay ciudad que ofrezca en sus
plazas, parques y avenidas un conjunto urbano más moderno. El
plano general de la ciudad sigue en su mayor parte el viejo sistema
cuadricular de los pueblos coloniales españoles, formado por
manzanas cuadradas y regulares que reciben el nombre de cuadras.
40 Una de las plazas más bellas de la capital argentina es la de Mayo,
situada en el centro de la ciudad, que conmemora el mes de la
independencia argentina. En esta plaza está situada la Casa
Rosada, residencia del Presidente da la República. Entre las
avenidas más conocidas figuran la de Mayo, que parte de la plaza
45 del mismo nombre, la de la Florida, donde se encuentran los
grandes comercios de la capital, y la de Rivadavia, una de las más
largas de América.

La vida de Buenos Aires va unida a la actividad de su puerto,
visitado diariamente por numerosos barcos de todos los países que
50 vienen a la Argentina a buscar sus productos principales y a dejar
allí los artículos manufacturados de Europa y los Estados Unidos.
En los muelles y dársenas de su puerto y en sus grandes aeropuertos es incesante el tráfico que da a Buenos Aires la sensación
de una de las ciudades más activas de nuestro hemisferio. ¡Ojalá
55 que Vd. también pudiera visitarla algún día!

EXPRESIONES ÚTILES

las comunicaciones marítimas y terrestres land and sea communications

el punto de partida the point of departure

una red de comunicaciones a network of communications

en sus orígenes in the beginning, originally

miles de millas thousands of miles

el actual territorio the present territory

a pasos agigantados in gigantic steps

convertirse en to turn into

en su mayor parte on the whole

da la sensación gives the impression

RESUMEN PRÁCTICO

1. Buenos Aires es el centro de las comunicaciones fluviales y del comercio de la América del Sur.
2. En sus orígines Buenos Aires era el puerto del Perú en el Atlántico y estaba unido a él por una larga carretera.
3. A fines del siglo XVIII el gobierno español estableció en Buenos Aires la capital del nuevo virreinato de la Plata.
4. Buenos Aires fue la primera ciudad de la América que se separó de España, proclamando su independencia el 25 de mayo de 1810.
5. A Buenos Aires vienen diariamente numerosos barcos de todos los países del mundo.
6. La ciudad es no sólo una de las más activas de nuestro hemisferio, sino una de las más bellas.
7. En extensión superficial, Buenos Aires es la ciudad más grande de la América latina.

EJERCICIOS

I. CONVERSACIÓN. Expliquen Vds. en forma completa las siguientes ideas delante de la clase:

1. ¿Cuál es la posición de Buenos Aires en el continente del sur?
2. ¿En qué aspecto son diferentes las dos mayores ciudades de los

dos continentes? 3. ¿Qué es el Río de la Plata y cuál es su importancia? 4. ¿Cuál ha sido la función histórica de Buenos Aires en el comercio de la América del Sur? 5. ¿Por qué se celebra el 25 de mayo en la Argentina? 6. ¿Por qué se considera Buenos Aires una de las ciudades más bellas del mundo? 7. ¿Cómo es el plano general de la ciudad? 8. Describa Vd. una de las plazas. 9. Describa Vd. la actividad del puerto de Buenos Aires.

II. Complétense las oraciones siguientes con frases interesantes:

1. Aunque Nueva York sea la metrópoli de la América del Norte . . . 2. Cuando yo visité a Buenos Aires . . . 3. Antes de que fuera el centro del comercio de la América del Sur, Buenos Aires . . . 4. Sin que su madre lo supiera, ella . . . 5. A menos que Vd. no quiera olvidar todo lo aprendido . . . 6. Aunque la ciudad ocupe un lugar muy importante . . . 7. Construyeron una carretera muy larga para que . . . 8. La vida allí es tan cómoda que . . . 9. Yo no sabía que el territorio . . . 10. Si es una de las ciudades más bellas es porque . . . 11. El plano general sigue en su mayor parte . . . 12. Ellos no quieren que . . . 13. ¿Sabía Vd. que la Casa Rosada . . . ? 14. Numerosos barcos llegan diariamente al puerto de Buenos Aires para . . . 15. No me parece que la ciudad . . .

III. Tradúzcase oralmente al español:

1. I sure wish that (Would that) you could accompany me! 2. Let them study the history of Peru. 3. May it be worth the time that I have spent. 4. Could you give her some advice? 5. It must have been (It was probably) ten o'clock. 6. I should like to learn. 7. It is not red, but green. 8. I do not want you to sing, but to be quiet. 9. The city is not large, but small. 10. She answered without their having spoken.

IV. Hagan Vds. preguntas empleando las frases siguientes:

1. en su mayor parte. 2. el centro de la ciudad. 3. a pasos agigantados. 4. una red de comunicaciones. 5. miles de millas. 6. un conjunto urbano. 7. en sus orígenes. 8. el punto de partida. 9. hasta convertirse. 10. una larga carretera.

V. CONVERSACIÓN

Tres estudiantes, (A) un newyorkino, (B) un mexicano, y (C) un argentino, discuten la mayor ciudad de cada país.

A dice que Nueva York es la metrópoli de la América del Norte y presenta sus razones.

B dice que ahora la Ciudad de México tiene una enorme población también, pero lo que tiene es importancia histórica y artística.

C dice que Buenos Aires va creciendo a pasos agigantados y que algún día no muy lejano será la mayor ciudad de las Américas.

B mantiene que la Ciudad de México y São Paulo en el Brasil van creciendo al mismo paso.

A dice que Nueva York es el centro del comercio mundial y que es la ciudad más completa del mundo.

C dice que Buenos Aires no sólo tiene gran comercio, sino que es una de las ciudades más bellas.

Y la discusión sigue así lo más que se pueda.

VI. Escríbase en español:

1. For a long time New York was the most important city in river communications as well as **(lo mismo que)** in other forms of transportation. 2. Although it is situated on the shores of the Plata River, Buenos Aires is the center of both land and sea communications. 3. Find me the point of departure of this whole network of communications, because I do not understand the map. 4. Originally Argentina depended on Peru, but now it is far more important than its neighbor to the northwest. 5. Although the Pan American highway passes through very high chains of mountains, it is very carefully constructed. 6. If Buenos Aires were not one of the most beautiful cities in the world, it would not be the center of Latin American culture. 7. The square which commemorates the date of the independence of the republic is situated in the heart of the city. 8. The docks and wharfs of New York have more traffic than those of the capital of Argentina, but the latter is still one of the most active cities in this hemisphere.

LECCIÓN 27

La civilización árabe en España

Review

Conjunctive Object Pronouns, 81–83.
Personal Pronouns after Prepositions, 61.

130. Inverted Word Order

The order in a Spanish sentence is generally the same as in English. However, when a word other than the subject begins a sentence, the order of the subject and verb may be inverted for special effects, particularly in dependent clauses.

En el momento en que invadieron la   At the moment when the Musulmans
península los musulmanes . . .   invaded the peninsula . . .

131. Exclamations

In an exclamation the indefinite article is omitted before a noun or an adjective.

¡Qué hermoso paisaje!   What a beautiful countryside!

     This same idea can be expressed by placing the noun first and following it with **tan** before the adjective.

¡Qué paisaje tan hermoso!

Court of Lions, La Alhambra, Granada, Spain

In an exclamation **cuánto** as an adverb or **cuánto** (–a, –os, –as) as an adjective means *how* (*much*) or *how many* and takes a written accent.

¡ **Cuánto me gusta vivir aquí!**	How I like to live here!
¡ **Cuántos monumentos que hay!**	How many monuments there are!

¡ **Qué!** preceding an adjective or an adverb corresponds to *how*.

¡ **Qué bonita me pareció!**	How beautiful she seemed to me!

¡ **Qué!** preceding a noun corresponds to *what, what a*.

¡ **Qué pobreza que había!**	What poverty there was!
¡ **Qué hombre!**	What a man!

132. Interjections

Some of the common, respectable interjections are:

¡ **Caramba!** Gosh! Hell!	¡ **Mire!** Look!
¡ **Claro!** Of course!	¡ **Oiga!** Listen!
¡ **Cuidado!** Look out!	¡ **Olé!** Hurrah!
¡ **Hombre!** Man alive!	

133. Intonation

Intonation refers to the rising and falling of the voice within a sentence, thereby giving a characteristic expression. Intonation is extremely important in a foreign language, because not only does each language have its own pattern, but the intonation differs within different regions speaking the same language. The intonation given to a Spanish sentence by a Mexican is different from that given to it by an Argentinean, and they are both completely different from English intonation, of course.

Study the following intonation patterns and then observe and imitate closely patterns as you hear them in native speakers.

La puerta está cerrada.	Tradúzcase al español.
¿A dónde va Vd.?	¡No me digas!
¡Qué niña tan bonita!	

La civilización árabe en España

Uno de los rasgos peculiares de la civilización española, que la distingue entre las otras de la Europa occidental, es la presencia en ella de numerosos elementos que recibió de los árabes en la época en que éstos dominaron la península ibérica. Pero esta influencia se reparte de una manera muy desigual por las varias regiones españolas: apenas existe en el norte, y es, en cambio, muy fuerte en las provincias del antiguo reino de Granada, en donde los árabes permanecieron casi ocho siglos. Las huellas de la civilización árabe en España son más profundas en Aragón, Valencia y Andalucía, en donde todavía se conservan muchos y muy bellos monumentos de esta época.

En realidad los árabes no eran un solo pueblo con una sola cultura, sino que constituían un conglomerado de naciones. Muchas de ellas, como Egipto, Persia, Siria, Líbano y Palestina, eran muy viejas en la civilización; y los árabes las unieron en una comunidad de fe y de lengua. Una de las viejas culturas que entró a formar parte de esta comunidad del mundo islámico fue la española, que, en el momento en que invadieron la península ibérica los musulmanes (711 A.D.), era una de las más avanzadas de la Europa occidental. La cultura española no desapareció con la invasión árabe, sino que se incorporó a las otras que formaban parte del mundo islámico y que los árabes iban trayendo a España; y fue el principal motor que animó, en los años de dominio musulmán, las creaciones culturales de los árabes españoles.

Los dos monumentos más notables que se conservan de esta cultura son la mezquita de Córdoba y la Alhambra de Granada, los dos en Andalucía. La mezquita de Córdoba — comenzada en el siglo VIII, no mucho después de la invasión árabe — es una de las más notables del mundo. En su construcción se emplearon materiales de iglesias cristianas visigóticas derribadas por los árabes. La vista interior de la mezquita, con más de ochocientas columnas, veinte y nueve naves transversales y diez y nueve longitudinales, es uno de los espectáculos más impresionantes, que da al visitante la sensación de encontrarse en medio de un bosque

35 de armoniosas construcciones artísticas. El Palacio de la Alhambra es más moderno — quizás del siglo XIV — y muestra la
influencia de la lejana Persia en la delicadeza de sus proporciones.
La Alfajería de Zaragoza, el Alcázar de Sevilla, las puertas de
Toledo, la torre de la Giralda en Sevilla, y centenares de castillos en
40 muchas de las provincias españolas son un recuerdo eternamente
presente del pasado musulmán.

La tradición árabe se conserva también en muchas pequeñas
industrias que son una de las mayores riquezas de la artesanía
española. Una de las más famosas es la cerámica, que tiene una
45 larga y brillante historia en España. Sevilla con sus azulejos y
Valencia con sus excelentes platos siguen siendo los herederos de
esta artesanía. Otra es la del cuero, principalmente la de Córdoba,
que es conocida en el mundo entero por su excelencia. En Toledo
y en Eibar se producen hoy una serie de objetos artísticos de varios
50 metales que revelan su clara ascendencia árabe. Esta artesanía
española, así como las huertas de Valencia y Murcia, y los jardines
de Andalucía y Castilla la Nueva, nos muestran que la herencia
árabe quedó incorporada de manera permanente a la cultura
española.

EXPRESIONES ÚTILES

de una manera desigual in an uneven
  manner, unevenly
en realidad in reality
comunidad de fe y de lengua community of faith and language

se incorporó a las otras became incorporated with the others
en medio de un bosque in the middle
  of a forest
centenares de castillos hundreds of
  castles

RESUMEN PRÁCTICO

1. La influencia árabe se reparte por muchas regiones de España,
   sobre todo por Andalucía, Valencia y Aragón.
2. La cultura española entró a formar parte del mundo islámico porque
   era una de las más avanzadas de la Europa occidental.

3. En los años del dominio musulmán las varias culturas del mundo islámico animaron las creaciones culturales de los árabes.
4. En muchas mezquitas se emplearon materiales de iglesias cristianas visigóticas derribadas por los árabes.
5. El Palacio de la Alhambra en Granada muestra la influencia de Persia en la delicadeza de sus proporciones.
6. La tradición árabe se conserva en muchas pequeñas industrias, como la cerámica y la industria del cuero.
7. La herencia árabe se encuentra en el campo, en la horticultura de Valencia y Murcia, y en los jardines de España.

EJERCICIOS

I. CONVERSACIÓN. Expliquen Vds. en oraciones completas las siguientes ideas delante de la clase:

1. ¿Cómo se reparte la influencia árabe en España? 2. ¿Dónde se conservan las huellas de la civilización árabe? 3. ¿Eran un solo pueblo los árabes? 4. ¿Cómo se incorporaron la cultura española y la cultura islámica? 5. ¿Desapareció la cultura española con la invasión árabe? 6. ¿Cuáles son los monumentos más notables de la cultura árabe? 7. Describa Vd. la mezquita de Córdoba. 8. Describa Vd. algo del Palacio de la Alhambra. 9. ¿Qué industrias se desarrollaron con la invasión árabe? 10. ¿Queda todavía en España la influencia árabe?

II. Háganse oraciones completas basadas sobre los conceptos siguientes:

1. elementos, árabes, dominar. 2. influencia, repartir, regiones. 3. p∢ovincias, permanecer, siglos. 4. huellas, conservar, monumentos. 5. conglomerado, naciones, comunidad. 6. musulmanes, invadir, siglo. 7. cultura, incorporarse, mundo islámico. 8. mezquita, columnas, bellas. 9. delicadeza, proporciones, mostrar. 10. industrias, riquezas, artesanía. 11. azulejos, platos, ciudades. 12. Toledo, producir, metales.

III. Dé Vd. una definición en español de cada una de las palabras siguientes:

1. artesanía. 2. heredero. 3. horticultura. 4. mezquita. 5. invasión. 6. construcción. 7. centenares. 8. conglomerado. 9. invadir. 10. huella.

IV. Pónganse las siguientes frases en el imperfecto de subjuntivo, empleándolas en oraciones completas:

1. Ellos distinguen. 2. Él recibió. 3. Se reparte. 4. Ellos permanecieron. 5. Ellos constituían. 6. Nosotros traemos. 7. Yo pongo. 8. Vosotros permitís. 9. Nosotros empleamos. 10. Él da. 11. Se encuentran. 12. Me recuerdo. 13. Ella conoce. 14. Ellos dicen. 15. Él fue.

V. Tradúzcase oralmente al español:

1. Listen, come here! 2. At a bullfight one shouts **Olé!** 3. Look out with that cup! 4. What a beautiful tower! 5. What an impressive spectacle! 6. How he likes to sleep! 7. The traces of Arab civilization. 8. There is a community of language. 9. In the middle of the room. 10. Hundreds and hundreds of monuments.

VI. Escríbase en español:

1. In the era in which the Arabs dominated the peninsula, Spain received many elements which were foreign to the rest of Europe. 2. The influence is spread over the various regions of the country, in some places more and in other places less. 3. We hope that the nations of the world will some day be united in a community of faith and language. 4. It is difficult to imagine how peoples can become united if they do not understand their languages. 5. Without the influence of the Islamic world, the Iberian peninsula would have had a different development. 6. The Christian churches torn down by the Arabs were smaller than the mosque of Cordova or the Alhambra of Granada. 7. If I could take a trip to Spain, I would not fail to see the hundreds of castles which are found in many of the provinces. 8. He who sees the world understands many languages and many countries, but most of all **(más que nada)** he understands himself better.

Façade of The Mosque in Córdoba, Spain

Miraflores Locks, Panama

LECCIÓN 28

Una carta de Panamá

Review

Conjugation of Irregular Verbs, see Appendix.

134. Family Names

In Spanish, people generally use the last name of the father together with the mother's maiden name as their last name.

Ramón (first name) **Cajal** (father's last name) **y Rodríguez** (mother's maiden name)

When a woman gets married, the mother's maiden name is dropped and the last name of the husband is used instead, preceded by **de.**

Rosa Cajal (father's last name) **de Camino** (husband's last name)

Frequently, for convenience, Spanish people will use only one last name, in which case they use the father's family name.

135. Letter Writing

In writing friendly letters the heading is very simple in Spanish, as in English. The date goes in the upper right hand corner, together with the place of writing.

Madrid, 20 de abril, 1972

The beginning of the letter is also quite simple:

Querido amigo:	Dear friend:
Muy querido —:	My dear —:
Estimado señor —:	Dear Mr. —:
Distinguido profesor —:	Dear professor —:
Reverendo padre —:	Reverend Father —:

The closing of a friendly letter is likely to be a little more affectionate and flowery than in English.

Con saludos cordiales,   Cordially yours,

Con mil recuerdos,   With best regards,
Su amigo   Cordially

Con un abrazo,   With cordial regards,
Su amigo   Sincerely

Con muchos recuerdos a Vd. y a su estimable esposa,
Su amigo
With best regards to you and your charming wife,
Cordially

The closing of an informal business letter may still contain the classic formula **Su atento y seguro servidor,** abbreviated into **Su atento y s.s.**

In the old-fashioned Spanish letters there were many set formulas, some of which were quite picturesque, but they have all been dropped in modern, friendly correspondence.

Una carta de Panamá

Panamá, 23 de diciembre, 1972

Querido Fernando:

Acabo de regresar de Costa Rica. Pasé el otoño en San José, huyendo de la lluvia que cae constantemente en Panamá desde
5 octubre hasta principios de diciembre. Ahora el cielo está despejado; y, aunque tenemos alguna vez que otra un aguacero, no se siente tanto la humedad.

Panamá, la capital de la nación, donde ahora resido, es una hermosa ciudad, situada en la costa del Océano Pacífico. Colón, la segunda ciudad panameña por su importancia y número de habitantes, está en la costa del Atlántico. Las dos ciudades se comunican por un ferrocarril construido hace ya un siglo por una empresa norteamericana. Y también entre ellas, aunque no para su servicio sino para el de la navegación internacional, corre el canal llamado de Panamá, obra de la iniciativa, de la ingeniería y de la sanidad norteamericana; pues para poder construirlo, los médicos y sanitarios de los Estados Unidos tuvieron que limpiar estas tierras de la fiebre amarilla.

A diferencia del Canal de Suez, excavado en la arena del desierto, el de Panamá corre entre montañas cubiertas de espesa vegetación, aprovechando en algunas partes el curso de los ríos, que fue ampliado, cortando en otras las montañas, y utilizando en ocasiones esclusas para salvar la diferencia de nivel entre las varias presas y los océanos. A ambos lados del canal hay una estrecha faja de tierra, administrada, conjuntamente con el canal, por la Dirección de la Zona del Canal. Los Estados Unidos pagan anualmente una crecida suma a Panamá por el arrendamiento de este territorio. La contribución norteamericana por este arrendamiento es la principal fuente de ingresos de la República de Panamá.

La Zona del Canal tiene dos ciudades de muy distinto carácter y las dos están a cada uno de los extremos del canal, como sus puertos de entrada: en el Atlántico, la pequeña ciudad de Cristóbal, unida casi a la panameña de Colón, que es más un puerto con sus instalaciones que una villa propiamente dicha; y en el Pacífico, la de Balboa, que es una de las ciudades más lindas del continente americano, con sus casas particulares y edificios públicos escondidos en parques de árboles tropicales.

En el límite de la Zona del Canal en el Pacífico, donde Balboa se encuentra con la ciudad de Panamá, se alza el cerro de Ancón, cubierto de espesa vegetación. Desde su cima se domina el extenso golfo de Panamá con sus encantadoras islas, entre ellas la de Taboga, de la que salió Pizarro para conquistar el Perú.

Estos días de Navidad la ciudad está muy animada. Los comercios están siempre llenos de gente que compra toda clase de cosas.

Yo he comprado varios regalos para los muchos amigos que
tenemos. Una de las costumbres más curiosas de la vida panameña
en estos días navideños es la de exhibir nacimientos en los portales
de las casas. Para que se puedan ver mejor, dejan abierta la media
50 puerta superior.
    Espero poder veros en la primavera. Mientras tanto os deseo
Felices Pascuas y un Próspero Año Nuevo, con un abrazo de tu
buen amigo.

JOSEPH

EXPRESIONES ÚTILES

alguna vez que otra from time to
  time
se comunican por are connected by
a diferencia de unlike
aprovechar algo to take advantage
  of something
en ocasiones occasionally

a ambos lados on both sides
días de Navidad (días navideños)
  Christmas season
Felices Pascuas Merry Christmas
Próspero Año Nuevo Happy New
  Year

RESUMEN PRÁCTICO

1. En Panamá la lluvia cae constantemente desde octubre hasta principios de diciembre.
2. Panamá, la capital, y Colón, la segunda ciudad panameña, se
   comunican por un ferrocarril y una carretera.
3. Entre las dos ciudades corre el canal llamado de Panamá, obra de
   la ingeniería norteamericana.
4. El canal corre entre montañas cubiertas de espesa vegetación,
   aprovechando en algunas partes el curso de los ríos.
5. La Dirección de la Zona del Canal administra no sólo el canal mismo
   sino la faja de tierra a sus dos lados.
6. Algunas de las calles de Balboa, que pertenece a la Zona, se comunican con las de la ciudad de Panamá, que pertenece a Panamá.
7. Una de las costumbres curiosas de la vida panameña en Navidad
   es la de exhibir nacimientos en los portales de las casas.

EJERCICIOS

I. CONVERSACIÓN. Contesten Vds. a las siguientes preguntas:

1. ¿Hay mucha lluvia en Panamá? 2. ¿Le gusta a Vd. un aguacero en el verano cuando hace mucho calor? 3. ¿Cuáles son las dos ciudades principales de Panamá? 4. ¿Quién construyó el ferrocarril por el cual se comunican las dos ciudades? 5. ¿Qué tuvieron que hacer los médicos y sanitarios de los Estados Unidos para poder construir el canal? 6. ¿Qué diferencia hay entre el Canal de Suez y el de Panamá? 7. ¿Tienen que pagar algo los Estados Unidos por el arrendamiento de la Zona del Canal? 8. ¿Qué dos ciudades tiene la Zona del Canal? 9. ¿Qué se domina desde la cima del cerro de Ancón? 10. ¿Hay mucha actividad en los días navideños?

II. PRÁCTICA ORAL. Mandatos Indirectos.

1. Pregúntele a un amigo si ha estado alguna vez en Panamá. 2. Pídale que le describa el tiempo que hace en Panamá desde octubre hasta principios de diciembre. 3. Pregúntele cómo se comunican las dos ciudades principales de Panamá. 4. Pídale que le diga lo que tuvieron que hacer los médicos y sanitarios de los Estados Unidos. 5. Pregúntele quién administra la Zona del Canal. 6. Pregunte a una muchacha cuál es la principal fuente de ingresos de la República de Panamá. 7. Pídale que le describa las dos ciudades de Cristóbal y Balboa. 8. Pídale que le describa el cerro de Ancón. 9. Pida a un amigo que le compre varios regalos, y le diga para qué sirven.

III. Estudie Vd. cuidadosamente la entonación de las siguientes oraciones, imitando la de su profesor:

1. Panamá, 23 de diciembre de 1972. 2. El Canal de Panamá es obra de la iniciativa, de la ingeniería y de la sanidad norteamericana. 3. Desde la cima del cerro de Ancón se domina el extenso golfo de Panamá con sus encantadoras islas. 4. ¿Cómo pudiera yo saber que había tanta lluvia en los trópicos? 5. ¡Hombre! ¡Oiga! ¡Cuidado con las cartas que escribe a las muchachas! 6. ¡Cuántos monumentos que hay! 7. Para mí el flamenco es el baile español más original e interesante.

IV. Escriba Vd. tres cartitas originales sobre los siguientes temas:

1. Un amigo de España va a visitar los Estados Unidos y Vd. le convida a pasar algunos días con su familia.
2. Vd. ha pasado una semana con algunos amigos en México y ahora les escribe una carta de agradecimiento.
3. Un estudiante argentino le pide información sobre la universidad a que Vd. asiste.

V. CONVERSACIÓN

Dos estudiantes, (A) y (B), acaban de volver de Panamá. Dos amigos, (C) y (D), les hacen preguntas sobre el viaje.

C pregunta cuántas horas tomó el avión para llegar a Panamá.
A contesta que el viaje tomó seis horas de Nueva York.
D pregunta cómo viajaron de Panamá a Colón.
B contesta que tomaron un viejo tren de una ciudad a la otra.
C quiere saber qué tal les pareció el canal.
A contesta que les pareció una obra sobresaliente de la ingeniería.
D quiere saber por qué los Estados Unidos siguen controlando la Zona.
B dice que la cuestión es política y mejor no discutirla.

Pero si los estudiantes quieren discutir la cuestión en la clase, que lo hagan en español.

VI. Escríbase en español:

Los Angeles, May 21, 1972

1. Dear Peter:

I have just finished my course in Spanish composition and conversation and I feel quite happy. 2. We have not only reviewed our grammar, but we have learned something about every country where Spanish is spoken. 3. For example, we know now that the Arabs exercised great influence on Spanish civilization. 4. We know that the Incas of Peru had an empire which extended over most of the west coast of South America. 5. We have studied about the great development of the oil industry in Venezuela and the wealth which has come to that country in the last thirty years. 6. Did you know that the northern coast of Spain has some of the most picturesque scenery in Europe? 7. Wouldn't you be interested in learning about the famous festivals of southern Spain? 8. For me, one of the favorite lessons was the one on tourism in Mexico, because I hope to get the old car ready and start traveling. 9. When I do travel, the course in Spanish will be worth while not only for the pleasure that it gives me, but for the money it will save me.

10. Remember me to your father and mother, and of course to your sister, who looks very pretty in the photograph you sent me.

As ever,

George

Appendix I

This Appendix provides long and informative selections of specialized interest, one on professional careers and one on foods. The words of these selections are included in the end vocabulary, but the student should learn to guess them from the context rather than translate. The questions on the facing pages provide the basis for a discussion of the content.

La elección de una carrera:
Carreras y profesiones liberales

Uno de los momentos más decisivos en la vida del hombre es la selección
de la carrera que será su profesión a lo largo de su vida. Antes solían ser
los padres los que escogían el marido para su hija, por ser entonces el
matrimonio la principal carrera de la mujer; y eran también los que
5 escogían la carrera del hijo. Por esta razón se pueden todavía encontrar,
en los hombres de las viejas generaciones, españoles con dos carreras:
la de abogado, que le fue impuesta por su padre; y la de letras, a la que
se dedicó el joven por vocación.

Esta selección de la carrera se puede producir en distintos momentos
10 de la vida del joven o de la joven interesados. Quizás los primeros en
escoger una carrera sean los que se van a dedicar al magisterio, a la
enseñanza primaria, en las escuelas públicas o privadas. Esta selección
suele ocurrir, en este caso, en un momento muy temprano en la vida del
muchacho o de la muchacha. Entre los 12 y 18 años cursan sus estudios,
15 en las Escuelas Normales o Escuelas de Magisterio, los que van a
dedicarse a enseñar las primeras letras; mientras todavía están, en esos
mismos años, en el bachillerato los jóvenes que se van a dedicar a otras
carreras profesionales.

Quizás después de los maestros sean los militares los que hacen su
20 elección en años mozos; pues los que van a ingresar en las academias
militares y navales de algunos países de lengua española toman un
examen de ingreso antes de que otros jóvenes terminen el bachillerato.

En general, es durante los años de la enseñanza secundaria, sobre
todo en los últimos en el Instituto de Segunda Enseñanza, en el Liceo o
25 en el Colegio Nacional, cuando los jóvenes eligen la carrera que van a
seguir más tarde.

PREGUNTAS

1. ¿Cuál era en otros tiempos la principal carrera de la mujer?
2. ¿Quién solía escoger el marido para las señoritas?
3. ¿Quién escogía también la carrera para los jóvenes?
4. ¿Por qué tenían dos carreras los hombres de las viejas generaciones?
5. ¿La selección de una carrera se produce siempre temprano en la vida?
6. ¿Qué carrera es la del magisterio?
7. ¿Se escoge temprano la carrera del magisterio?
8. ¿Entre qué años se cursan los estudios en las Escuelas Normales?
9. ¿Entre qué años están los jóvenes en el bachillerato?
10. ¿Es el bachillerato la preparación normal para otras carreras profesionales?
11. ¿Tienen que escoger temprano su carrera los militares?
12. ¿Hay que tomar un examen de ingreso para ingresar en las academias militares y navales?
13. ¿El Instituto de Segunda Enseñanza, el Liceo, y el Colegio Nacional vienen todos después del bachillerato?

TEMAS PARA DISCUSIÓN

1. Carreras ahora disponibles para las mujeres.
2. Maneras de resolver el conflicto entre una carrera y el matrimonio.
3. La carrera de maestros de escuelas primarias.
4. La diferencia entre el bachillerato y el A. B.
5. La vida militar como carrera en los Estados Unidos.

Todavía a principios de este siglo las carreras más importantes en todos los países hispánicos eran la de derecho y la de medicina, que constituían las dos profesiones liberales más numerosas. La carrera de derecho no era entonces en estos países, como lo es todavía hoy en los
5 Estados Unidos, una carrera profesional para la formación de abogados, sino que los seis años de estudios eran una especie de humanidades en ciencias morales, políticas y económicas. La tomaban los que se iban a dedicar a servir la administración del Estado (magistrados, secretarios de ayuntamiento, cónsules, embajadores, abogados del Estado, etc.), a
10 intervenir en la vida política del país (gobernadores, ministros, diputados a cortes, senadores, etc.), o, por ser de familias ricas, no pensaban ejercer la profesión y se contentaban sólo con el título.

La medicina, en cambio, era una carrera profesional que atraía un gran número de jóvenes, en algunos países mucho más que la de
15 derecho. Entonces eran pocos los que se iban a dedicar a las ciencias o a las letras, a la ingeniería, a la arquitectura, y a otras distintas actividades profesionales.

En los últimos años ha cambiado mucho la situación. Uno de los fenómenos más característicos de nuestro tiempo es el gran aumento del
20 número de estudiantes que hay en todas las facultades o escuelas universitarias. El aumento es sobre todo visible en las Facultades de Filosofía y Letras, antes poco concurridas, y hoy llenas de estudiantes, particularmente mujeres, que aspiran a enseñar en los Institutos de Segunda Enseñanza y Universidades de su respectivo país; y también
25 fuera de él, enseñando lengua y literatura española en alguna universidad europea o de los Estados Unidos.

Es también muy numerosa la concurrencia de estudiantes a las Facultades o Escuelas de Ciencias. Pero el aumento mayor en la matrícula de estudiantes se ha registrado en las Escuelas de Ingenieros,
30 que son las que cuentan, en algunos países hispánicos, con un mayor número de alumnos.

PREGUNTAS

1. ¿Cuáles eran las dos profesiones más numerosas a principios de este siglo?
2. ¿La carrera de derecho era sólo para la formación de abogados?
3. ¿Qué ciencias se estudiaban en la carrera de derecho?
4. ¿Sabe Vd. lo que hace un secretario de ayuntamiento?
5. ¿Sabe Vd. lo que hacen los abogados del Estado?
6. ¿Ejercían siempre su profesión los de familias ricas?
7. ¿Eran muchos los que se iban a dedicar a las ciencias o a las letras?
8. ¿En los últimos años hay muchos estudiantes en todas las facultades universitarias?
9. ¿Hay estudiantes de ambos los sexos, o sólo hombres?
10. ¿A qué aspiran las mujeres que estudian en las Facultades de Filosofía y Letras?
11. ¿Sabe Vd. lo que son los Institutos de Segunda Enseñanza?
12. ¿Se enseña mucho la lengua y literatura española?
13. ¿Hay gran concurrencia de estudiantes en las Escuelas de Ciencias?
14. ¿Hay muchos estudiantes en las Escuelas de Ingeniería?

TEMAS PARA DISCUSIÓN

1. La diferencia en la carrera de derecho entre los países hispánicos y los Estados Unidos.
2. Las profesiones que pueden resultar de la carrera de derecho.
3. El valor del título universitario en la sociedad moderna.
4. La medicina como carrera profesional para las mujeres.
5. La razón por el aumento en la matrícula de estudiantes en nuestros tiempos.

Los grandes cambios producidos en los últimos años en la vida académica de los países hispánicos y en las carreras que sigue la gente joven han afectado de una manera directa a la carrera de derecho. La antigua Facultad de Derecho y Ciencias Sociales se ha transformado
5 últimamente en algunos países en tres distintas facultades o escuelas: de Derecho, de Ciencias Políticas, y de Ciencias Económicas.

La transformación que ha experimentado la sociedad de los países de lengua española en los últimos años, sobre todo en Venezuela, España, México, la Argentina, el Uruguay, y Colombia, ha afectado de una
10 manera singular a la matrícula universitaria en las varias escuelas. El desarrollo sensible de la economía en esos países ha hecho descender, sobre todo en España, el número de estudiantes de derecho y aumentar de una manera sensible los que cursan sus estudios en las escuelas de ingeniería.

15 Antiguamente había en España cinco diferentes escuelas de ingenieros que, con la de arquitectura, componían las llamadas escuelas especiales, aparte de la universidad: de ingenieros de caminos, canales y puertos, que equivale a lo que se designa en los Estados Unidos con el nombre de ingeniería civil; de ingenieros agrónomos, de ingenieros industriales, de
20 ingenieros de minas, y de ingenieros de montes, a las que se añadió más tarde la de ingenieros de telecomunicación. Aparte de ellas estaba la de ingenieros navales, que dependía entonces del Ministerio de Marina y formaba parte de los estudios de la Marina de Guerra.

De todas estas escuelas era la de ingenieros industriales la que atraía
25 mayor número de estudiantes, porque servía las necesidades del desarrollo industrial de España y de los países hispanoamericanos. Antes eran muchos los estudiantes de lengua española que cursaban sus estudios en las escuelas de ingenieros más famosas de Europa (París, Lieja, Zurich). Hoy, en cambio, son pocos los estudiantes españoles e
30 hispanoamericanos que salen de sus respectivos países para cursar estudios en las escuelas de ingeniería extranjeras.

PREGUNTAS

1. ¿Los cambios en la vida académica han afectado a la carrera de derecho?
2. ¿Cómo se divide ahora la antigua Facultad de Derecho y Ciencias Sociales?
3. ¿En qué países hispánicos se nota la transformación indicada?
4. ¿Cuáles diferentes escuelas de ingenieros había antiguamente?
5. ¿De qué se ocupan los ingenieros de caminos, canales y puertos?
6. ¿Cómo se designan esos ingenieros en los Estados Unidos?
7. ¿De qué se ocupan los ingenieros agrónomos? los ingenieros industriales?
8. ¿Por qué es necesaria la carrera de ingenieros de montes en los países hispanos?
9. ¿Le parece importante la carrera de ingeniero de telecomunicación?
10. ¿Qué carrera formaba parte de los estudios de la Marina de Guerra?
11. ¿Por qué había tantos ingenieros industriales?
12. ¿Cuáles eran algunas de las escuelas famosas de Europa en la ingeniería industrial?
13. ¿Qué cambio han subido los estudios de ingeniería industrial en los países de habla española?

TEMAS PARA DISCUSIÓN

1. Los cambios en la vida académica de los Estados Unidos.
2. El desarrollo de la economía en los países hispanoamericanos.
3. Los varios tipos de ingenieros y sus funciones.
4. La importancia de la Marina en el mundo de hoy.
5. La importancia de la telecomunicación.

El desarrollo industrial en los países de lengua española, con las nuevas oportunidades que ofrecen en carreras profesionales, ha estimulado la creación, sobre todo en España, de una serie de Escuelas de Administración o Dirección, donde se estudia todo lo relativo a la
5 gestión de negocios e industrias.

Así es que los estudiantes eligen la carrera que los acompañará de por vida. Unos serán ingenieros, otros médicos, maestros, profesores, arquitectos, farmacéuticos, etc. Pero no todos ellos, a pesar del desarrollo industrial y cultural de los países de lengua española, ejercerán su
10 profesión en el lugar de su nacimiento; muchos saldrán al extranjero. Los primeros en número son los profesores de lengua y literatura española e hispanoamericana, que enseñan su lengua y cultura en las universidades extranjeras. Estos profesores son cada día más numerosos en el profesorado de los Colegios y Universidades norteamericanos.
15 Pero no son ellos solos los profesionales de lengua española llegados a los Estados Unidos para ejercer su carrera. Cada día más médicos e ingenieros españoles e hispanoamericanos vienen a los Estados Unidos en busca de mayores oportunidades para su vida profesional. Uno de los fenómenos más importantes y significativos de las últimas olas
20 emigratorias llegadas a los Estados Unidos, que proceden sobre todo de la América española, es la presencia entre los emigrantes de numerosos profesionales, médicos principalmente.

Estas gentes profesionales que vienen a ejercer su carrera en los Estados Unidos tuvieron en su vida dos momentos decisivos en la
25 elección de su carrera: uno, en su juventud, para elegir la carrera a la que se iban a dedicar toda su vida; y otro, ya más entrados en años, encaminada ya su carrera, cuando eligieron los Estados Unidos como el país que les ofrecía mayores oportunidades para ejercerla.

PREGUNTAS

1. ¿Qué se estudia en las Escuelas de Administración o Dirección?
2. ¿Qué quiere decir la « gestión de negocios e industrias »?
3. ¿Qué trabajo hacen los arquitectos?
4. ¿Qué futuro tiene la carrera de farmacéutico, según lo que piensa Vd.?
5. ¿Quedan en el lugar de su nacimiento todos los que escogen una carrera?
6. ¿Tienen su preparación en las letras todos los profesores de lengua y literatura española?
7. ¿Por qué vienen a los Estados Unidos los médicos e ingenieros españoles e hispanoamericanos?
8. ¿Qué es una ola emigratoria?
9. ¿De qué país de habla española es la más reciente ola emigratoria?
10. ¿Hay muchas oportunidades en los Estados Unidos para los profesionales de habla española?

TEMAS PARA DISCUSIÓN

1. Las nuevas oportunidades que ofrece el desarrollo industrial.
2. La influencia de las Escuelas de Administración en los negocios.
3. La preparación profesional de los profesores de español.
4. El efecto de la emigración en las profesiones.
5. Las oportunidades profesionales que ofrecen los Estados Unidos.

Comida en un restaurante

CAMARERO. — Buenas noches, señores. ¿Prefieren una mesa hacia el centro, o a un lado? Al lado se está más fresco, por el aire acondicionado.

SEÑOR. — Hoy hace muchísimo calor. Mejor una mesa al lado, ¿no
5   te parece, querida?

CAMARERO. — Pasen por aquí, por favor. ¿Está bien esta mesa?

SEÑORA. — Muy bien, gracias. Todavía no hay mucha gente.

CAMARERO. — Es tempranito para la mayoría aquí. Vds. en América comen más temprano, ¿verdad?

10 SEÑOR. — En nuestra casa tomamos la cena a las seis y media. Las nueve y media ya es muy tarde para nosotros; pero nos vamos acostumbrando.

CAMARERO. — Les dejo el menú y vuelvo en seguida.

SEÑORA. — ¿Qué hay de entremés? ¿Hay jugo de tomate?

15 CAMARERO. — Sí, señora. Hay también jugo de uvas, canapés variados, sandía, jamón, o lo que quisiera.

SEÑORA. — Hay una buena selección. ¿Y de sopas, por favor?

CAMARERO. — Podrían empezar con una sopa de cebolla, o una sopa de pescado. Algunos prefieren una sopa de ajo con huevo,
20   que es la especialidad de la casa. O tal vez les gustaría un gazpacho andaluz, o un consomé frío, si prefieren una sopa fría.

SEÑOR. — La sopa poco me interesa a mí. ¿Qué hay de pescado?

CAMARERO. — Tenemos filetes de lenguado fresquísimo. Hay centro de
25   merluza, medallón de mero, lubina asada en parrilla, langosta, calamares.

SEÑORA. — Pues, para mí un jugo de tomate y una sopa de pescado.

SEÑOR. — Y para mí jamón serrano con sandía y lubina asada. Nada de sopa. A ver, ¿como carne, qué vamos a tomar?

LISTA DE COMESTIBLES   LIST OF FOODS

ENTREMESES   HORS D'OEUVRES

aceitunas rellenas stuffed olives
canapés variados assorted canapés
  (**fríos o calientes** cold or hot)
entremeses variados assorted hors
  d'oeuvres
jamón de Jabugo smoked ham
jugo de tomate tomato juice

jugo de uvas grape juice
jugo de toronja grapefruit juice
lubina ahumada smoked bass
salmón ahumado smoked salmon
salpicón de mariscos marinated seafood
melón honeydew melon

SOPAS   SOUPS

consomé frío cold consommé
consomé natural consommé
crema de legumbres cream of vegetable soup
crema de tomate cream of tomato
  soup
crema de yema consommé with egg

gazpacho andaluz Andalusian cold
  soup
sopa de ajo garlic soup
sopa de cebolla onion soup
sopa parisienne Parisian potato soup
sopa de pescado fish chowder

HUEVOS   EGGS

huevos escalfados poached eggs
huevos pasados por agua soft boiled
  eggs
huevos revueltos scrambled eggs
huevos fritos fried eggs
  (**con jamón** with ham)
  (**con tocino** with bacon)

tortilla jamón ham omelet
tortilla champiñon (hongo) mushroom omelet
tortilla espinacas spinach omelet
tortilla espárragos asparagus omelet

PESCADOS   FISH

bacalao dried codfish
calamares squids
centro de merluza codfish steak
filetes de lenguado filet of sole

lubina bass
langosta lobster
medallón de mero grouper steak
mariscos seafood

TEMAS

1. DIÁLOGO: *A* toma la parte de mozo y *B* la parte de un señor que
     pide su almuerzo.
2. DIÁLOGO: *A* toma la parte del esposo y *B* la parte de la esposa.
     Tratan de decidir lo que van a pedir para la comida
     antes de que llegue el mozo.
3. COMPOSICIÓN: Preparen un menú para un buen almuerzo en un
     restaurante modesto.

CAMARERO. — Puedo ofrecerles un solomillo al carbón, muy sabroso. Hay también escalopes de ternera, chuletas de cerdo, pollo asado, jamón serrano y jamón cocido. Si quieren algo muy especial, les ofrezco una perdiz toledana, que es una delicia.

SEÑORA. — Para mí, escalopes de ternera. ¿ Qué verduras hay con los escalopes?

CAMARERO. — Puede Vd. escoger guisantes a la mantequilla, espinacas, o judías verdes. Claro que hay también un excelente puré de patatas.

SEÑORA. — Bueno, déme Vd. guisantes y espinacas.

SEÑOR. — Yo tomo un solomillo al punto. ¡ Cuidado que no me lo traiga pasado! Veo aquí en la lista que hay alcachofas salteadas y espárragos. Y para mí, patatas fritas, por favor.

CAMARERO. — Bueno. Ahorita les traigo la lista de los postres. ¿ Quieren agua mineral, o vino?

SEÑOR. — Sí, sí. Un buen vino tinto de la región, y una botella de agua mineral.

CAMARERO. — Tenemos un vino excelente, especialidad de la casa. Se lo traigo en seguida, con hielo.

SEÑORA. — No, señor, sin hielo, por favor.

SEÑOR. — A ver estos postres: flan de caramelo, tarta de chocolate, tarta de fresa, pastel de manzana o de crema al limón, helado variado, melocotón en almíbar, frutas, y queso. Hay de todo.

SEÑORA. — Querido, no olvides tu dieta. Tomamos sólo café.

SEÑOR. — Sí, mi querida. Sólo café, y sin azúcar. En estos viajes hay que tener siempre cuidado con el peso.

CARNES MEATS

chuleta de cerdo pork chop

entrecote a la parrilla grilled rib steak

escalope de ternera veal scaloppine

higado de ternera calf's liver

jamón cocido boiled ham

jamón serrano cured ham

perdiz toledana partridge, Toledo style

pollo asado roast chicken

rosbif roast beef

solomillo al carbón charcoal broiled sirloin steak

(al punto rare)

(pasado well done)

(entre al punto y pasado medium)

VERDURAS VEGETABLES

alcachofas salteadas sautéed artichokes

champiñon (hongo) mushroom

espárragos asparagus

espinacas spinach

guisantes green peas

judías verdes string beans

patatas a la inglesa potato chips

patatas fritas French fries

patatas paja shoestring potatoes

puré de patata mashed potatoes

pimientos peppers

POSTRES DESSERTS

churros fritters

flan de caramelo caramel custard

fruta variada fruit salad

helado (vainilla, chocolate, fresa) ice cream (vanilla, chocolate, strawberry)

melocotón en almíbar peaches in syrup

pastel de manzana apple pie

(de crema al limón lemon cream)

tarta de chocolate chocolate cake

(de fresa strawberry)

(de yema Boston cream)

quesos cheeses

TEMAS

1. DIÁLOGO: *A* es el mozo, *B* la señora, y *C* el señor. Los señores tratan de escoger los varios platos de la comida y *A* los ayuda.

2. DIÁLOGO: *A* y *B* son los padres, *C* es la hija, y *D* es el mozo en un pequeño restaurante donde la familia va a almorzar. Preguntas y contestaciones entre todos.

3. COMPOSICIÓN. Preparen un menú para una comida completa en un restaurante de lujo.

Appendix II

VERBS

REGULAR VERBS

SIMPLE TENSES

I	II	III

INFINITIVE

hablar *to speak*   **aprender** *to learn*   **vivir** *to live*

PRESENT PARTICIPLE

hablando *speaking*   **aprendiendo** *learning*   **viviendo** *living*

PAST PARTICIPLE

hablado *spoken*   **aprendido** *learned*   **vivido** *lived*

INDICATIVE MOOD

PRESENT

I speak, do speak, am speaking, etc.	*I learn, do learn, am learning, etc.*	*I live, do live, am living, etc.*
hablo	aprendo	vivo
hablas	aprendes	vives
habla	aprende	vive
hablamos	aprendemos	vivimos
habláis	aprendéis	vivís
hablan	aprenden	viven

IMPERFECT

I was speaking, used to speak, spoke, etc.	*I was learning, used to learn, learned, etc.*	*I was living, used to live, lived, etc.*
hablaba	aprendía	vivía
hablabas	aprendías	vivías
hablaba	aprendía	vivía
hablábamos	aprendíamos	vivíamos
hablabais	aprendíais	vivíais
hablaban	aprendían	vivían

<table>
<tr><td colspan="3" align="center">PRETERITE</td></tr>
</table>

I spoke, did speak, etc.	*I learned, did learn, etc.*	*I lived, did live, etc.*
hablé	aprendí	viví
hablaste	aprendiste	viviste
habló	aprendió	vivió
hablamos	aprendimos	vivimos
hablasteis	aprendisteis	vivisteis
hablaron	aprendieron	vivieron

<table>
<tr><td colspan="3" align="center">FUTURE</td></tr>
</table>

I shall (will) speak, etc.	*I shall (will) learn, etc.*	*I shall (will) live, etc.*
hablaré	aprenderé	viviré
hablarás	aprenderás	vivirás
hablará	aprenderá	vivirá
hablaremos	aprenderemos	viviremos
hablaréis	aprenderéis	viviréis
hablarán	aprenderán	vivirán

<table>
<tr><td colspan="3" align="center">CONDITIONAL</td></tr>
</table>

I should (would) speak, etc.	*I should (would) learn, etc.*	*I should (would) live, etc.*
hablaría	aprendería	viviría
hablarías	aprenderías	vivirías
hablaría	aprendería	viviría
hablaríamos	aprenderíamos	viviríamos
hablaríais	aprenderíais	viviríais
hablarían	aprenderían	vivirían

IMPERATIVE MOOD

Speak, etc.	*Learn, etc.*	*Live, etc.*
habla (tú)	aprende (tú)	vive (tú)
hable Vd.	aprenda Vd.	viva Vd.
hablemos (nosotros)	aprendamos (nosotros)	vivamos (nosotros)
hablad (vosotros)	aprended (vosotros)	vivid (vosotros)
hablen Vds.	aprendan Vds.	vivan Vds.

SUBJUNCTIVE MOOD

PRESENT

I may speak, etc.	*I may learn, etc.*	*I may live, etc.*
hable	aprenda	viva
hables	aprendas	vivas
hable	aprenda	viva
hablemos	aprendamos	vivamos
habléis	aprendáis	viváis
hablen	aprendan	vivan

IMPERFECT (–se form)

I might speak, etc.	*I might learn, etc.*	*I might live, etc.*
hablase	aprendiese	viviese
hablases	aprendieses	vivieses
hablase	aprendiese	viviese
hablásemos	aprendiésemos	viviésemos
hablaseis	aprendieseis	vivieseis
hablasen	aprendiesen	viviesen

IMPERFECT (–ra form)

hablara	aprendiera	viviera
hablaras	aprendieras	vivieras
hablara	aprendiera	viviera
habláramos	aprendiéramos	viviéramos
hablarais	aprendierais	vivierais
hablaran	aprendieran	vivieran

COMPOUND TENSES

The compound tenses of all verbs, regular or irregular, are formed by adding their past participle to the proper form of the auxiliary verb **haber.**

PERFECT INFINITIVE

haber hablado *to have spoken*

haber aprendido *to have learned*

haber vivido *to have lived*

PERFECT PARTICIPLE

habiendo hablado *having spoken*

habiendo aprendido *having learned*

habiendo vivido *having lived*

INDICATIVE MOOD

PRESENT PERFECT

I have spoken (learned, lived), etc.

he
has
ha
hemos } hablado (aprendido, vivido)
habéis
han

PLUPERFECT

I had spoken (learned, lived), etc.

había
habías
había
habíamos } hablado (aprendido, vivido)
habíais
habían

PRETERITE PERFECT

I had spoken (learned, lived), etc.

hube
hubiste
hubo
hubimos } hablado (aprendido, vivido)
hubisteis
hubieron

FUTURE PERFECT

I shall have spoken (learned, lived), etc.

habré
habrás
habrá
habremos } hablado (aprendido, vivido)
habréis
habrán

CONDITIONAL PERFECT

I should have spoken (learned, lived), etc.

habría
habrías
habría
habríamos } hablado (aprendido, vivido)
habríais
habrían

SUBJUNCTIVE MOOD

PRESENT PERFECT

I may have spoken (learned, lived), etc.

haya
hayas
haya
hayamos } hablado (aprendido, vivido)
hayáis
hayan

PLUPERFECT (–se, –ra)

I might have spoken (learned, lived), etc.

hubiese *or* hubiera
hubieses *or* hubieras
hubiese *or* hubiera
hubiésemos *or* hubiéramos } hablado (aprendido, vivido)
hubieseis *or* hubierais
hubiesen *or* hubieran

RADICAL-CHANGING VERBS

See the complete summary of radical-changing verbs in Lesson 24. Common radical-changing verbs of the first class:

acordarse (de) *to remember*
acostar(se) *to put (go) to bed*
apretar *to tighten*
ascender *to rise, advance*
atender *to attend*
atravesar *to cross*
calentar *to warm*
cerrar *to close*
comenzar *to begin*
confesar *to confess*
contar *to count, relate*
costar *to cost*
defender *to defend*
descender *to descend*

desenvolver *to develop*
despertar(se) *to wake (up)*
devolver *to give back*
doler *to ache*
empezar *to begin*
encontrar *to meet*
entender *to understand*
extender(se) *to extend*
jugar *to play*
llover *to rain*
mostrar *to show*
mover *to move*
nevar *to snow*
pensar *to think*

perder *to lose*
probar *to demonstrate, test; taste*
recordar(se) *to remember*
resolver *to solve*
sentarse *to sit*

soler *to be accustomed to*
soñar *to dream*
volar *to fly*
volver *to return*

Common radical-changing verbs of the second class:

adquirir *to acquire*
arrepentirse (de) *to repent*
convertir *to convert, change*
divertir(se) *to amuse (oneself)*
dormir(se) *to sleep (fall asleep)*

morir *to die*
preferir *to prefer*
referir *to refer*
sentir(se) *to feel*

Common radical-changing verbs of the third class:

competir *to compete*
conseguir *to earn*
despedirse (de) *to say good-bye (to)*
elegir *to choose*
medir *to measure*
pedir *to ask for*

reñir *to quarrel, scold*
repetir *to repeat*
seguir *to follow*
servir *to serve*
vestir(se) *to dress (get dressed)*

ORTHOGRAPHIC-CHANGING VERBS

(1) Verbs ending in –**guir** change **gu** to **g** before **a** and **o**.

seguir *to follow*

PRES. IND.   **sigo, sigues, sigue,** seguimos, seguís, **siguen**
PRES. SUBJVE.   **siga, sigas, siga, sigamos, sigáis, sigan**

(2) Verbs ending in –**gar** change **g** to **gu** before **e**.

llegar *to arrive*

PRET. IND.   **llegué,** llegaste, llegó, llegamos, llegasteis, llegaron
PRES. SUBJVE.   **llegue, llegues, llegue, lleguemos, lleguéis, lleguen**

(3) Verbs ending in –**guar** change **gu** to **gü** before **e.**

averiguar *to ascertain, find out*

PRET. IND.   **averigüé,** averiguaste, etc.
PRES. SUBJVE.   **averigüe, averigües, averigüe, averigüemos, averigüéis, averigüen**

(4) Verbs ending in –**ger** and –**gir** change **g** to **j** before **a** and **o.**

coger *to catch, seize*

PRES. IND.   **cojo,** coges, coge, cogemos, cogéis, cogen
PRES. SUBJVE.   **coja, cojas, coja, cojamos, cojáis, cojan**

corregir *to correct*

PRES. IND.   **corrijo,** corriges, etc.
PRES. SUBJVE.   **corrija, corrijas, corrija, corrijamos, corrijáis, corrijan**

(5) Verbs ending in –**car** change **c** to **qu** before **e.**

buscar *to look for*

PRET. IND. **busqué,** buscaste, etc.
PRES. SUBJVE.   **busque, busques, busque, busquemos, busquéis, busquen**

(6) Verbs ending in –**zar** change **z** to **c** before **e.**

comenzar *to begin*

PRET. IND.   **comencé,** comenzaste, etc.
PRES. SUBJVE.   **comience, comiences, comience, comencemos, comencéis, comiencen**

(7) Verbs ending in –**cer** or –**cir** preceded by a vowel usually change **c** to **zc** before **a** or **o.**

conocer *to know*

PRES. IND.   **conozco,** conoces, etc.
PRES. SUBJVE.   **conozca, conozcas, conozca, conozcamos, conozcáis, conozcan**

(8) Verbs ending in **–cer** or **–cir** preceded by a consonant usually change **c** to **z** before **a** or **o.**

vencer *to win*

PRES. IND.   **venzo,** vences, etc.
PRES. SUBJVE.   **venza, venzas, venza, venzamos, venzáis, venzan**

(9) Some verbs ending in **–iar** or **–uar** take a written accent on the weak vowel when it is stressed.

enviar *to send*

PRES. IND.   **envío, envías, envía,** enviamos, enviáis, **envían**
PRES. SUBJVE.   **envíe, envíes, envíe,** enviemos, enviéis, **envíen**

continuar *to continue*

PRES. IND.   **continúo, continúas, continúa,** continuamos, continuáis, **continúan**
PRES. SUBJVE.   **continúe, continúes, continúe,** continuemos, continuéis, **continúen**

(10) Verbs in which an unstressed **i** would fall between two vowels change the **i** to **y.**

leer *to read*

PRES. PART.   **leyendo**
PRET. IND.   leí, leíste, **leyó,** leímos, leísteis, **leyeron**
IMPERF. SUBJVE.   **leyese,** etc. or **leyera,** etc.

concluir *to conclude*

PRES. IND. **concluyo, concluyes, concluye,** concluímos, concluís,
        concluyen
PRES. SUBJVE. **concluya,** etc.
PRET. IND. concluí, concluíste, **concluyó,** concluímos, concluísteis,
        concluyeron
IMPERF. SUBJVE. **concluyese,** etc. or **concluyera,** etc.
IMPERATIVE **concluye**   PRES. PART. **concluyendo**

(11) Verbs whose stems end in –**ll** or –**ñ** lose the **i** of the ending before
another vowel.

bullir *to boil*

PRES. PART. **bullendo**
PRET. IND. bullí, bulliste, **bulló,** bullimos, bullisteis, **bulleron**
IMPERF. SUBJVE. **bullese,** or **bullera,** etc.

reñir *to quarrel*

PRES. PART. **riñendo**
PRET. IND. reñí, reñiste, **riñó,** reñimos, reñisteis, **riñeron**
IMPERF. SUBJVE. **riñese,** etc. or **riñera,** etc.

IRREGULAR VERBS

(*Tenses not given are perfectly regular.*)

andar *to walk, go*

PRET. IND. anduve, anduviste, anduvo, anduvimos, anduvisteis, andu-
        vieron
IMPERF. SUBJVE. anduviera, etc.   anduviese, etc.

caber *to fit in(to), hold*

PRES. IND. quepo, cabes, cabe, cabemos, cabéis, caben
PRES. SUBJVE. quepa, quepas, quepa, quepamos, quepáis, quepan

FUTURE cabré, etc.   CONDITIONAL cabría, etc.
PRET. IND. cupe, cupiste, cupo, cupimos, cupisteis, cupieron
IMPERF. SUBJVE. cupiera, etc.   cupiese, etc.

caer *to fall*

PRES. PART. cayendo   PAST PART. caído
PRES. IND. caigo, caes, cae, caemos, caéis, caen
PRES. SUBJVE. caiga, caigas, caiga, caigamos, caigáis, caigan
PRET. IND. caí, caíste, cayó, caímos, caísteis, cayeron
IMPERF. SUBJVE. cayera, etc.   cayese, etc.

conducir *to lead, drive*

PRES. IND. conduzco, conduces, conduce, conducimos, conducís, con-
　　　　　　　ducen
PRES. SUBJVE. conduzca, conduzcas, conduzca, conduzcamos, con-
　　　　　　　duzcáis, conduzcan
PRET. IND. conduje, condujiste, condujo, condujimos, condujisteis,
　　　　　　　condujeron
IMPERF. SUBJVE. condujera, etc.   condujese, etc.

dar *to give*

PRES. IND. doy, das, da, damos, dais, dan
PRES. SUBJVE. dé, des, dé, demos, deis, den
PRET. IND. di, diste, dio, dimos, disteis, dieron
IMPERF. SUBJVE. diera, etc.   diese, etc.

decir *to say, tell*

PRES. PART. diciendo   PAST PART. dicho
PRES. IND. digo, dices, dice, decimos, decís, dicen
IMPERATIVE   di   decid
PRES. SUBJVE. diga, digas, diga, digamos, digáis, digan
FUTURE diré, etc.   CONDITIONAL diría, etc.
PRET. IND. dije, dijiste, dijo, dijimos, dijisteis, dijeron
IMPERF. SUBJVE. dijera, etc.   dijese, etc.

estar *to be*

PRES. IND estoy, estás, está, estamos, estáis, están
PRES. SUBJVE. esté, estés, esté, estemos, estéis, estén

PRET. IND.   estuve, estuviste, estuvo, estuvimos, estuvisteis, estuvieron
IMPERF. SUBJVE.   estuviera, etc.   estuviese, etc.

haber *to have* (auxiliary)

PRES. IND.   he, has, ha, hemos, habéis, han
PRES. SUBJVE.   haya, hayas, haya, hayamos, hayáis, hayan
FUTURE.   habré, etc.   CONDITIONAL   habría, etc.
PRET. IND.   hube, hubiste, hubo, hubimos, hubisteis, hubieron
IMPERF. SUBJVE.   hubiera, etc.   hubiese, etc.

hacer *to do, make*

PRES. PART.   haciendo   PAST PART.   hecho
PRES. IND.   hago, haces, hace, hacemos, hacéis, hacen
IMPERATIVE   haz   haced
PRES. SUBJVE.   haga, hagas, haga, hagamos, hagáis, hagan
FUTURE   haré, etc.   CONDITIONAL   haría, etc.
PRET. IND.   hice, hiciste, hizo, hicimos, hicisteis, hicieron
IMPERF. SUBJVE.   hiciera, etc.   hiciese, etc.

ir *to go*

PRES. PART.   yendo   PAST PART.   ido
PRES. IND.   voy, vas, va, vamos, vais, van
IMPERATIVE   ve   id
PRES. SUBJVE.   vaya, vayas, vaya, vayamos, vayáis, vayan
IMPERF. IND.   iba, ibas, iba, íbamos, ibais, iban
PRET. IND.   fui, fuiste, fue, fuimos, fuisteis, fueron
IMPERF. SUBJVE.   fuera, etc.   fuese, etc.

oír *to hear*

PRES. PART.   oyendo   PAST PART.   oído
PRES. IND.   oigo, oyes, oye, oímos, oís, oyen
IMPERATIVE   oye   oíd
PRES. SUBJVE.   oiga, oigas, oiga, oigamos, oigáis, oigan
PRET. IND.   oí, oíste, oyó, oímos, oísteis, oyeron
IMPERF. SUBJVE.   oyera, etc.   oyese, etc.

poder *to be able*

PRES. PART. pudiendo   PAST PART. podido
PRES. IND. puedo, puedes, puede, podemos, podéis, pueden
PRES. SUBJVE. pueda, puedas, pueda, podamos, podáis, puedan
FUTURE podré, etc.   CONDITIONAL podría, etc.
PRET. IND. pude, pudiste, pudo, pudimos, pudisteis, pudieron
IMPERF. SUBJVE. pudiera, etc.   pudiese, etc.

poner *to put, place*

PRES. PART. poniendo   PAST PART. puesto
PRES. IND. pongo, pones, pone, ponemos, ponéis, ponen
IMPERATIVE   pon   poned
PRES. SUBJVE. ponga, pongas, ponga, pongamos, pongáis, pongan
FUTURE pondré, etc.   CONDITIONAL pondría, etc.
PRET. IND. puse, pusiste, puso, pusimos, pusisteis, pusieron
IMPERF. SUBJVE. pusiera, etc.   pusiese, etc.

querer *to wish, want*

PRES. IND. quiero, quieres, quiere, queremos, queréis, quieren
PRES. SUBJVE. quiera, quieras, quiera, queramos, queráis, quieran
FUTURE querré, etc.   CONDITIONAL querría, etc.
PRET. IND. quise, quisiste, quiso, quisimos, quisisteis, quisieron
IMPERF. SUBJVE. quisiera, etc.   quisiese, etc.

saber *to know*

PRES. IND. sé, sabes, sabe, sabemos, sabéis, saben
PRES. SUBJVE. sepa, sepas, sepa, sepamos, sepáis, sepan
FUTURE sabré, etc.   CONDITIONAL sabría, etc.
PRET. IND. supe, supiste, supo, supimos, supisteis, supieron
IMPERF. SUBJVE. supiera, etc.   supiese, etc.

salir *to go out*

PRES. IND. salgo, sales, sale, salimos, salís, salen
IMPERATIVE   sal   salid
PRES. SUBJVE. salga, salgas, salga, salgamos, salgáis, salgan
FUTURE saldré, etc.   CONDITIONAL saldría, etc.

ser *to be*

PRES. PART. siendo PAST PART. sido
PRES. IND. soy, eres, es, somos, sois, son
IMPERATIVE sé sed
PRES. SUBJVE. sea, seas, sea, seamos, seáis, sean
IMPERF. IND. era, eras, era, éramos, erais, eran
PRET. IND. fui, fuiste, fue, fuimos, fuisteis, fueron
IMPERF. SUBJVE. fuera, etc. fuese, etc.

tener *to have*

PRES. IND. tengo, tienes, tiene, tenemos, tenéis, tienen
IMPERATIVE ten tened
PRES. SUBJVE. tenga, tengas, tenga, tengamos, tengáis, tengan
FUTURE tendré, etc. CONDITIONAL tendría, etc.
PRET. IND. tuve, tuviste, tuvo, tuvimos, tuvisteis, tuvieron
IMPERF. SUBJVE. tuviera, etc. tuviese, etc.

traer *to bring*

PRES. PART. trayendo PAST PART. traído
PRES. IND. traigo, traes, trae, traemos, traéis, traen
PRES. SUBJVE. traiga, traigas, traiga, traigamos, traigáis, traigan
PRET. IND. traje, trajiste, trajo, trajimos, trajisteis, trajeron
IMPERF. SUBJVE. trajera, etc. trajese, etc.

valer *to be worth*

PRES. IND. valgo, vales, vale, valemos, valéis, valen
IMPERATIVE val(e) valed
PRES. SUBJVE. valga, valgas, valga, valgamos, valgáis, valgan
FUTURE valdré, etc. CONDITIONAL valdría, etc.

venir *to come*

PRES. PART. viniendo PAST PART. venido
PRES. IND. vengo, vienes, viene, venimos, venís, vienen
IMPERATIVE ven venid
PRES. SUBJVE. venga, vengas, venga, vengamos, vengáis, vengan

FUTURE vendré, etc.   CONDITIONAL   vendría, etc.
PRET. IND.   vine, viniste, vino, vinimos, vinisteis, vinieron
IMPERF. SUBJVE.   viniera, etc.   viniese, etc.

ver *to see*

PRES. PART.   viendo   PAST PART.   visto
PRES. IND.   veo, ves, ve, vemos, veis, ven
IMPERATIVE   ve   ved
PRES. SUBJVE.   vea, veas, vea, veamos, veáis, vean
IMPERF. IND.   veía, veías, veía, veíamos, veíais, veían
PRET. IND.   vi, viste, vio, vimos, visteis, vieron
IMPERF. SUBJVE.   viera, etc.   viese, etc.

Vocabulary

SPANISH-ENGLISH VOCABULARY

In general we have omitted from the Spanish-English vocabulary articles, numerals under twenty, simple personal pronouns, cognates which are unmistakable, regular adverbs in **-mente** and regular superlatives in **-ísimo,** when the adjective is included.

A

a *prep.* to; at; in; by; on; *not translated when used before a direct object*

abanico *m.* fan; **en —,** like a fan

abarrote: tienda de abarrotes *f.* grocery store

abierto, -a (*p.p. of* **abrir**) open

abogado *m.* lawyer

abrazo *m.* embrace; greeting

abrigo *m.* overcoat

abril *m.* April

abrir to open (*p.p.* **abierto**)

abuela *f.* grandmother

abuelo *m.* grandfather; *pl.* grandparents

acá *adv.* here (*near speaker*)

acabar to end, finish; **— con** to put an end to; **— de** to have just (*accomplished an action*)

académico-a academic

academia *f.* academy

Acapulco *Mexican city on the Pacific*

accesible accessible; attainable

accidentado, -a indented

aceite *m.* oil

aceptar to accept

acera *f.* sidewalk

acerca de about, concerning

acercarse (a) to draw near, approach

acompañar to accompany

Aconcagua *highest peak in the Andes, on the border between Argentina and Chile*

acondicionado *see* **aire**

aconsejar to advise

acontecimiento *m.* event

acordarse (ue) (de) to remember

acostarse (ue) to go to bed

acostumbrarse to become accustomed

actividad *f.* activity

activo, -a active

actual actual; present

actualidad *f.* present time

acuerdo *m.* agreement; **estar de —,** to be in agreement

además (de) besides, moreover

adiós good-bye (*for good*)

admiración *f.* admiration

admirar to admire

adónde (a dónde) where

adornado, -a decorated, adorned

adornar to adorn

aéreo, -a *adj.* aerial, air

aeroplano *m.* airplane
aeropuerto *m.* airport
afectar to affect
afecto *m.* affection
afectuosamente affectionately
aficionado *m.* fan; — **a los deportes** sports fan
afirmar to affirm, state
agigantado, –a gigantic
agosto *m.* August
agradable agreeable, pleasant
agradar to please, be agreeable
agradecer to appreciate; be grateful (for)
agradecimiento *m.* gratitude
agricultor *m.* farmer
agricultura *f.* agriculture
agrónomo *m.* agronomist
agruparse to group oneself
agua *f.* water; — **mineral** mineral water
aguacero *m.* shower
ahí there
ahora now; — **mismo** just now, right now
ahorita in a moment
aire *m.* air;— **acondicionado** air-conditioning; **al** — **libre** in the open air
ajo *m.* garlic
alba *f.* dawn
Albéniz, Isaac *Spanish composer (1860–1909)*
Alberto Albert
alcachofa *f.* artichoke; —**s salteadas** sautéed artichokes
alcanzar to reach, attain
alcázar *m.* castle; — **de Sevilla** *famous structure in Arab style in Seville*
aldea *f.* village, hamlet
alegórico, –a allegorical
alegrarse (de) to be happy
alegre happy, glad, gay

alegría *f.* rejoicing, gaiety
alemán *m.* German; *adj.* **alemán, –ana** German
Alfajería *Moorish palace in Zaragoza, Spain*
algo *pron.* something, some; *adv.* somewhat
algodón *m.* cotton
alguien someone
algún, alguno, –a *adj.* some, any; *pl.* a few; *pron.* someone, some
Alhambra (Palacio de la) *famous palace in Granada*
Alicante *a city and a province of southeastern Spain, on the Mediterranean*
alma *f.* soul
Almagro, Diego de *Spanish conqueror of Chile*
almendro *m.* almond tree
almíbar *m.* syrup
almorzar (ue) to have lunch, eat lunch
almuerzo *m.* lunch
alquilar to rent; hire
alrededor (de) around, about
alto, –a tall, high
altura *f.* height; altitude
alumna *f.* pupil
alumno *m.* pupil
alzarse to rise
allá there, over there
allí there
ama *f.* mistress of the house
amabilidad *f.* kindness
amable kind; lovely
amante *adj.* loving, fond of
amarillo, –a yellow
Amazonas *m.* Amazon River
ambiente *m.* atmosphere
ambos, –as both
América *f.* America; **la** — **Central** Central America; **la** — **del Sur**

South America; **la — española**
Spanish America
americano, –a American
amiga *f.* friend
amigo *m.* friend
amiguito *m.* little friend
amistad *f.* friendship; *pl.* acquaintances
amor *m.* love
ampliar to widen
amplio, –a ample, roomy
Ana Anna
ancho, –a wide, broad; **cara ancha** full face
Andalucía *f. region in the south of Spain*
andaluz, -uza *adj.* Andalusian
andar to walk
Andes *m.pl. mountain range in South America*
anfitrión *m.* host
animación *f.* animation, liveliness
animar to animate, enliven
anoche last night
anterior preceding, prior
antes *adv.* before, formerly; **— de** *prep.* before; **— (de) que** *conj.* before
antiguamente anciently, in ancient times
antiguo, –a ancient; former
Antonio Anthony
antropológico, –a anthropological
anualmente annually
añadir to add
año *m.* year; **¿Cuántos años tiene Vd?** How old are you?
apartado, –a distant, secluded
apartamento *m.* apartment
aparte de apart from
apenas scarcely, hardly, as soon as
apoderarse (de) to take possession of
aportar to bring

apóstol *m.* apostle
apoyar to support
apreciar to appreciate
aprender to learn
apretar (ie) to fit snugly, fit tightly
aprieto *m.* fix, difficult position
apropiado, –a appropriate
aprovechar to be useful, profit; take advantage of
aquel, aquella *adj.* that; *pl.* those
aquél, aquélla, aquello *pron.* that (one), the former; *pl.* those; the former
aquí here; **por —,** this way; around here
árabe *m.* Arab
Aragón *a Spanish region northeast of Madrid*
Aranjuez *city to the south of Madrid, formerly one of the residences of the royal family*
araucano *m.* Araucanian
árbol *m.* tree
arco iris *m.* rainbow
arena *f.* sand
argentino, –a Argentinean, Argentine
aristocrático, –a aristocratic
armonioso, –a harmonious
armonizar to harmonize
arquitectura *f.* architecture
arreglar to arrange
arrendamiento *m.* rental
arrepentirse (ie) (de) to repent, regret
arriba up, above
arroyo *m.* stream
arroz *m.* rice
arte *m.* art
arteria *f.* artery, main line
artesanía *f.* workmanship
artículo *m.* article; *pl.* goods, products

Artigas, José *leader of the Uruguayan gauchos in the Uruguayan independence*
artista *m. or f.* artist
artístico, –a artistic
asado, –a roast, broiled
ascendencia *f.* origin
ascender (ie) to advance (*in rank*)
asegurar to insure; assure; **—se** to take out insurance
asentar to settle
así thus; so; like that; **así que** so that; **así pasa con** that's how it is with; **así lo espero** I hope so
asiento *m.* seat
asilo *m.* asylum, refuge
asistir (a) to be present (at)
asnillo *m.* little donkey
aspecto *m.* appearance, aspect
aspirar to aspire
asturiano, –a Asturian
Asturias *a region in northern Spain*
Asunción *capital of Paraguay*
asunto *m.* matter, topic
asustarse to become frightened
Atacama *desert in northern Chile*
ataque *m.* attack
atender (ie) to attend (to), look after
atómico, –a atomic
atracción *f.* attraction
atractivo *m.* attraction; *adj.* attractive
atraer to attract
atravesar (ie) to cross, go through
atreverse (a) to dare (to), venture
aumentar to increase
aumento *m.* increase
aun, aún even, still
aunque although, even though
auto *m.* automobile; one-act play; **— sacramental** religious play
autobús *m.* bus
automóvil *m.* car

automovilismo *m.* automobilism
autopista *f.* speedway, highway
autor *m.* author
autovía *m.* beeliner
avance *m.* advance
avanzar to advance
avenida *f.* avenue
averiguar to find out, inquire
aviación *f.* aviation
avión *m.* airplane, plane; **en (por) —,** by plane
ayer yesterday
ayuda *f.* help
ayudar to help
ayuntamiento *m.* township; town hall
azteca *m. or adj.* Aztec
azúcar *m.* sugar
azul blue
azulejo *m.* glazed tile

B

bachillerato *m.* European baccalaureate
bahía *f.* bay, harbor
bailar to dance
baile *m.* dance
bajar to go down; descend, land
bajo, –a *adj.* low, short; *adv.* underneath, below; *prep.* under
balada *f.* ballad
Balboa *a city in Panama*
Baleares *f.pl.* Balearic Islands
banana *f.* banana
banco *m.* bank; bench
bañarse to take a bath
barato, –a cheap
barbero *m.* barber
barca *f.* rowboat
barco *m.* boat, ship
Barranquilla *Colombian city on the Magdalena River*

barrio *m.* city district
basar to base
base *f.* base, basis
bastante enough
bastar to be sufficient
beber to drink
bebida *f.* beverage, drink
beca *f.* scholarship
béisbol *m.* baseball
belleza *f.* beauty
bello, –a beautiful
Benavente, Jacinto *Spanish dramatist (1866–1954)*
bien well
bienestar *m.* welfare, well-being
blanco, –a white
bloque *m.* block
blusa *f.* blouse
boda *f.* marriage, wedding
Bogotá *capital of Colombia*
Bolívar, Simón *(1783–1830) greatest leader in the South American Revolution*
bolsillo *m.* pocket, purse, pocketbook
bomba *f.* bomb
bondad *f.* kindness, goodness; mildness; **tenga la —,** please
bonísimo, –a very good
bonito, –a pretty, beautiful
bosque *m.* forest, woods
botella *f.* bottle
Brasil *m.* Brazil
brazo *m.* arm
breve brief, short
brillante brilliant, bright
brisa *f.* breeze
broma *f.* joke, jest; **en —,** jokingly
Buen Retiro *old royal palace in Madrid whose garden is now the municipal park of Madrid*
buen(o), –a good; *adv.* fine, all right
Buenos Aires *capital of Argentina*

Buero Vallejo, Antonio Spanish playwright (1916–   )
bufón *m.* clown
bullir to boil; bustle
buque *m.* ship
burlarse (de) to make fun (of)
buscar to look for

C

caballero *m.* man, gentleman
caballerote *m.* unpolished gentleman
caballote *m.* big horse
caber to fit; **no cabe duda** there is no doubt
cabeza *f.* head
cabo *m.* end, completion; **al — de** after, at the end of; **se están llevando a —,** there are being carried on
cada each, every
Cádiz *city and Province in Andalusia, southern Spain*
caer to fall; **—se** to fall (down), drop
café *m.* coffee; coffeehouse; **—solo** black coffee
cafetería *f.* snack bar
cajita *f.* little box; basket
calamar *m.* squid
Calderón de la Barca, Pedro *Spanish dramatist (1600–1681)*
calentar (ie) to warm, heat
Cali *Columbian city*
calidad *f.* kind, quality
caliente hot
califa *m.* caliph
calificar to rate, class
calor *m.* heat; **hace —,** it is warm
calvicie *f.* baldness
callarse to be silent, keep quiet
calle *f.* street

callejón *m.* narrow street
cama *f.* bed
cámara *f.* hall
camarote *m.* cabin, stateroom
cambiar to change; **cambiarse de ropa** to change clothes
cambio *m.* change; **en —,** on the other hand
camino *m.* road
camisa *f.* shirt
camisería *f.* shirt store
campesino *m.* peasant, farmer
campestre *adj.* country; **jira —,** picnic
campo *m.* field, country
canal *m.* canal
canapé *m.* canape, appetizer
canción *f.* song
cansado, –a tired; boring
cansarse to get tired
cantar to sing
canto *m.* song, singing
capa *f.* cape
capital *f.* capital (*city*); capital
capítulo *m.* chapter
cara *f.* face
Caracas *capital of Venezuela*
carácter *m.* character
característico, –a characteristic
¡caramba! gosh! hell!
caramelo *m.* caramel
carbón *m.* charcoal
cargar to load
caribe *adj.* Caribbean
carmen *m. garden in the houses of Granada*
carne *f.* meat
carrera *f.* career
carretera *f.* highway
carro *m.* cart, wagon; car (*Mexico*)
carruaje *m.* vehicle, carriage; float
carta *f.* letter
casa *f.* house; **a su —,** home; **en —,** at home; **Casa Rosada**

Presidential Palace in Buenos Aires
casado, –a married; **vida de casado, –a** married life
casarse (con) to marry, get married
caseta *f.* small house, hut
casi almost, nearly
casita *f.* pretty little house
caso *m.* case; **en — (de) que** in case
Casona, Alejandro *Spanish playwright (1900–1967)*
castaño, –a brown
castellano, –a Castilian
Castilla la Nueva *region around and south of Madrid*
castillo *m.* castle
casucha *f.* run-down hut
Cataluña Catalonia, *a region in the northeast of Spain*
catedral *f.* cathedral
caudillo *m.* leader
causa *f.* cause; **a — de** on account of
causar to cause
cebolla *f.* onion
celebrado, –a famous
celebrar to take place; celebrate
cenar to dine; have supper
centavo *m.* cent
centenar *m.* hundred
centímetro *m.* centimeter (*0.39 of an inch*)
centro *m.* center, middle
cerámica *f.* ceramic art; pottery
cerca (de) about, near
cerdo *m.* pork
cerezo *m.* cherry tree
cerrar (ie) to close
Cerro de Ancón Ancon peak (*in Panama City*)
Cervantes Saavedra, Miguel de *greatest Spanish writer (1547–1616)*
cerveza *f.* beer

césped *m.* lawn (*singular only*)
cielo *m.* sky
ciencia *f.* science
cien(to) a hundred
cierto, –a (a) certain; **cierto** *adv.* sure; **por —,** certainly
cigarra *f.* cicada
cigarrillo *m.* cigarette
cigarrón *m.* great big cicada
cima *f.* top, summit
cine *m.* movie
circular to circulate
círculo *m.* club
cita *f.* appointment; **darse —,** to make an appointment
citar to cite, to mention
ciudad *f.* city; **Ciudad de México** Mexico City
ciudadano *m.* citizen
civilización *f.* civilization, culture
claro, –a clear, light; **— (que)** of course
clase *f.* class, classroom; type, kind; **compañero de —,** classmate
cliente *m.* customer
clima *m.* climate
cobrar to charge
cobre *m.* copper
cocido, –a cooked, boiled
cocina *f.* kitchen
coche *m.* car; coach
cofradía *f.* confraternity, brotherhood
coger to seize
coincidir to coincide
colegiado: gobierno —, government by council
colegio *m.* boarding school; college
colocación *f.* position
colombiano, –a Colombian
Colón *a city in Panama*
colonización *f.* colonization
coloso *m.* colossus

columna *f.* column
combinar to combine
comedia *f.* comedy; **— de capa y espada** cloak and dagger drama
comedor *m.* dining room
comenzar (ie) to begin, start; **al —,** at the beginning
comer to eat
comercio *m.* business; commerce; store
comestibles *m.pl.* groceries, food
comida *f.* meal; dinner
como as; how; since; **— no sean** unless they (it) be
¿cómo? how is that? how?
comodidad *f.* comfort, convenience
cómodo, –a comfortable
compañero *m.* companion; **— de clase** classmate; **— de estudios** school friend
compañía *f.* company, society; **hacer — a** accompany, keep (someone) company
comparar to compare
compenetración *f.* compenetration
complejo, –a intricate, complex
completar to complete
completo, –a complete
complicado, –a complicated
componer to compose; **componerse (de)** to consist (of)
composición *f.* composition
compositor *m.* composer
compra *f.* purchase; **ir de —s** go shopping
comprar to buy
comprender to understand
comprobar (ue) to verify, confirm
comprometerse to pledge (oneself); vow
común common, public; current
comunicación *f.* communication
comunicarse: — con: to lead into; **— por** be connected by

comunidad *f.* community
comunión *f.* communion
comunismo *m.* Communism
con with
concebir (i) to conceive
concluir to finish, end, conclude
conclusión *f.* conclusion
concurrencia *f.* attendance, crowd
concurrir to frequent
concurso *m.* contest
condición *f.* condition
conducción *f.* pipe, pipeline
conducir to carry, lead
confesar (ie) to confess, admit
conflicto *m.* conflict
confuso, –a confused
conglomerado *m.* conglomerate
conjuntamente together
conjunto *m.* whole; unit
conmemorar to commemorate
conmigo (con + mí) with me
conocer to know, be acquainted
with; meet
conque and so
conquista *f.* conquest
conquistar to conquer
conseguir (i) to earn
consejo *m.* council; **Consejo de Castilla** Council of Castile
conserva *f.* preserve
conservar to preserve, keep, maintain; have
considerablemente considerably
considerar to consider
consigo (con + sí) with oneself; along
constantemente constantly
constar to consist of, be composed of
constitucional *adj.* constitutional
constituir to constitute
construcción *f.* building, construction

construir to construct, build
consultar to consult
consumir to consume
contar (ue) to tell; count; **— con** count (on), reckon; have
contemporáneo, –a contemporary
contentar(se) to satisfy (oneself)
contento, –a happy
contestación *f.* answer, reply
contestar to answer, reply
contigo (con + ti) with you
continente *m.* continent
continuar to continue, keep on
continuo, –a continuous, uninterrupted
contra against
contrario, –a contrary; **en —,** to the contrary; **por lo (el) —,** on the other hand, on the contrary
contraste *m.* contrast
contribución *f.* contribution
controlar to control, check
convencerse to become convinced
convenir to suit; agree with
conversación *f.* conversation
convertir (ie) to convert, change; **convertirse (ie)** to be converted, become
convidar to invite
copia *f.* copy
corazón *m.* heart
corbata *f.* necktie
cordillera *f.* range (chain) of mountains
Córdoba Cordova, *a city and a province in Spain; also a city in Argentina*
cordobés *of or belonging to Cordova*
corral *m.* corral, ancient playhouse
correo *m.* mail
correr to run; flow
corresponder to correspond; go to

corrida (de toros) *f.* bullfight; bullfighting

Corrientes *a large city in northern Argentina*

cortar to cut (through)

corte *f.* court

cortesano *m.* courtier; *adj.* court-like

cortesía *f.* courtesy

corto, –a short

La Coruña *a city and a province in northern Spain*

cosa *f.* thing

cosecha *f.* harvest

cosmopolita cosmopolitan

costa *f.* coast; shore

costar (ue) to cost

costoso, –a expensive, costly

costumbre *f.* custom, habit

creación *f.* creation

creador *m.* creator

crear to create, found

crecer to grow

crecido, –a considerable

creciente increasing, growing

crecimiento *m.* growth

creer to believe, think

crema *f.* cream

criada *f.* maid

criado *m.* servant

crisis *f.* crisis

cristal *m.* crystal; glass

cristalino, –a crystalline; clear

cristiano *m.* Christian

Cristóbal *a city in the Panama Canal Zone*

Cristóbal Colón Christopher Columbus

crítica *f.* criticism

crucero *m.* cruise

cruzar to cross; go across

cuadra *f.* block (*of houses*)

cuadrado, –a square

cuadricular *adj.* square

cuadro *m.* painting, picture

cual which; like; **el (la, lo) cual, los (las) cuales** who, which, whom

¿cuál? (¿cuáles?) *interr. pron.* which (one, ones)?

cualquier, –a (*pl.* **cualesquiera**) any (whatever)

cuando when; **¿cuándo?** when? **¿desde cuándo?** how long? since when?

cuanto, –a as much as (*pl.* as many as); as; all that (who); **en cuanto a** as for; concerning

¿cuánto, –a? how much? (*pl.* how many?) **¿a cuánto?** how much?; **¿a cuántos estamos?** what is the date today?; **¿cuántos años tiene Vd.?** how old are you?

cuarenta forty

cuarto *m.* room; quarter

cuatrocientos, –as four hundred

cubrir to cover (*p.p.* **cubierto**)

cuenta *f.* bill

cuentista *m.* storyteller

cuento *m.* story, tale

Cuernavaca *Mexican city near the capital*

cuerno *m.* horn

cuero *m.* leather; rawhide

cuestión *f.* question

cueva *f.* cave

Cuevas de Altamira *prehistoric caves in Santander province, famous for their mural paintings*

cuidado *m.* care; **dar —,** worry (someone); **¡cuidado!** watch out!; **¡pierda Vd. —!** don't worry!; **sin —s** without worry

cuidar (de) to take care (of)

cultivar to cultivate, farm

cultivo *m.* farming, cultivation

cultura *f.* culture, civilization

(la) Cumparsita *a popular tango*
cumplir to fulfill, keep (*a promise*)
cura *m.* priest
curiosidad *f.* curiosity
cursar to take (a course of study)
curso *m.* course; **cursos de verano** summer session
curva *f.* curve
cuyo, –a whose
Cuzco *Peruvian city, capital of the ancient Inca empire*

Ch

Chanchán *old Peruvian city now in ruins*
chaqueta *f.* jacket
charlar to chat
chica *f.* girl
chico *m.* boy; youngster, "kid"; *adj.* small, little
Chile *m.* Chile
chileno, –a Chilean
Chimú *old Peruvian civilization*
chiquito *m.* little boy
chocolate *m.* chocolate
chuleta *f.* cutlet

D

dado que since
dama *f.* lady
dar to give; strike; — **cuidado** to worry (someone); — **miedo** to frighten; — **un rodeo** take a roundabout way
dársena *f.* pier, wharf
de of; from; with; as; than
debajo (de) under
deber to owe; ought to; must; — **de** must
deberse a to be due to

debido, –a appropriate
débil weak
decir to say, tell; **es —,** that is to say
decisivo, –a decisive
declararse to propose
dedicar to dedicate
defender (ie) to defend, protect
definición *f.* definition
dejar to leave, leave behind; allow, let
delante (de) in front (of)
delgado, –a thin, slender
delicadeza, *f.* delicacy, fineness
delicia *f.* delight
demás: lo —, the rest; **los (las) —,** others
demasiado, –a too much; *pl.* too many; *adv.* too, too much
democracia *f.* democracy
dentro (de) within
dependencia *f.* dependence; branch office
depender (de) to depend (on)
dependiente *m.* clerk
deporte *m.* sport
derecho *m.* right; law; **en su —,** within your rights
derecho, –a right; **a la derecha** to the right
derribar to throw down, tear down
desaparecer to disappear
desarrollar to develop
desarrollo *m.* development
desayunar to have breakfast
desayuno *m.* breakfast
descansar to rest
descanso *m.* rest
descender to diminish, decrease
descifrar to decipher, decode
describir to describe
descubrir to discover, find out
desde since; from; — **luego** of course; **¿— cuándo?** how long?

desear to wish, desire, want
desembarcar to land, disembark
desembocar to flow (into), empty
desempeñar to perform
desenvolver (ue) to develop
deseo *m.* wish, desire
desfile *m.* parade
desierto *m.* desert
designarse to be called
desigual uneven
despacio slowly
despacho *m.* office
despedida *f.* departure
despedirse (i) (de) to say good-bye (to)
despejado, –a clear
despertarse (ie) to wake up
después after, afterwards, then; **— de** after
destacado, –a outstanding, prominent
detener to stop, detain; **—se** stop
detrás (de) behind
deuda *f.* debt
día *m.* day; **buenos días** good morning; **de —,** by day; **de — en —,** from day to day; **por el —,** during the day
diálogo *m.* dialogue, conversation
diapositiva *f.* lantern slide
diario, –a daily
dibujo *m.* drawing; design
diciembre *m.* December
dictado *m.* dictation
dicho (*p.p. of* **decir**) said; called
dichoso, –a lucky, fortunate
dieta *f.* diet
diferencia *f.* difference; **a — de** unlike
diferente different; **algo —,** something else
difícil difficult
dificultad *f.* difficulty
dificultar to make difficult

dinero *m.* money
Dios *m.* God
diplomático *m.* diplomat
diputado *m.* deputy, representative
dirección *f.* direction; address; management
directamente directly
directo, –a direct
dirigir to direct; address; turn
discusión *f.* discussion
discutir to discuss
disfrutar to enjoy
dispensar to excuse
disponible available
disposición *f.* disposal
distancia *f.* distance
distinguido, –a dear; distinguished
distinguir to distinguish
distinto, –a distinct; different
divertirse (ie) to have a good time, amuse oneself
dividir to divide, split
divinamente divinely
doblar to turn (*a corner*)
docena *f.* dozen
dólar *m.* dollar
doloroso, –a painful; pitiful
dominar to rule, govern; control; dominate
domingo *m.* Sunday; **Domingo de Ramos** Palm Sunday
dominio *m.* domination, rule
donde where; **¿dónde? ¿a dónde (adónde)?** where?
dondequiera wherever
dormir (ue) to sleep; **—se** to fall asleep; **dormirse en los laureles** to rest on one's laurels
dormitorio *m.* dormitory; bedroom
doscientos, –as two hundred
dramático, –a dramatic
dramaturgo *m.* playwright

duda *f.* doubt; **no cabe** —, there is
no doubt; **sin** —, undoubtedly
dudar to doubt
dulce sweet; *m.* sweet; *m.pl.* candy,
sweets
durante during
durar to last
duro, –a hard

E

economía *f.* economy
económico, –a economic; **ciencias
económicas** *f.pl.* economics
echar to throw; — **de menos** miss
Echegaray, José *Spanish dramatist
(1833–1916)*
Echeverría, Esteban *Argentine romantic poet (1809–1851)*
edad *f.* age
edificio *m.* building
educativo, –a educational
efecto *m.* effect
eficiencia *f.* effectiveness, efficiency
Egipto *m.* Egypt
Eibar *city in the Basque province*
ejemplo *m.* example
ejercer to exercise, practice
ejercicio *m.* exercise
ejército *m.* army
ejote *m.* string bean *(Mexico)*
el que the one who, that which
elección *f.* election, selection
elegante elegant
elegir (i) to elect
elemental *adj.* elementary
elemento *m.* element
Elena Helen
elevado, –a high
emancipador *m.* emancipator
emancipar to liberate
embajador *m.* ambassador
embargo: sin —, nevertheless, and
yet

emigrado *m.* émigré, political
refugee
emigrante *m.* emigrant
emigratorio, –a emigratory
eminente eminent, prominent
emocionado, –a stirring
emparedado, –a walled
empeñarse to undertake
empezar (ie) to begin, start
emplear to employ, use
empleo *m.* job
emprendedor, –ora enterprising
empresa *f.* concern; firm
en in; into; at; on
enamorarse (de) to fall in love
with
encaminado, –a set on its way
**encantador,   –ora   enchanting,
charming
encantar to   enchant,   charm;
"send"
encanto *m.* enchantment, charm
(por) encima (de) on top (of)
encontrar (ue) to find; meet; **—se
(con)** find oneself; meet; be
found
enérgico, –a energetic, lively
enero *m.* January
enfermo, –a ill
engañarse to be mistaken
enorgullecerse to be proud
enorme enormous, imposing
enormidad *f.* enormity, tremendous
amount
ensalada *f.* salad; — **de papas**
potato salad; — **de verduras**
green salad
ensayista *m. or f.* essayist
enseñanza *f.* education, teaching;
— **elemental** elementary education; — **primaria** primary education; — **secundaria** secondary education; — **superior**
higher education

enseñar to show; teach
entender (ie) to understand; hear
enterarse (de) to find out
entero, –a entire, whole
entierro *m.* funeral procession, burial
entonar to harmonize; fit in
entonces then, at that time
entrada *f.* entrance, door; mouth (*of river*), entry; ticket
entrado, –a advanced
entrar (en) to enter, get into
entre between; among
entregar to hand over
entremés *m.* hors d'oeuvre; interlude
entretenido, –a entertaining, amusing
entrevista *f.* interview
entusiasmar to make one enthusiastic, enthuse
entusiasmo *m.* enthusiasm
enviar to send
época *f.* period, time, age
equilibrado, –a balanced
equivaler to be equivalent to
equivocarse to be mistaken
escalera *f.* staircase
escalonado, –a graded, scaled
escalope *f.* scaloppine
escarpado, –a steep, craggy
esclusa *f.* lock (*in a canal*)
escoger to choose, select
esconder to hide
(El) Escorial *royal monastery and palace to the north of Madrid*
escribir (*p.p.* **escrito**) to write
escritor *m.* writer
escuchar to listen (to)
escuela *f.* school; — **de verano** summer school
escultura *f.* sculpture
ese, –a, –os, –as *adj.* that; *pl.* those (*near person addressed*)

ése, –a, –os, –as *pron.* that, that one; *pl.* those
esmeralda *f.* emerald
eso *pron.* that (*indef.*)
espacio *m.* space
espada *m.* bullfighter
España *f.* Spain
español, –ola Spanish; *m.* Spaniard; Spanish
espárrago *m.* asparagus
especial special
especialidad *f.* specialty
especie *f.* kind
espectáculo *m.* spectacle, show
espejo *m.* mirror
espera *f.* wait, waiting
esperanza *f.* hope
esperar to wait for; hope
esperpento *m.* distortion, the absurd
espeso, –a thick
espina dorsal *f.* backbone
espinaca *f.* spinach
espíritu *m.* spirit, soul
esposa *f.* bride; wife
esposo *m.* husband; bridegroom
esquina *f.* corner
estable firm, steady
establecer to settle, establish
estación *f.* season; station
estado *m.* state; government
(los) Estados Unidos *m.pl.* United States
estancia *f.* stay; large state farm
estar to be
este *m.* east
este, –a, –os, –as *adj.* this; *pl.* these
éste, –a, –os, –as *pron.* this (one), the latter; *pl.* these, the latter
estético, –a aesthetic
estimable worthy
estimado, –a dear; appreciated
estimar to estimate; value
estimular to stimulate

estímulo *m.* stimulus
esto *pron.* this (*indef.*)
estómago *m.* stomach; **mal de —,** upset stomach
estrecho, –a narrow
estrenar to give a première
estreno *m.* opening night; **día del —,** opening day
estuario *m.* estuary
estudiante *m. or f.* student
estudiar to study
estudio *m.* study
estupendo, –a stupendous, extraordinary
eterno, –a eternal
Europa *f.* Europe
europeo, –a European
evidentemente of course, evidently
evolución *f.* evolution, change
exactamente exactly
examen *m.* examination; **— ingreso** entrance examination
excavar to excavate
excelencia *f.* excellence; **por —,** par excellence
excelente excellent
excepción *f.* exception
exclusivamente exclusively
excursión *f.* excursion; trip
exhibir to exhibit
exilio *m.* exile
existir to exist; live
experiencia *f.* experience
experimentar to experience
explicar to explain
exportador, –ora exporter, exporting
exportar to export
exposición *f.* exhibition
expresionista expressionistic
exquisito, –a exquisite
extender (ie) to extend; **—se hasta** to reach

extensión *f.* extension, area; extent
extenso, –a extensive
exterior *adj.* outside
extranjero, –a foreign; *m.* foreigner; foreign countries
extraño, –a strange
extraordinario, –a extraordinary
extremo *m.* extreme; terminal
exuberante luxuriant, exuberant

F

facción *f.* feature
fácil easy
facilidad *f.* facility, ease
factor *m.* factor, element
facultad *f.* faculty; school; **— de medicina** medical school
faja *f.* strip
falda *f.* skirt
falta *f.* mistake; fault
Falla, Manuel de *Spanish composer* (*1876–1946*)
falla (valenciana) *f. monumental statue made for the occasion, bonfire*
familia *f.* family
familiar familiar, family (*adj.*)
famoso, –a famous
fantástico, –a fantastic
farmacéutico *m.* druggist
favor *m.* favor; **por —,** please
favorecer to favor, help
fe *f.* faith
febrero *m.* February
fecha *f.* date
felicidad *f.* happiness
felicitaciones *f.pl.* congratulations
feliz happy
femenino, –a feminine
fenómeno *m.* phenomenon
feo, –a homely

feria *f.* fair, market; holiday
Fernando Ferdinand
ferrocarril *m.* railroad
fértil fertile
festividad *f.* festivity
fiebre *f.* fever
fiesta *f.* feast, party; — **familiar** house party
figura *f.* figure
figurar to figure; make a showing, stand out
figurarse to imagine
filete *m.* filet
filosofía *f.* philosophy
fin *m.* end; **a — de que** so that; **a fines de** toward the end of; — **de semana** weekend; **hasta fines de** toward the end of
final *m.* end; *adj.* final, ultimate
fino, –a fine, delicate
firme solid
flamenco *m. Andalusian dance (song and music)*
flan *m.* custard
flor *f.* flower, blossom
florecer to flourish, bloom
(la) Florida *f.* Florida; *a street in Buenos Aires*
flotante floating
flotar to float
fluvial *adj.* river
forastero *m.* outsider, foreigner
forma *f.* form
formación *f.* formation, making
formar to form, develop
fortaleza *f.* fortress
fragancia *f.* fragrance
francés –esa French; *m.* French, Frenchman, *f.* Frenchwoman
franco, –a frank, open
frase *f.* phrase, sentence
frente *f.* forehead; — **a** facing; **en — de** opposite
fresa *f.* strawberry

fresco, –a fresh, cool; **hace —,** it is cool
frío *m.* cold; **hace —,** it is cold
frío, –a cold
frito, –a fried
frontera *f.* frontier, border
fruta *f.* fruit
frutal *adj.* fruit-bearing
fuente *f.* source; fountain
fuera out, outside; — **de** outside of; besides
fuerte strong
fuerza *f.* strength; **a — de** by dint of, by means of, through
fumar to smoke
función *f.* function, affair, event
fundación *f.* foundation
fundar to found, build
funeral *m.* funeral
fútbol *m.* football
futuro *m.* future

G

gaita gallega *f.* bagpipe
Galeoto *m.* go-between (*a reference to Dante's Inferno V*)
galería *f.* balcony, porch
Galicia *a Spanish region in the northwest*
gallego, –a Galician
gama *f.* gamut; — **de colores** symphony of colors
gana *f.* wish; **le da la —,** feels like; **tener —s de** to have a strong desire to
ganadería *f.* cattle raising
ganar to earn
garantir to guarantee
García-Lorca, Federico *Spanish poet and dramatist (1898–1936)*
gasolina *f.* gasoline
gato *m.* cat

gaucho *m.* gaucho; *Argentine cowboy*

gazpacho *m.* cold soup

generación *f.* generation

Generalife *m. summer residence of the Moorish Kings of Granada*

generalmente generally

generosamente generously

genio *m.* genius

gente *f.* people

gestión *f.* management

gigantesco, –a gigantic

Gijón *harbor in the province of Oviedo*

(la) Giralda *tower of the cathedral of Seville*

girar to turn

Girardot *city on the Magdalena River*

gitana *f.* gipsy woman

gitano *m.* gipsy; *adj.* gipsy

glorioso, –a glorious

gobernador *m.* governor

gobierno *m.* government

golf *m.* golf

golfo *m.* gulf; **Golfo Pérsico** *m.* Persian Gulf

gordo, –a fat

gozar (de) to enjoy

gracia *f.* grace

gracias *f.pl.* thanks, thank you

grado *m.* degree; rank

gramaticalmente grammatically

Granada *f. city and province in southern Spain*

Granados, Enrique *Spanish composer* (*1868–1916*)

gran(de) large, great

grandeza *f.* size; grandeur, greatness

(la) Granja *royal palace on the mountains of the Guadarrama range near Madrid*

gris grey, gray

grupo *m.* group

Guadalajara *a city in Mexico, northwest of Mexico City*

La Guaira *Venezuelan harbor*

guante *m.* glove

guapo, –a pretty

guardar to keep, guard; **— silencio** to keep silent

guerra *f.* war

guía *m.* guide; *f.* guide-book

guisantes *m.pl.* peas

guitarra *f.* guitar

guitarrista *m. or f.* guitarrist

gustar to please (like)

gusto *m.* pleasure; taste

H

haber to have

habichuelas verdes *f.pl.* string beans

habitación *f.* home, dwelling; room

habitante *m.* inhabitant

habla *f.* speech; **de — española** Spanish-speaking

hablar to speak

hacendado *m.* landholder, rancher

hacer to do; make; **— calor** be warm; **— frío** be cold; **— un viaje** take a trip; **—se** become; take place; **— viento** be windy

hacia toward

hacienda *f.* farm

hambre *f.* hunger; **tener —,** be hungry

hasta until; to; as far as; **— luego, — la vista** good-bye (*until I see you again*); **— mañana** good-bye (*until tomorrow*); **— que** until

hay there is (are); **— que** one must, it is necessary

hecho (*p.p. of* **hacer**) done

helado *m.* ice cream

hemisferio *m.* hemisphere

heredar to inherit
heredero *m.* heir
herencia *f.* inheritance
hermana *f.* sister
hermano *m.* brother
hermoso, –a beautiful
hermosura *f.* beauty
hidalgo *m.* squire
hielo *m.* ice
hierba *f.* grass
hierro *m.* iron
hija *f.* daughter
hijo *m.* son
hispánico, –a Hispanic
hispanoamericano, –a Spanish American
historia *f.* history; story
histórico, –a historical
hoja *f.* leaf
hombre *m.* man; ¡**Hombre!** Man alive!
hombrón great big man
hora *f.* hour; time
hoy today; — **como ayer** today as in the past; — **en día** nowadays
huella *f.* trace, track
huerta *f.* vegetable garden, truck garden; orchard
hueso *m.* bone
huevo *m.* egg
huir to flee
humanidades *f.pl.* humanities
humedad *f.* humidity
húmedo, –a humid

I

ibérico, –a Iberian
idioma *m.* language
iglesia *f.* church
igual equal, the same; *m.* match
igualar to match, equal
ilusión *f.* illusion

imagen *f.* image; statue
imaginación *f.* imagination
imaginar to imagine; suspect
impedir (i) to prevent
impenetrable impenetrable, impervious
imperfecto *m.* imperfect
imperio *m.* empire
imponer to impose
importancia *f.* importance
importante important
importar to matter
impresión *f.* impression
impresionante imposing, impressive
impuesto *m.* tax; (*p.p. of* **imponer**) imposed
impulso *m.* impulse
inauguración *f.* inauguration
inca *m. or adj.* Inca
incaico, –a *adj.* Inca
incesante endless, continual
incomparable unmatched
incorporar to incorporate
independencia *f.* independence
indicar to indicate
indigestión *f.* indigestion
indio, –a Indian; *m.* Indian
indomable indomitable
industria *f.* industry
inferior inferior, lower
infinito, –a infinite, unbounded
influencia *f.* influence
ingeniería *f.* engineering
ingeniero *m.* engineer
inglés, –esa English; *m.* English
ingresar to enter
ingreso *m.* income
iniciativa *f.* initiative
insigne noted, famous, distinguished
inspirar to inspire
instalación *f.* installation
institución *f.* institution

instituto *m.* institute
integración *f.* integration
integrar to integrate
intelectual intellectual
interés *m.* interest
interesante interesting
interesar to interest
interior *m.* inland, interior
interpretar to interpret
intérprete *m.* interpreter
intervenir to take part
íntimo, –a innermost, intimate
invadir to invade
invasión *f.* invasion, attack
inventar to invent
investigación *f.* investigation; *pl.*
  research
invierno *m.* winter
invitación *f.* invitation
invitado *m.* guest
invitar to invite
ir to go; — **bien con** to match;
  agree; — **de compras** go shopping; **irse** go away, leave
Isabel *f.* Elizabeth, Isabella
isla *f.* island; **Islas Canarias**
  Canary Islands
islámico, –a Islamic
islote *m.* small barren island, islet
istmo *m.* isthmus
Italia *f.* Italy
italiano, –a Italian; *m.* Italian
Ixtaccíhuatl *mountain near Mexico
  City*
izquierdo, –a left; **a la izquierda** to
  the left; **izquierda** *f.* left hand

J

jamás ever; never
jamón *m.* ham
jardín *m.* garden
jardincito *m.* tiny little garden

jefe *m.* boss
jerez *m.* sherry
jira (campestre) *f.* picnic
jornada *f.* act of a play; journey
Josefa Josephine
jota *f. dance of Aragon, Navarra
  and Valencia*
joven *adj.* young; *m.* young man
joya *f.* jewel
Juan John
Juana Joan
judía *f.* (string) bean
juego *m.* game, play
jueves *m.* Thursday
jugar (ue) to play (*a game*)
jugo *m.* juice
Julieta Juliet
julio *m.* July; **Julio** Julius
junio *m.* June
juntar to join, unite
junto, –a near; *pl.* together; — **a**
  next to
juventud *f.* youth

K

kilo *m.* kilogram (*2.2 lbs.*)
kilómetro *m.* kilometer

L

la que the one who; that which
labor *f.* task, work
ladera *f.* slope
lado *m.* side; **a cada** —, on each
  side; **al** — **de** alongside; **por
  otro** —, on the other hand
lago *m.* lake
langosta *f.* lobster
largo, –a long; *m.* length; **a lo** —
  de alongside, throughout; in
  the course of

lástima *f.* pity, shame; **es —**, it's a pity, it's too bad; **¡qué —!** too bad!

laurel *m.* laurel; *pl.* triumphs; laurels

lavar(se) to wash (oneself)

lección *f.* lesson

leche *f.* milk

leer to read

legislación *f.* legislation

legumbres *f.pl.* vegetables

lejano, –a distant

lejos (de) far (from); **de —**, from afar, in the distance

lengua *f.* language

lenguado *m.* sole

lento, –a slow

león *m.* lion

letra *f.* letter; *pl.* letters; literature; **primeras letras** first rudiments

letrado *m.* literary figure

levantar to raise, build; **—se** get up, rise

Levante *m.* Levant, East

levantino *m.* Levantine

libertad *f.* liberty

libra *f.* pound

libraco *m.* horrid book

libre free; **al aire —**, in the open air

libro *m.* book

Liceo *m. institution of higher learning*

Lima *capital of Peru*

limitar to limit; bound

límite *m.* boundary

limón *m.* lemon

limpiar to clean

limpio, –a clean

lindo, –a pretty, neat

línea *f.* line

lista *f.* list; menu

literatura *f.* literature

litro *m.* liter (*1.026 quart*)

lo que what; which; **los que** those which

lobo *m.* wolf

lograr to achieve, accomplish; manage

lona *f.* canvas

Lope de Vega, Félix *Spanish playwright (1562–1635)*

lubina *f.* bass

lucir to shine

luego then; **— que** as soon as; **desde —**, of course; **hasta —**, good-bye

lugar *m.* place; **en — de** instead of; **tener —**, to take place

lujo *m.* luxury

luna *f.* moon

lunar lunar, moon *adj.*

lunes *m.* Monday

luz *f.* light

Ll

llamar to call; **llamado, –a** so-called ; **llamarse** be called

llegada *f.* arrival

llegar to reach, arrive at, get to

llenar to fill

lleno, –a full

llevar to take; bring; wear; carry away; **— a cabo** carry out

llover (ue) to rain

lluvia *f.* rain

M

Macarena, Virgen de la *famous statue of the Virgin, venerated in Seville*

Machu-Picchu *old Inca Peruvian city*

madre *f.* mother

Madrid *m. capital of Spain*
madrileño, –a Madrilenian
maduro, –a ripe, mature
maestro *m.* master, leader; teacher
Magdalena (Río) *river in Colombia*
magisterio *m.* teaching career
magistrato *m.* magistrate, official
magnífico, –a perfect, magnificent
magnitud *f.* magnitude
majestad *f.* majesty
majestuoso, –a majestic
mal *m.* evil, harm; — **de estómago** upset stomach; *adv.* badly
Málaga *a city and province of Spain, on the Mediterranean*
maleta *f.* suitcase
mal(o), –a bad
malquerido, –a disliked
mamá *f.* mother
Mancha *a region in central Spain*
mandar to ask; — **entrar** to show someone in
manera *f.* manner; **de — que** so that; **de ninguna —,** not at all; **de una — fantástica** fantastically
mano *f.* hand
mantequilla *f.* butter
manufacturado, –a manufactured
manzana *f.* apple; block (*of houses*)
manzanilla *f. a strongly-flavored Andalusian wine*
mañana *adv.* tomorrow; *f.* morning
mapa *m.* map
máquina (para escribir) *f.* typewriter; **escribir a —,** to typewrite
mar *m. or f.* sea; **Mar Caribe** Caribbean Sea
Maracaibo *city and lake in Venezuela, near the Colombian border*
maravilla *f.* marvel, wonder
maravilloso, –a marvellous

marcar to mark
marchar to walk; march; —**se** go away, leave
marearse to get seasick; get dizzy, become nauseated
María Mary; **María Luisa** Marie Louise
marido *m.* husband
marina *f.* marine; seashore; seascape; **ministerio de —,** naval ministry
marisco *m.* shellfish
marítimo, –a maritime; *adj.* sea
Mármol, José *Argentine novelist and poet (1818–1871)*
marrón *adj.* brown
martes *m.* Tuesday
Martí, José *Cuban patriot, essayist and poet (1853–1895)*
marzo *m.* March
mas but
más more, most; — **bien** rather; — **o menos** more or less; **no . . . —,** not . . . any more; **sin — ni —,** without further ado
masculino, –a masculine
material *m.* stuff, material
matrícula *f.* registration
matrimonio *m.* (married) couple; marriage
máximo, –a largest; maximum
maya *adj. and n.* Maya
mayo *m.* May
mayor major, bigger; older; **la — parte de** most of
mayoría *f.* majority
mecánico, –a mechanical
mecanógrafa *f.* typist, stenographer
media *f.* stocking
mediados: a — de toward the middle of
medianoche *f.* midnight
medicina *f.* medicine

médico *m.* doctor, physician
medida *f.* measure; size; **a — que**
as, in pace with
Medina Azahara *ruins of old Arab
palace near Cordova*
medio, –a half
medio *m.* middle; **en — de** in the
midst of, in the middle of; **por
— de** by means of
mediodía *m.* midday, noon
mediterráneo, –a Mediterranean
mejor better; best; **— dicho** better
said, rather
melocotón *m.* peach
melodía *f.* melody
melodioso, –a melodious
memoria *f.* memory; **de —,** by
heart
mencionar to mention, point out
menor smaller; younger
menos less; minus; **a — que** unless; **el —,** the least; **por (a) lo
—,** at least
menú *m.* menu
menudo: a —, often, frequently
mercado *m.* market
mercancía *f.* merchandise
merecer to deserve
merienda *f.* lunch
merluza *f.* cod, hake
mero *m.* grouper; **medallón de —,**
grouper steak
mes *m.* month
mesa *f.* table
meseta *f.* plateau
metrópoli *f.* metropolis
mexicano, –a Mexican
México *m.* Mexico
mezquita *f.* mosque
mi(s) my
mí me
miedo *m.* fear; **dar —,** to frighten;
tener —, to be afraid
miembro *m.* member

mientras (que) while, meanwhile;
— tanto meanwhile
miércoles *m.* Wednesday
mil a thousand; **miles y miles**
thousands upon thousands
militar military
milla *f.* mile
millón *m.* million
mina *f.* mine
minería *f.* mining
mínimo, –a least, smallest
ministerio *m.* ministry
ministro *m.* minister
minuto *m.* minute
mío, –a my, mine; **el mío, la mía**
mine
mirar to look at
mismo, –a self, oneself, itself;
same; **ahora —,** right now
misterio *m.* mystery
mitad *f.* half; middle
Mitre, Bartolomé *Argentine statesman, poet and scholar (1821–
1906)*
moda *f.* fashion; **ponerse de —,** be
in fashion
modelo *m.* model; pattern
modernidad *f.* modernity
modernista *adj.* modernist
modernización *f.* modernization
moderno, –a modern
modesto, –a humble, modest
modo: de — que so that, in such a
manner that
molestar to bother, disturb; **—se**
to bother
molestia *f.* bother
momento *m.* moment; particular
time; **en un momentito** in just a
moment
momia *f.* mummy
monasterio *m.* monastery
monolítico, –a monolithic
montaña *f.* mountain

montañoso, –a mountainous
monte *m.* mountain
Montefrío *royal palace in the Segovia province, not far from Madrid*
Montevideo *capital of Uruguay*
monumento *m.* monument
moral moral; **ciencias morales** *f.pl.* ethics
Morelia *Mexican city, near the capital*
morir (ue) to die
mosca *f.* fly
mostrar (ue) to show, point out
motivo *m.* motive; **con — de** on the occasion of; for the purpose of
motor *m.* motor; **— a petróleo** gasoline engine; **principal —,** motivating force
movido, –a (a) run (by)
mozo, –a young; *m.* waiter
muchacha *f.* girl
muchacho *m.* boy
muchachote *m.* big boy
muchedumbre *f.* crowd
mucho much, a great deal; **muchazo** quite a bit
muchos, –as many
mueble *m.* piece of furniture
muelle *m.* dock
muerte *f.* death
mujer *f.* woman; **mujerona** *f.* great big woman; **mujeruca** *f.* wench
multicolor many-colored
multiplicar to multiply
mundial *adj.* world
mundo *m.* world; **todo el —,** everybody
muiñeira *f. Galician dance*
muralla *f.* wall
Murcia *a region in the southeast of Spain*
museo *m.* museum

música *f.* music
músico *m.* musician
musulmán *m.* Mussulman, Moslem
muy very

N

nacer to be born; rise
nacimiento *m.* crèche; birth
nación *f.* nation
nacional national
nada nothing; anything; *adv.* at all; **— de —,** nothing at all
nadar to swim
nadie no one, nobody, (not) anyone
naranja *f.* orange
naranjo *m.* orange tree
natación *f.* swimming
naturaleza *f.* nature
Navarra *Spanish region near the French border*
nave *f.* aisle; nave (*of a cathedral*)
navegable navigable
navegación *f.* navigation
Navidad *f.* Christmas
navideño, –a of the Christmas season
nazca *old Peruvian civilization*
necesario, –a necessary
necesidad *f.* necessity, need
necesitar to need
negocio *m.* business; **por negocios** on business
negro, –a black
neoyorkino *m.* New Yorker
(no) ni . . . ni . . . , neither . . . nor . . . ; **ni tampoco** nor
nieve *f.* snow
ningún, ninguno, –a no, not any, none
niña *f.* girl, child
niño *m.* boy; *pl.* children

nivel *m.* level; — **de vida** standard of living

nocturno *m.* nocturne

noche *f.* night, evening; **de —**, at night; **por la —**, in the evening, at night; **buenas noches** good evening (night)

nombrar to name

nombre *m.* name

normal normal; **escuela —**, teachers' college

norte *m.* north

norteamericano *m.* North American

nos us; to us; ourselves

nosotros we; us

nota *f.* note

notable remarkable, notable

notar to note, mark

noticia *f.* news, piece of news

novecientos, –as nine hundred

novedad *f.* novelty, newness

novela *f.* novel

noventa ninety

novia *f.* fiancée

noviembre November

novio *m.* fiancé

novísimo, –a most new, most recent

nube *f.* cloud

nuestro, –a our; **el —, la nuestra** ours

nuevo, –a new

número *m.* number

numeroso, –a numerous

nunca ever; never

O

o or

Oaxaca *f. Mexican city founded by Cortés*

obedecer to obey

objeto *m.* object; thing

obra *f.* work; — **dramática** play; **obras públicas** public works

o(b)scuro, –a dark

obstáculo *m.* obstacle

Oca *old Galician manor in the Pontevedra province*

ocasión *f.* occasion, opportunity

occidental *adj.* western

occidente *m.* occident, west

océano *m.* ocean

octavo, –a eighth

octubre *m.* October

ocupado, –a busy, occupied

ocupar to occupy; —**se (de)** be busy with, occupy oneself with; attend to

ocurrir to occur, happen, take place

ochenta eighty

ochocientos, –as eight hundred

oeste *m.* west

oficial official

oficina *f.* office

ofrecer to offer

oír to hear

ojalá I wish that, would that

ola *f.* wave

¡olé! hurrah!

olivo *m.* olive tree

olvidar(se) (de) to forget

opinión *f.* opinion

oportunidad *f.* opportunity

optimismo *m.* optimism

óptimo, –a best

opuesto, –a opposite

oración *f.* sentence

orden *f.* order; **a sus órdenes** at your service, if you please

organización *f.* organization

organizar to organize

orgullo *m.* pride

oriental *adj.* eastern

oriente *m.* east, orient; **Plaza de Oriente** *square in Madrid where the royal palace is located*

origen *m.* origin; **en sus orígenes**
originally
originalidad *f.* originality
orilla *f.* bank (*of a river*); shore
Orinoco *Venezuelan river*
Orizaba *Mexican mountain near
Vera Cruz*
ornamento *m.* ornament, decora-
tion
oro *m.* gold
os you; to you
oscuro, –a dark
otoño *m.* autumn, fall
otro, –a other, another; **otra vez**
again
Oviedo *a city and a province in
northern Spain*

P

Pablo *m.* Paul
pacer to graze
Pacífico *m.* Pacific
padrazo *m.* good-hearted father
padre *m.* father; *pl.* parents
pagar to pay
país *m.* country; **país de sol** sunny
country; **País Vasco** Basque
Provinces
paisaje *m.* countryside, landscape
paja *f.* straw
pajarillo *m.* tiny little bird
pájaro *m.* bird
palabra *f.* word
Palacete de la Moncloa *royal
palace in the outskirts of Madrid*
palacio *m.* palace
Palestina Palestine
pan *m.* bread
panameño, –a belonging to Panama
pantalón *m.* or **pantalones** *m.pl.*
trousers

papa *f.* potato
papá *m.* dad
papel *m.* paper; part (*role*)
paquete *m.* package
para for, to, in order to; — **que** so
that, in order that
Paracas *peninsula on the Peruvian
shore*
paraguas *m.* umbrella
paraíso *m.* paradise
Paraná *river which serves in part as
a border between Argentina and
Paraguay*
parar(se) to stop
(el) Pardo *royal palace near Madrid*
parecer to appear, seem; —**se** look
like, resemble
parecido, –a alike, similar
parque *m.* park
párrafo *m.* paragraph
parrilla *f.* grill, grate
parte *f.* part; side (*of a discussion*);
en gran —, to a great extent; **en
su mayor** —, on the whole; **la
mayor** — **de** most of; **por su** —,
on their part; **por todas partes**
everywhere
participación *f.* participation, contribution
particular particular, private
partida *f.* departure; **punto de** —,
starting point
partir to leave, start out
pasado, –a past; well done (*of
meat*)
pasajero *m.* passenger, traveler
pasar to come in, pass; spend; **así
pasa con** that's how it is with;
— **a mejor vida** to pass away;
— **de** to exceed
Pascuas: Felices —, Merry Christmas
pasearse to take a walk
paseo *m.* walk; ride; **dar un** —, to

take a walk; **dar un — en auto**
go for a ride; **Paseo de la Reforma** *one of the main avenues in
Mexico City*
paso *m.* pace, step; statue; **al — de**
along with
pasta seca *f.* cookie
pastel *m.* cake, tart, pie
patata *f.* potato
patio *m.* yard
patria *f.* fatherland, motherland
patrona *f.* landlady
paz *f.* peace
pazo *m.* Galician manor
peculiar peculiar, characteristic
pedir (i) to ask for; order
Pedro Peter
pegar to hit
peinado *m.* hairdo
peinarse to comb one's hair
película *f.* film
peligro *m.* danger
pelo *m.* hair
pelota *f.* ball
peluca *f.* wig
pena *f.* trouble; **vale la pena** it is
worth while
penetrar to penetrate
península *f.* peninsula
pensamiento *m.* thought
pensar (ie) to think; expect
pensión *f.* boardinghouse, home
hotel
peor worse
pequeñito, –a tiny
pequeño, –a small, little
pera *f.* pear
perder (ie) to lose; **— cuidado** not
to worry; **— (el) tiempo** waste
time
perdiz *f.* partridge
perdonar to forgive, pardon
peregrinación *f.* pilgrimage
perezoso, –a lazy

perfecto, –a perfect
periódico *m.* newspaper
permanecer to remain, stay
permanente permanent
permitir to permit, allow
pero but
perro *m.* dog
Persia *f.* Iran
pérsico, –a Persian
persona *f.* person
personaje *m.* personage, character
perspectiva *f.* perspective, view
pertenecer (a) to belong (to)
Perú *m.* Peru
peruano, –a Peruvian
pesar: a — de in spite of
pesca *f.* fishing
pescado *m.* fish; **sopa de —,** fish
chowder
peseta *f. Spanish monetary unit (70
to the dollar in 1970)*
peso *m.* weight; *Spanish American
monetary unit whose value varies
in different countries*
petróleo *m.* petroleum, oil
petrolero, –a *adj.* oil
petrolífero, –a oil-bearing
pianista *m. or f.* pianist
pico *m.* peak, top
pie *m.* foot
piedra *f.* stone
Pilcomayo *m. river which serves in
part as border between Paraguay
and Argentina*
pimiento *m.* pepper
pintar to paint
pintor *m.* painter
pintoresco, –a picturesque
pintura *f.* painting
pipa *f.* pipe
piso *m.* floor, story
placa *f.* sign
plan *m.* plan
planeta *m.* planet

plano *m.* plan, map; *adj.* flat
planta *f.* plant
plástico *m.* plastic
plata *f.* silver
plátano *m.* banana
platense *adj., on the Plata River*
plato *m.* plate, dish; — **combinado** blue plate special
playa *f.* beach
plaza *f.* square; **plazuela** *f.* little square
pleno, –a full, complete
pluma *f.* pen
población *f.* population
poblacho *m.* shabby old town
poblachón *m.* big, shabby old town
poblador *m.* settler
poblar (ue) to people, settle
pobre poor
pobrecita *f.* poor little girl
pobrecito *m.* poor little fellow
pobretón *m.* one who is quite poor
pobreza *f.* poverty
poco, –a little, small; *pl.* a few; **a — de** shortly after; **hace —,** a short while ago; **un —,** somewhat
poder (*irr.*) to be able, can, may
poderoso, –a powerful
poema *m.* poem
poesía *f.* poetry
poeta *m.* poet
poético, –a poetical
política *f.* politics
político *m.* politician; *adj.* political
pollo *m.* chicken
poner to put, lay, place; **—se** to become, get, put on; **—se a** start; **—se de moda** be in fashion
Pontevedra *province in north-western Spain*
Popocatépetl *volcano near Mexico City*

(un) poquito a bit, a tiny bit
por by, during, for, over, along, per, through, because of, in exchange for, for the sake of
¿por qué? why?
porque because
portal *m.* doorway; entrance
posible possible; **lo más —,** as much as possible
posición *f.* position
postguerra *f.* postwar period
postre *m.* dessert
pozo *m.* well; — **petrolífero** oil-well
practicar to practice, exercise
prado *m.* meadow
preciado, –a valued, priced
precio *m.* price
precioso, –a beautiful, delightful
preciso, –a necessary; **es —,** it is necessary
predilecto, –a preferred, favorite
preferente *adj.* preferential; prominent
preferido, –a preferred, favorite
preferir (ie) to prefer
pregunta *f.* question; **hacer preguntas** ask questions
preguntar to ask
preincaica *adj.* before the Incas, preincaic
premio *m.* prize; — **Nobel** Nobel Prize
prenda *f.* article (*of clothing*)
preocuparse (de) (por) to worry (about)
preparar to prepare
presa *f.* dam
presencia *f.* presence
presentar to present, introduce, show
presente present (one)
presidente *m.* president
prestar to lend

pretensión *f.* pretention, ambition
prima *f.* cousin
primario, –a primary
primavera *f.* spring
primer(o), –a first, foremost; *adv.* first
primitivo, –a first; primitive
primo *m.* cousin
principal main, principal
principio *m.* beginning; **a principios** in the beginning
prisa *f.* hurry, haste; **de —**, in a hurry; **tener —**, be in a hurry
privado, –a private
probablemente probably
probar (ue) to taste
problema *m.* problem
proceder to proceed, come from
procesión *f.* procession
proclamar to proclaim, cheer
producción *f.* production
producir to produce, yield, bear
producto *m.* product
productor *m.* producer
profesión *f.* profession
profesional professional; *m.* professional person
profesor *m.* professor, teacher
profesora *f.* professor, teacher
profesorado *m.* faculty
profundo, –a deep
programa *m.* program
progresar to progress
progreso *m.* progress
promesa *f.* promise
pronombre *m.* pronoun
pronto, –a quick, speedy; **pronto** *adv.* immediately, quickly, soon; **lo más — posible** as soon as possible
propiamente properly
propicio, –a favorable
propio, –a proper, suitable, very, own; himself, oneself

proporción *f.* proportion
propósito *m.* purpose; **a — de** as regards
prosperidad *f.* prosperity, boom
próspero, –a prosperous, favorable
proteger to protect
provincia *f.* province
próximo, –a next, nearest
público, –a public
Puebla *Mexican city between Vera Cruz and Mexico City*
pueblo *m.* town; people
puerta *f.* door; gate
puerto *m.* port, harbor
pues for, because, since, well
puesto *m.* position
punto *m.* point; **en —**, exactly, on the dot; **al —**, rare (*of meat*)
puré *m.* puré; **— de patatas** mashed potatoes

Q

que *rel. pron.* who, which, that; *adv.* than; *conj.* that, for
¿qué? *interrog. adj. and pron.* what? which? **¡qué!** *exclam.* how!
quedar(se) to remain, be situated
quejarse (de) to complain (about)
quemar to burn
querer (ie) (*irr.*) to like, love; wish, want
querido, –a dear
queso *m.* cheese
quien who, whom; he who, the one who; **—quiera** whoever
¿quién? (¿quiénes?) who? whom?
quinientos, –as five hundred
Quiroga, Horacio *Uruguayan storyteller (1878–1937)*
quitar(se) to take off
quizá(s) perhaps

R

radio *f.* radio
ramal *m.* branch, ramification
ramo *see* **domingo**
rápido, –a rapid
raro, –a rare, unusual
rasgo *m.* feature
rato *m.* while
Ravel, Maurice *French composer (1875–1937)*
razón *f.* reason; **tener —**, be right; **no tener —**, be wrong
real royal
realce *m.* lustre, splendor; **dar —**, to emphasize, enhance
realeza *f.* royalty, royal dignity
realidad *f.* reality; **en —**, actually, in fact
rebaja *f.* reduction
recibir to receive
reciente recent
recoger to collect, gather, pick
reconocer to recognize
recordar (ue) to remember, recall
recorrer to travel, go over
recorrido *m.* tour, run
recuerdo *m.* souvenir, regard
red *f.* net, network
redondo, –a round
referir (se) (ie) to refer
refinamiento *m.* refinement
refugio *m.* refuge
regalo *m.* present
región *f.* region
regir (i) to rule, govern
registrar to note, record
regla *f.* rule; **como (por) — general** as a general rule
regresar to return
regularmente regularly
reino *m.* kingdom
reír(se) (de) to laugh (at)
relativo, –a relative

religión *f.* religion
religioso, –a religious
reloj *m.* watch, clock
remador *m.* rower
remedio *m.* remedy
Renacimiento *m.* Renaissance; rebirth
reñir (i) to quarrel, scold
repartir to divide, distribute
repetición *f.* repetition
repetir (i) to repeat
representación *f.* show, performance
representar to perform, represent
representativo, –a representative
república *f.* republic
reserva *f.* reserve
residencia *f.* residence, domicile
residencial residential
residir to reside, live; remain
resolver (ue) to solve
respectivo, –a respective
respirar to breathe
responder to answer, respond
restaurante *m.* restaurant
resto *m.* remainder, rest; *pl.* remains
resultado *m.* result
resultar to turn out, result, follow
retirarse to withdraw
reunirse to get together
revelar to reveal, show
reverendo *m. or adj.* reverend
rey *m.* king; **Reyes Católicos** *Ferdinand and Isabella*
ría *f.* sound (*of sea*), inlet, bay
Ribadeo *a small harbor in Galicia*
rico, –a rich, wealthy
Rimsky-Korsakov, Nicolas *Russian composer (1844–1908)*
rincón *m.* corner, nook
río *m.* river; **Río de la Plata** Estuary of the Plata River
riqueza *f.* wealth

ritmo *m.* rhythm, pace
Rivadavia, Bernardino *Argentine statesman; an avenue in Buenos Aires*
rivalizar con to rival
rodear to surround, encircle
rodeo *m.* turn, detour; **dar un —,** take a roundabout way
Rodó, José *Uruguayan essayist (1872–1917)*
rojo, –a red
romance *m.* ballad; romance
romanticismo *m.* Romanticism
romántico, –a romantic
romería *f.* pilgrimage; picnic
ropa *f.* clothing; **— interior** underwear; **tienda de —,** clothing store
rosado, –a rose-colored
Rosario *the second largest city in Argentina*
rotisería *f.* rotisserie
rubio, –a blond
ruido *m.* noise
ruina *f.* ruin

S

sábado *m.* Saturday
saber (*irr.*) to know, know how
sabroso, –a tasty
sacar to take out, take off
Sacromonte *a hill in the outskirts of Granada*
Sacsahuaman *old preincaic fortress near Cuzco*
saeta *f. Andalusian song*
sala *f.* room; wing (*of a museum*)
Salado *m. Argentine river*
salir (de) to leave, go out (of)
salteado, –a sautéed
salud *f.* health
saludo *m.* greeting; *pl.* regards

Salvador *m.* Saviour
salvar to equalize
salvo except(ing)
San José *the capital of Costa Rica*
Sánchez, Florencio *Uruguayan dramatist (1875–1910)*
sandía *m.* watermelon
sanidad *f.* sanitation
sanitario *m.* health officer
Santa Cruz de Ribadulla *old Galician manor in La Coruña province*
Santa Fe *a big city in Argentina*
Santander *a city and a province in northern Spain*
Santiago Saint James; **Santiago de Chile** *capital of Chile;* **Santiago de Compostela** *city in Galicia*
Santillana del Mar *an old city in Santander province*
san(to), –a saint; **Santo Entierro** Holy Entombment
sardana *f. Catalan dance*
Sarmiento, Domingo Faustino, *Argentine statesman, essayist and scholar (1811–1888)*
satírico, –a satirical
se himself, herself; yourself, yourselves; themselves; to him, etc.
sección *f.* section
seco, –a dry
secretaria *f.* secretary
secretario *m.* secretary
sed *f.* thirst; **tener —,** be thirsty
seguida: en —, immediately, at once
seguidita: en —, right away
seguir (i) to continue, go on; follow
según according to
segundo, –a second; secondary
seguro, –a sure, safe
seiscientos, –as six hundred

selección *f.* selection, choice
selva *f.* forest
semana *f.* week; **fin de —,** weekend; **Semana Santa** Holy Week
semejante similar, like that
senador *m.* senator
sencillo, –a simple
sensible noticeable
sentarse (ie) to sit down
sentir (ie) to feel; regret; **—se** feel; **lo siento** I am sorry
señal *f.* sign
señalar to point out, mark
señor Mr., sir, gentleman; **señores** Mr. and Mrs.; **Señor del Gran Poder** Lord All-powerful
señora *f.* lady, Mrs., madam
señorita *f.* young lady, Miss
señorón *m.* important gentleman
separar to separate, divide; **—se** secede, withdraw
septiembre *m.* September
sepulcro *m.* sepulcher, grave
ser (*irr.*) to be; **lo que va a — de mí** what is to become of me
serie *f.* series
serio, –a serious
serrano, –a cured (*of ham*)
servicio *m.* service
servir (i) to serve; be used as; **¿En qué puedo servirles?** What can I do for you?
sesenta sixty
setecientos, –as seven hundred
setenta seventy
Sevilla *city in southwestern Spain*
sevillano, –a Sevillian
sexo *m.* sex
si if
sí yes; himself, etc.
sidra *f.* cider
siempre always; **— que** whenever
sierpe *f.* snake

sierra *f.* range of mountains
siglo *m.* century; **Siglo de Oro** Golden Age
significativo, –a significant
siguiente following
silencio *m.* silence
silenciosamente silently
Silvia Sylvia
silla *f.* chair
simbólico, –a symbolical
símbolo *m.* symbol
simpatía *f.* friendliness
simpático, –a attractive; pleasant
sin without; **sin que** *conj.* without
sinfonía *f.* symphony
singular singular, unique
sino but, except; **— que** but rather
síntesis *f.* synthesis
siquiera: ni —, not even
Siria *f.* Syria
sistema *m.* system
sitio *m.* place
situación *f.* situation
situar to place, locate
sobre upon, above; **— todo** especially, above all
sobresaliente outstanding
sobrino *m.* nephew
sociedad *f.* society
socio *m.* member
sol *m.* sun; sunshine
soleado, –a sunny
solemnidad *f.* solemnity
soler (ue) to be in the habit of, used to
sólido, –a solid, firm
solitario, –a solitary
solo, –a alone; **solito, –a** all alone
sólo *adv.* only
solomillo *m.* sirloin steak
sombra *f.* shade
sombrerería *f.* hat shop
sombrero *m.* hat

sopa *f.* soup
sorprendente surprising
sorpresa *f.* surprise
su his, her, its, your (*pol.*), their
suave soft, mild, sweet
subida *m.* ascent
subir to go up, walk up, get into
suceder to happen
sucursal *f.* branch office
sud *m.* south; **Sud América (Sud-américa)** *f.* South America
sueldo *m.* salary, pay
suelo *m.* soil, ground
sueño *m.* sleep; **tener —**, be sleepy
suerte *f.* luck
suéter *m.* sweater
sufrir to suffer, get
Suiza *f.* Switzerland
suma *f.* sum
superar to excel, surpass
superficial *adj.* surface
superior superior, upper, higher
supuesto: por —, of course
sur *m.* south; **América del Sur** South America
el suyo, la suya his, hers, its, yours (*pol.*), theirs

T

tabaco *m.* tobacco
Taboga *f. an island in the Pacific*
tal such; **con tal que** provided that; **¿qué tal?** how are you?
tal vez perhaps
Talgo *m. Spanish speed train*
también also, too
tampoco either; neither
tan so, as
tanto, –a so (as) much; *pl.* so (as) many; **un —**, somewhat; *adv.* so much

tardar to take (time)
tarde *f.* afternoon; **buenas tardes** good afternoon; **por la —**, in the afternoon; *adv.* late
tarea *f.* task
tarjeta *f.* card; **— postal** postcard
tarta *f.* cake, tart
Taxco *old colonial Mexican city, near the capital*
te you (*fam.*), to you
té *m.* tea
teatral theatrical
teatro *m.* theater
técnica *f.* technical skill
tejido *m.* texture, fabric
telecomunicación *f.* telecommunication
telefonear to telephone
teléfono *m.* telephone
telégrafo *m.* telegraph
televisión *f.* television
tema *m.* topic, plot
temeroso, –a afraid
temperamento *m.* temperament
templado, –a mild, moderate
templo *m.* temple
temporada *f.* season, length of time, spell
tempranito quite early
temprano early
tenazmente stubbornly, tenaciously
tener (*irr.*) to have; **— lugar** to take place; **— que** have to
tenis *m.* tennis
tenso, –a tense, intense
tercer(o), –a third
terminar to end, finish
ternera *f.* calf; veal; **ternero** *m.* calf
terraza *f.* terrace
terrestre terrestrial, land (*adj.*)
terriblemente terribly
territorio *m.* territory

tesoro *m.* treasure
ti you (*fam.*), to you
tiempo *m.* time; weather; tense;
　hace mal —, the weather is bad
tienda *f.* shop, store; — **de ropa**
　clothing store
tierra *f.* earth; land; country
tinto, –a red (*of wine*)
típico, –a characteristic
tipo *m.* kind, type
Tirso de Molina *Spanish play-*
　wright (*1571?–1648*)
Titicaca *lake on the border of Peru*
　and Bolivia
título *m.* title; degree
tocado *m.* headdress, hairdo
tocar to play (*an instrument*)
todavía still, yet
todo, –a all, whole, every; *pron.*
　all, everything; **todos** everyone,
　everybody
toledano, –a from Toledo, Toledo
　style
Toledo *city and province in Spain,*
　near Madrid
tomar to take; drink; eat
tomate *m.* tomato
tonto, –a foolish
toque *m.* playing
toros *m.pl.* bullfight
torre *f.* tower
tortilla *f.* omelet
trabajar to work
trabajo *m.* work
tradición *f.* tradition
traducir to translate
traer to bring; wear
tráfico *m.* traffic, trade
tragedia *f.* tragedy
traje *m.* suit
tranquilo, –a quiet, calm
transformación *f.* transformation
transformar to transform, become
tránsito *m.* traffic

transportación *f.* transportation
transportar to carry, transport
transporte *m.* transportation
transversal *adj.* transversal, cross
tranvía *m.* trolley
trasladar to move, transfer
tratar (de) to treat; try (to)
a través de across, through
travesía *f.* passage, crossing
treinta thirty
tremendo, –a tremendous
tren *m.* train
trescientos, –as three hundred
triste sad
tú you (*fam.*)
tu your (*fam.*)
Tucumán *city in Argentina*
Tupungato *high mountain on the*
　border between Chile and Argen-
　tina
turismo *m.* tourism
turista *m.* tourist
el tuyo, la tuya yours (*fam.*)

U

últimamente lately, recently
último, –a last, latter; *pl.* last few
Ulla (río) *river which separates the*
　provinces of Pontevedra and La
　Coruña in Spain
único, –a only, only one, only thing
unidad *f.* unity
unido, –a united; — **a** together
　with
unir to unite, be joined with
universidad *f.* university
universitario, –a college (*adj.*),
　university (*adj.*)
un(o), –a a, an; one; *pl.* some, a
　few
urbanización *f.* city development,
　urbanization

urbano, -a urban
urbe *f.* metropolis
Uruguay Uruguay; *river which serves partly as border between Argentina and Uruguay*
uruguayo, -a Uruguayan
usar to use
uso *m.* use
usted (Vd., Ud.), ustedes (Vds., Uds.) *pron.* you
útil useful
utilizar to use, utilize
uvas *f.pl.* grapes

V

vaca *f.* cow
vacaciones *f.pl.* vacation
Valdivia, Pedro de *Spanish conqueror of Chile*
Valencia *a city and region in the eastern part of Spain*
valer to be worth; **— la pena** be worth while
valor *m.* value
valle *m.* valley
Valle-Inclán, Ramón María de *Spanish writer (1866–1936)*
variado, -a varied; assorted
variedad *f.* variety, differences
varios, -as various, several
vaso *m.* glass
vecina *f.* neighbor
vecino *m.* neighbor
vegetación *f.* vegetation
veintisiete twenty-seven
vencer to conquer, defeat
vender to sell
venezolano, -a Venezuelan
venir to come
ventana *f.* window
ventanilla *f.* window (*of train or plane*)

ver to see; **a —,** let's see
verano *m.* summer
veras: de —, really, in truth
verbo *m.* verb
verdad *f.* truth; **en —,** in fact; **es —,** it is true; **¿no es —?** isn't it so?
verdadero, -a true, real
verde green
verduras *f.pl.* vegetables; **ensalada de —,** vegetable salad
versión *f.* translation, version
vestido *m.* dress, clothing, costume
vestir (i) to dress; **—se** get dressed
vez *f.* time; **a veces** at times; **alguna —,** sometimes; **alguna — que otra** occasionally; **de — en cuando** from time to time; **en — de** instead of; **unas veces** sometimes
vía *f.* way, lane
viajar to travel
viaje *m.* trip
viajero *m.* traveler
vid *f.* grapevine
vida *f.* life, living
viejecito *m.* little old man
viejo, -a old
viento *m.* wind; **hace —,** it is windy
viernes *m.* Friday
villa *f.* village; city
Villagarcía (de Arosa) *city in Galicia*
vino *m.* wine
Virgen *f.* Virgin
virreinato *m.* viceroyship
visible visible, evident
visigodo *m.* Visigoth
visigótico, -a Visigothic
visita *f.* visit; **hacer una —,** to pay a visit, visit; **ir de —,** go for a visit

visitante *m.* visitor
visitar to visit
víspera *f.* eve, day before
vista *f.* view, sight
visto (*p.p. of* **ver**) seen
vivir to live
vivo, –a alive, bright, live
vocación *f.* vocation, inclination
volcán *m.* volcano
volver (ue) to return, go back; — **a**
do something again; —**se** turn,
become
vosotros you (*fam. pl.*)
voz *f.* voice
vuelta *f.* return; turn, revolution;
dar una —, take a walk, take
a trip; make a revolution
(*earth*)
vuelto (*p.p. of* **volver**) returned
vuestro, –a your (*fam. pl.*); **el
vuestro, la vuestra** yours

X

Xochimilco *floating gardens, not
far from Mexico City*

Y

ya already, as soon as; — **es todo**
that's all
yacimiento *m.* deposit, field

Z

zapato *m.* shoe
Zaragoza *a city in northeastern
Spain*
Zarzuela *royal palace near Madrid;* **zarzuela** *f.* musical comedy
zona *f.* zone

ENGLISH-SPANISH VOCABULARY

A

a, an un, uno, una
about acerca de, sobre, de; **be — to** estar para
above arriba, encima
accomplish llevar a cabo, lograr
account relato *m.;* cuenta *f.;* **on — of** a causa de
accustomed acostumbrado, –a; **become, get — (to)** acostumbrarse (a); **be — (to)** estar acostumbrado (a)
across a través de
act acto *m.;* jornada *f.*
active activo, –a
activity actividad *f.*
admire admirar
admit confesar (ie), reconocer
advice consejo *m.*
advise aconsejar
aerial aéreo, –a
afar: from —, de lejos
affinity afinidad *f.*
afraid: be —, tener miedo
after después (de), al cabo de; **soon —,** a poco de
afternoon tarde *f.;* **in the —,** por la tarde
again otra vez
against contra
age edad *f.*
ago *construction with* **hace**
agree estar de acuerdo (con)
agriculture agricultura *f.*

air aire *m.;* **in the open —,** al aire libre; **by —,** por avión; **air-conditioned** con aire acondicionado
airline línea aérea *f.;* compañía de aviación comercial *f.*
alive vivo, –a
all todo, –a; **most of —,** lo más importante, lo principal; **not at —,** de ninguna manera; **— of you** todos Vds.; **that's —,** ya es todo
allegorical alegórico, –a
alone solo, –a
along (with) al paso de
alongside a lo largo de
also también
although aunque (+ *subjunctive*)
always siempre
ambition aspiración; ambición; pretensión *f.*
America América *f.*
American americano, –a
among entre
and y, e (*before words beginning with* **i** *or* **hi**)
Andalusian andaluz, –uza
Andes Andes *m.pl.;* **of the —,** andino, –a
animation animación *f.*
another otro, –a; **one to —,** los unos a los otros
answer contestación *f.; verb* contestar, responder
any alguno (algún), –a; *after*

negative ninguno (ningún), –a;
  any (whatever) cualquier(a)
anybody alguien; *after negative*
  nadie
anyone alguno (algún), –a; cual-
  quier(a); *after negative* nadie
anything algo; *after negative* nada
apartment apartamento *m.*
apparently al parecer
appetite hambre *f.*
appreciate estimar
Arab árabe *adj. or n.*
Arabic árabe
Argentina Argentina *f.*
armchair sillón *m.*
around alrededor (de); — **here** por
  aquí
arrival llegada *f.*
arrive llegar
art arte *m.;* **fine arts** Bellas Artes
  f. pl.
artistic artístico, –a
as como; cuando; mientras; a
  medida que; **as** (*adj.*) **. . . as**
  tan . . . como; — **far** —, hasta;
  — **for** en cuanto a; — **if,** como
  si; — **long** —, mientras; —
  much —, tanto como; — **many**
  —, tantos como; — **soon** —, en
  cuanto, tan pronto como; — **a**
  general rule como (por) regla
  general
ask preguntar; — **for** pedir (i)
asleep dormido, –a; durmiendo;
  fall —, dormirse (ue)
assorted variado, –a
at a; en; — **the end of** al cabo de;
  — **once** en seguida
Atlantic atlántico, –a
attend asistir; cuidar, ocuparse
  (de)
attract atraer
attractive atractivo, –a; agradable
author autor *m.*

auto automóvil *m.;* auto (*play*) *m.;*
  — **highway** autopista *f.*
Aztec azteca *adj. or n.*

B

backbone espina dorsal *f.*
bad mal(o), –a; **too** —! ¡lástima!
  ¡qué lástima!
badly mal, malamente
baldness calvicie *f.*
banana banana *f.*, plátano *m.*
basis base *f.*
bath baño *m.;* **take a** —, bañarse
be ser; estar; — **about to** estar
  para; — **for** optar por; — **left**
  quedar; — **to** deber
beach playa *f.*
beautiful hermoso, –a; bonito, –a;
  bello, –a
beauty belleza *f.*
because porque
become hacerse, volverse (ue),
  ponerse, llegar a ser; — **accus-**
  tomed acostumbrarse; — **fright-**
  ened asustarse; — **quiet** callarse
beeliner autovía *m.*
beer cerveza *f.*
before *adv.* (*time*) antes (de);
  (*place*) delante de; *conj.* antes
  de que; *prep.* antes
begin empezar (ie), comenzar (ie)
beginning principio *m.;* **in the** —,
  en sus orígines
behind detrás de
believe creer
belong pertenecer
below inferior; por debajo de
beside al lado de; **besides** además
  de
best el (la) mejor; *adv.* mejor
better mejor
between entre
big grande (gran)

bird pájaro *m.*
(a) bit (un) poquito
black negro, –a
block bloque *m.;* manzana (*of houses*) *f.*
blood sangre *f.;* **royal** —, realeza *f.*
blossom flor *f.*
blue azul
boardinghouse pensión *f.*
boat barco *m.,* barca *f.,* buque *m.*
boil bullir
bone hueso *m.*
book libro *m.*
born: be —, nacer
boss patrono *m.,* jefe *m.*
both los (las) dos; — . . . **and** . . ., lo mismo . . . que . . .
bother molestar
boy muchacho *m.*
Brazil Brasil *m.*
breakfast desayuno *m.;* **have** —, desayunarse
bright brillante, preciado, –a
bring llevar, traer
brother hermano *m.*
build construir
bull toro *m.;* —**fight** corrida (de toros) *f.;* —**fighter** torero *m.;* espada *m.;* — **ring** plaza de toros *f.*
bus autobús *m.*
business negocio *m.;* **on** —, por negocios
busy ocupado, –a
but pero, sino (que)
buy comprar
by por, de, en; — **the side of** al lado de

C

cabin cabina *f.;* camarote *m.*
café café *m.*
call llamar
can poder (*irr.*)

canal canal *m.*
capital (*city*) capital *f.*
car automóvil *m.,* auto *m.,* carro *m.,* coche *m.*
care cuidado *m.;* *verb* importar (a alguien)
carefully con cuidado
carry llevar; — **on** continuar; — **out** llevar a cabo
case caso *m.;* causa *f.;* **in** —, en caso (de) que; **in any** —, en todo caso
Castilian castellano, –a
castle castillo *m.*
cat gato *m.*
cathedral catedral *f.*
celebrate celebrar
celebration celebración *f.*
center centro *m.*
century siglo *m.*
chain (*of mountains*) cordillera *f.*
chair silla *f.*
change cambiar
character carácter *m.*
characteristic característico, –a
charm encanto *m.;* atractivo *m.*
chat charlar
cheap barato, –a
child niño *m.;* **as a** —, de niño; **children** niños *m.pl.*
Chilean chileno, –a
China China *f.*
chocolate chocolate *m.*
Christian cristiano *m.*
church iglesia *f.*
city ciudad *f.;* — **life** vida urbana
civilization civilización *f.*
class clase *f.*
classify clasificar
clean limpio, –a
clearly claramente
clerk dependiente *m.*
climate clima *m.*
close cerrar (ie)
cloud nube *f.*

coast costa *f.*
coffee café *m.*
cold frío, –a; frío *m.;* **it is —,** hace frío
Colombian colombiano, –a
colonial colonial
color color *m.*
colossus coloso *m.*
combine combinar
come venir; **— back** volver (ue); **— down** bajar; **— in style** ponerse de moda; **— out** salir
comedy comedia *f.*
commemorate conmemorar
commercial comercial
common común
communication comunicación *f.;* **maritime and land communications** comunicaciones marítimas y terrestres
communion comunión *f.*
Communism comunismo *m.*
community comunidad *f.*
companion compañero *m.*
company compañía *f.;* **keep (someone) —,** hacer compañía a
compare comparar
complain quejarse (de)
complete completo, –a
complicated complicado, –a
composition composición *f.*
conclude concluir
conclusion conclusión *f.*
connect comunicar con
conquer conquistar, vencer
conqueror conquistador *m.*
consider considerar
consideration consideración *f.*
constitute constituir
construct construir, fabricar
consult consultar
contemporary contemporáneo, –a; de actualidad
contest concurso *m.*

continent continente *m.*
continue seguir (i)
convenience comodidad *f.*
conversation conversación *f.*
convinced: become —, convencerse (de)
cool fresco, –a; **it is —,** hace fresco
cool off refrescarse
cordially (*in letters*) atento y seguro servidor
corner esquina *f.;* rincón *m.*
cost costar (ue)
costly costoso, –a
count contar (ue)
country país *m.*
countryside paisaje *m.*
couple par *m.;* matrimonio *m.*
course: of —, claro, por supuesto
cousin primo *m.;* prima *f.*
cover cubrir (*p.p.* cubierto)
cow vaca *f.*
cross atravesar (ie)
crossing travesía *f.*
crowd muchedumbre *f.*
cruise crucero *m.*
cultivate cultivar
cultural cultural
culture cultura *f.*
cup taza *f.*
curious curioso, –a
curve curva *f.*
customer cliente *m.*

D

dance baile *m.; verb* bailar
dancer bailador *m.;* bailarina *f.;* **professional —,** profesional del baile *m.*
danger peligro *m.*
dare atreverse (a)
date fecha *f.*
daughter hija *f.*

day día *m.;* **from — to —**, de día
en día; **opening —**, día del
estreno
deal: a great —, mucho, –a
deal tratar, negociar
dear querido, –a; estimado, –a;
distinguido, –a
decipher descifrar
decorate adornar
defend defender (ie)
degree grado *m.;* título *m.*
democracy democracia *f.*
departure partida *f.;* **point of —**,
punto de partida
depend (on) depender (de)
desert desierto *m.*
desire gana *f.;* **to have a —**, tener
ganas
dessert postre *m.*
detain (oneself) detenerse (en)
develop desarrollarse
development desarrollo *m.*
different diferente
difficult difícil
difficulty dificultad *f.*
direct dirigir
disappear desaparecer
discover descubrir
discovery descubrimiento *m.*
discuss discutir
discussion discusión *f.*
disembark desembarcar
distance distancia *f.;* **in the —**, de
lejos
distinguish distinguir
distinguished distinguido, –a
divide dividir
do hacer; **How do you do?** ¿Cómo
está Vd.?
dock dársena *f.;* muelle *m.*
doctor médico *m.*
dog perro *m.*
dominate dominar
domination dominación *f.*

dot: on the —, en punto
doubt duda *f.;* *verb* dudar
dozen docena *f.*
dramatic dramático, –a
dramatist dramaturgo *m.*
draw near acercarse
dress vestir (i); **get dressed** vestirse
drink beber, tomar
drink bebida *f.*
drive (*to a place*) ir en auto
drop dejar caer; **— (one) a few
lines** poner(le) (a uno) unas
letras
during durante

E

each cada; **— one** cada uno; **—
other** el uno al otro
early temprano; **quite —**, tempranito
easily fácilmente
east este *m.*
easy fácil
eat comer
economic económico, –a
education enseñanza *f.* **higher —**,
enseñanza superior, enseñanza
universitaria
eight ocho
(not) either tampoco
element elemento *m.*
emancipator emancipador *m.*
emigrant emigrante *m.*
empire imperio *m.*
empty vacío, –a; *verb* desembocar
(*of a river*)
enchanting encantador, –ora
encircle rodear
enclose incluir
end fin *m.*
endless incesante
engine motor *m.*

English inglés *m.;* inglés, –esa
enjoy gozar
enormous enorme
enthusiasm entusiasmo *m.*
enthusiastic entusiástico, –a; entusiasmado, –a; **make one —,** entusiasmar
equal igual; *verb* igualar
era época *f.*
essayist ensayista *m.*
eternally eternamente
Europe Europa *f.*
European europeo, –a
even aun; hasta
evening noche *f.*
event función *f.*
ever nunca, jamás
every todos, –as; cada; **—thing** todo; **—where** en todas partes
exactly en punto
example ejemplo *m.*
excellence excelencia *f.;* **par —,** por excelencia
excellent excelente
except salvo; con excepción de
excursion excursión *f.*
exercise ejercicio *m.*
exercise ejercitar, practicar
exile exilio *m.*
exist existir
expect esperar; **can one — more?** ¿se le puede pedir más?
expectation esperanza *f.*
expensive costoso, –a
experience experiencia *f.*
explorer explorador *m.*
export exportar
express expresar
extend extender (ie), extenderse (ie)
extensive extenso, –a
extreme extremo, –a
extremely muy + *adj. or adv., or use superlative*

F

fabric tejido *m.*
face cara *f.;* *verb* dar a
facing frente a
fact hecho *m.;* **in —,** en verdad
fair feria *f.*
faith fe *f.*
fail dejar de
fall otoño *m.*
fall caer, caerse; **— asleep** dormirse (ue); **— down** caerse; **— in love with** enamorarse de
family familia *f.*
famous famoso, –a
fan (*sports*) aficionado *m.;* **like a —,** en abanico
fantastically de una manera fantástica
far lejos; **— from** lejos de
farmer campesino *m.*
fashion moda *f.;* **come into —,** ponerse de moda
father padre *m.*
favor favorecer, preferir (ie)
favorable favorable; **is — to** es propicio para
favorite favorito, –a; predilecto, –a
fearful temeroso, –a
feast fiesta *f.*
February febrero *m.*
feel sentir (ie), sentirse (ie)
fertility fertilidad *f.*
festival fiesta *f.*
festivity festividad *f.*
few pocos, –as; **a —,** algunos, unos pocos
fiancée novia *f.*
field campo *m.*
fifty-six cincuenta y seis
figure figurar
film película *f.*

find encontrar (ue), hallar; buscar; — **out** enterarse de, descubrir
fine fino, –a
finish terminar, acabar
firm compañía *f.*, empresa *f.*
first primer(o), –a
fishing pesca *f.*
five cinco
flamenco flamenco *m.* (*Andalusian dance*)
float carruaje *m.; verb* flotar
floor piso *m.*
flourish florecer
flower flor *f.*
fly mosca *f.; verb* volar (ue)
follow seguir (i)
fond (of) amante (de)
foolish tonto, –a
foot pie *m.*
for *conj.* porque; *prep.* para, por, durante
foreign extranjero, –a; extraño, –a
foreigner extranjero *m.*
foremost primero, –a
forest bosque *m.*, selva *f.*
forget olvidar, olvidarse
forgive perdonar
form forma *f.; verb* formar
fortress fortaleza *f.*
fortunate afortunado, –a; **be —,** tener la suerte (de)
forty cuarenta
found: be —, encontrarse (ue)
foundation fundación *f.*, base *f.*
four cuatro
fourth cuarto, –a
fragrance fragancia *f.*
frankly francamente
freight carga *f.*
frequently a menudo
Friday viernes *m.;* **Good —,** Viernes Santo
friend amigo *m.*, amiga *f.*

frightened asustado, –a; **become —,** asustarse
from de, desde; — **day to day** de día en día; — **time to time** de vez en cuando
front: in — of delante de
fruit fruta *f.;* — **tree** árbol frutal *m.*
full lleno, –a
fun broma *f.*, burla *f.;* **make — of** burlarse de
furniture muebles *m.pl.*

G

Galician gallego, –a
game juego *m.*
garden jardín *m.*
gasoline petróleo *m.;* gasolina *f.;* — **engine** motor a petróleo
gate puerta *f.*
general general; **as a — rule** como (por) regla general
generally generalmente
generation generación *f.*
genius genio *m.*
gentleman caballero *m.*, señor; **an important —,** un señorón
George Jorge
get llegar; conseguir (i), lograr, obtener; ponerse, volverse (ue), hacerse; — **dressed** vestirse (i); — **frightened** asustarse (de); — **married (to)** casarse (con); — **ready** preparar; — **tired (of)** cansarse (de); — **up** levantarse
girl muchacha *f.*, joven *f.*, señorita *f.*
give dar; — **in** ceder, dejarse vencer
glad alegre, contento, –a; **be — (of) (to),** alegrarse (de)
glove guante *m.*

go ir; — **away** irse; — **back**
  volver (ue); — **in** entrar; — **on**
  continuar; — **out** salir; —
  shopping ir de compras; —
  through recorrer; — **up** subir;
  — **well** ir bien
God Dios *m.*
good buen(o), –a
good-bye hasta la vista, hasta
  luego; adiós
gosh! ¡caramba!
government gobierno *m.;* — **by**
  council gobierno colegiado
grace gracia *f.*
gracefully con gracia
grammar gramática *f.*
grandfather abuelo *m.*
grandmother abuela *f.*
graze pacer, pastorear
grazing pastoreo *m.*
great gran(de); **a** — **deal** mucho,
  –a
greatness grandeza *f.*
green verde
grey, gray gris
group grupo *m.*
grow crecer

H

hair pelo *m.*
hairdo peinado *m.*, tocado *m.*
half medio, –a; mitad *f.;* — **an**
  hour media hora
hall cámara *f.*, sala *f.*
ham jamón *m.*
hand mano *f.;* **on the other** —, en
  cambio, por otra parte
happy contento, –a; **to be** —,
  alegrarse
harbor bahía *f.*, puerto *m.*

hardly apenas, difícilmente
hat sombrero *m.*
have haber; tener; — **a good time**
  divertirse (ie); — **to** tener que;
  — **just** acabar de + *infinitive*
he él
head cabeza *f.*
hear oír
heart corazón *m.*
heaven cielo *m.*
help ayuda *f.*
help ayudar, **cannot** — **but** no
  poder menos de
her su, sus; la
here aquí, acá
hers el suyo, la suya
hide esconder
high alto, –a; elevado, –a
highway carretera *f.*, autopista *f.;*
  four-lane —, carretera de cuatro
  vías
him le, lo; (*after prep.*) él; **himself**
  se, sí, él mismo
his *adj.* su; *pron.* el suyo, la suya
history historia *f.*
hold tener
holiday día de fiesta *m.*
holy santo, –a; **Holy Week** Semana
  Santa
home casa *f.*, hogar *m.;* **at** —, en
  casa
hope esperar
hot caliente
hotel hotel *m.*
hour hora *f.*
house casa *f.;* **run-down** —, casucha
how? ¿cómo? — **long?** ¿cuánto
  tiempo? ¿desde cuándo?; —
  much? ¿cuánto?; — **many?**
  ¿cuántos?; *exclam.* ¡qué!
hundred cien, ciento; **hundreds**
  centenares *m.pl.*

hurry prisa *f.;* **be in a** —, tener prisa
husband esposo *m.,* marido *m.*
hut casucha *f.*

I

Iberian ibérico, –a
idea idea *f.*
if si
imagination imaginación *f.*
imagine imaginar, imaginarse
immediately en seguida, pronto
immense inmenso, –a
important importante
impression impresión *f.,* sensación *f.*
impressive impresionante
improvement avance *m.,* mejora *f.*
in en, a, de, por; — **front of** delante de; — **the midst of** en medio de; — **spite of** a pesar de
inauguration inauguración *f.*
Inca inca *adj.;* incaico, –a
incorporate incorporar
independence independencia *f.*
industrial industrial
industry industria *f.*
infinite infinito, –a
influence influencia *f.*
inhabitant habitante *m.*
inherit heredar
inside of dentro de
instead of en vez de, en lugar de
institution institución *f.*
integration integración *f.*
intellectual intelectual
interest interés *m.; verb* interesar; **be interested in** tener interés por
interesting interesante
interview entrevista *f.*
intimate íntimo, –a

into en
invasion invasión *f.*
investigation investigación *f.*
invite invitar
islamic islámico, –a
island isla *f.*
islet islote *m.*
it lo, la; **its** su; **itself** se, sí; propio, –a

J

jewel joya *f.*
job empleo *m.*
John Juan
join: be joined with unirse con
joy alegría *f.;* — **of living** alegría de vivir
jungle selva *f.*
just: have —, acabar de + *infinitive*

K

keep guardar; — **quiet** callar(se); — **silent** guardar silencio; — **on** seguir (i) + *pres. part.*
keep (someone) company hacer compañía a
kind especie *f.*
know conocer; saber

L

laden cargado, –a
lady señora *f.;* **young** —, señorita
lake lago *m.*
land tierra *f.; adj.* terrestre
landlady patrona *f.*
landscape paisaje *m.*

lane vía *f.;* **six-lane highway** carretera de seis vías *f.*
language idioma *m.*, lengua *f.*
large gran(de)
last pasado, –a; último, –a; **— few**
últimos, –as
last durar, llevar
Latin American hispanoamericano, –a
(the) latter éste, ésta, esto
laugh reír (í); **— at** reírse (í) de
laurels triunfos *m.pl.*, **laureles** *m.
pl.*
lawn césped *m.* (*singular only*)
lawyer abogado *m.*
lead conducir; **— into** comunicarse
con
leader caudillo *m.*
learn aprender
least menos; **at —**, por lo menos,
al menos
leave irse, partir, salir; dejar
lemon limón *m.*
lend prestar, dar
less menos
lesson lección *f.*
lest para que no, por miedo de,
no fuera (sea) que
letter carta *f.;* letra *f.*
life vida *f.;* **city —**, vida urbana
like gustar; querer (ie), agradar;
adv. como; **just —**, lo mismo
que
line línea *f.*
listen escuchar
literature literatura *f.*, letras *f.pl.*
little pequeño, –a; poco, –a; **a —**,
un poco
live vivir
lively animado, –a
living vivo, –a
load carga *f.;* *verb* cargar
long largo, –a; **as — as** mientras;
— before mucho antes; **how —?**

¿cuánto tiempo? ¿desde cuándo?; **very —**, larguísimo, –a
look (at) mirar; **— for** buscar; **—
out!** ¡cuidado!; **to —** (*appear*)
parecer
lose perder (ie)
love amor *m.;* *verb* amar, querer
(ie); **fall in — with** enamorarse
de
lover amante *m.*, aficionado *m.*
low bajo, –a
lunar lunar
lunch almuerzo *m.;* **have —**, almorzar (ue)

M

magnitude magnitud *f.*
majestic majestuoso, –a
make hacer
man hombre *m.;* **— alive!**
¡hombre!
many muchos, –as; **as — as**
tantos como
map mapa *m.*
March marzo *m.*
married casado, –a; **— life** vida de
casado, –a
marry casar; **get married (to)**
casarse (con)
Mary María
matter asunto *m.;* **no —**, no importa; **no — how** como quiera
que sea, **no — how poor** por
pobre que sea
me me, mí; **with —**, conmigo
meal comida *f.*
means: by all —, sin duda; **by —
of** por medio de
medicine medicina *f.*
Mediterranean mediterráneo, –a
meet encontrar (ue), encontrarse
(ue), reunirse

melody melodía *f.*
mention mencionar, citar
Mexico México *or* Méjico *m.*
Mexico City Ciudad de México *f.*
middle medio *m.*, mitad *f.* **in the —**
of a mediados de
midst medio *m.*, centro *m.; in the**
— of en medio de
mildness bondad *f.*
mile milla *f.*
million millón *m.*
mine el mío, la mía
minute minuto *m.*
mirror espejo *m.*
Miss señorita *f.*
miss echar de menos
mistake falta *f.*, error *m.; verb* **be
mistaken** equivocarse, enga-
ñarse
mix mezclar(se)
model modelo *m.*
modern moderno, –a
modernization modernización *f.*
moment momento *m.; in a —,*
ahorita; ahora mismo
money dinero *m.*
month mes *m.*
monument monumento *m.*
Moor moro *m.*
more más; **— than** más que, más
de
morning mañana *f.; in the —,* por
la mañana
mosaic mosaico *m.*
most *def. art.* + más; muy; **— of**
la mayoría de, la mayor parte de
mother madre *f.*
motherland patria *f.*
motor motor *m.*
mountain montaña *f.;* **— side**
ladera *f.;* **— range** sierra *f.*, cordillera *f.*
movie(s) cine *m.*
Mr. señor *m.*

Mrs. señora *f.*
much mucho, –a; *adv.* mucho;
as — as tanto cuanto; **so —,**
tanto; **too —,** demasiado
mummy momia *f.*
music música *f.*
must deber de, tener que
my mi, mis; **— own** el mío, la mía
mystery misterio *m.*

N

name nombre *m.;* **What is your
name?** ¿Cómo se llama Vd.?
narrow estrecho, –a
nation nación *f.*
national nacional
native indígena *adj.;* natural *m.*
navigable navegable
near cerca (de)
neat limpio, –a
necessary necesario, –a
necktie corbata *f.*
need necesitar
neighbor vecino *m.*, vecina *f.*
neighborhood vecindad *f.*, cerca-
nías *f.pl.*
neither . . . nor no . . . ni . . . ni
network red *f.*
never nunca, jamás
nevertheless sin embargo
New Yorker neoyorquino *m.*
news noticia *f.*
newspaper periódico *m.*
next próximo, –a; siguiente; **— to**
junto a
nine nueve
no *adv.* no; *adj.* ninguno (ningún), –a
nocturne nocturno, *m.*
noise ruido *m.*
north norte *m.*
northern del norte

northwest noroeste *m.*
not no; — **at all** nada
notable notable
nothing nada; — **at all** nada
now ahora; **right** —, ahora mismo;
   up to —, hasta ahora
nowadays en nuestros días, hoy
   en día
numerous numeroso, –a

O

object objeto *m.*
occasion ocasión *f.*
occupied ocupado, –a
occupy ocupar
occur ocurrir
ocean océano *m.*
o'clock (*omitted in translation*): **it
   is ten** —, son las diez
of de
office oficina *f.*, despacho *m.*
official oficial
often a menudo
oil aceite *m.;* petróleo *m.;* — **well**
   pozo de petróleo *m.*, yaci-
   miento *m.*
old viejo, –a; antiguo, –a
olive tree olivo *m.*
on en, a, sobre, acerca de;
   — **account of** a causa de; —**to,**
   — **top of** encima de, sobre
one un, uno; **the** — **who** el que, la
   que
only sólo, solamente
open abrir
opening day día del estreno *m.*
opportunity oportunidad *f.*
opposite en frente de, frente a
orange naranja *f.;* — **tree** naranjo
   m.
order: in — **to** para + *inf.*
organize organizar

origin origen *m.*
original original
originally en sus orígenes
other otro, –a; **each** —, el uno al
   otro
ought deber
our nuestro, –a; **ours** el nuestro, la
   nuestra
out: go —, salir
outside fuera (de)
outstanding destacado, –a
over sobre; por; — **there** allá
overcoat abrigo *m.*
own propio, –a

P

pace paso *m.;* **in** — **with** a medida
   que
painter pintor *m.*
painting pintura *f.*
palace palacio *m.*
Pan American panamericano, –a
paper papel *m.*
parents padres *m.pl.*
park parque *m.*
part parte *f.;* (*role*) papel *m.*
particular: in —, de una manera
   señalada
particularly particularmente
pass pasar
passenger pasajero *m.*
patio patio *m.*
pay pagar
peace paz *f.*
peacefully tranquilamente, placi-
   damente
peak pico *m.*, cima *f.*
pear pera *f.*
penetrate penetrar
peninsula península *f.*
people gente *f.*, pueblo *m.*, nación
   f.; personajes *m.pl.*

per cent por ciento
perfectly perfectamente
perform actuar, presentar
performance representación *f.*, función *f.*
perhaps tal vez, quizá(s)
period período *m.;* — **of time** temporada *f.*
permit permitir
perpetual perpetuo, –a
person persona *f.*
personality personalidad *f.*
Peru el Perú *m.*
Peter Pedro
photograph fotografía *f.*
piano piano *m.*
picturesque pintoresco, –a
pipeline conducción *f.*
place lugar *m.*, punto *m.;* **take —,** celebrarse; *verb* poner
plane avión *m.*, aeroplano *m.*
planet planeta *m.*
plant planta *f.*
plateau meseta *f.*
play comedia *f.*, drama *m.*
play jugar (ue); tocar
pleasant agradable
please gustar, agradar; **please!** por favor, tenga la bondad (de)
pleased contento, –a; **I am — to know you** mucho gusto en conocerle
pleasure gusto *m.*, placer *m.*
poem poema *m.*
poetry poesía *f.*
point punto *m.;* — **of departure** punto de partida *m.*
political político, –a
politics política *f.*
poor pobre
popular popular
population población *f.*
port puerto *m.*
position colocación *f.*, plaza *f.*

possess poseer, contar (ue) con
possession posesión *f.;* **take — of** apoderarse de
possible posible; **it is —,** es posible, puede ser
powerful poderoso, –a
practice practicar, ejercitar
precede preceder
prefer preferir (ie)
prepare preparar
present presente, actual; **at —,** en la actualidad
present presentar
pretty bonito, –a; bello, –a
price precio *m.*
principal principal
principally principalmente
prior (to) anterior (a)
prize premio *m.;* **Nobel Prize** Premio Nobel
probably probablemente
problem problema *m.*
procession procesión *f.*, desfile, *m.*
produce producir
product producto *m.*
production producción *f.*
professional dancer profesional del baile *m.*
professor profesor *m.*
progress progreso *m.*
prominent destacado, –a; prominente
proportion proporción *f.*
prosperity prosperidad *f.*
prosperous próspero, –a
protect proteger
provided (that) con tal que, siempre que
province provincia *f.*
public público, –a
purpose propósito *m.;* **for the — of** con motivo de
put poner, colocar; — **on** ponerse

Q

quality calidad *f.*
quarrel reñir (i), pelear
quarter cuarto *m.*
quiet tranquilo, –a; quieto, –a;
  keep (be, become) —, callarse
quite: — a bit muchazo; **— poor**
  pobretón

R

rain llover (ue)
rainy lluvioso, –a; de lluvia
range (*mountains*) sierra *f.,* cordillera *f.*
rapid rápido, –a
rare raro, –a
rather sino que; más bien
reach llegar (a), alcanzar
read leer
ready listo, –a; preparado, –a
reality realidad *f.*
really de hecho, verdaderamente,
  en realidad
reason razón *f.,* causa *f., **for that**
  —,* por eso
receive recibir
red rojo, –a
refer referir (ie), referirse (ie)
refinement refinamiento *m.*
refuge refugio *m.*
regards saludos *m.pl.,* recuerdos
  m.pl.; **with regard to** con
  respecto a
region región *f.*
religious religioso, –a; sacramental
rely contar (ue) con, confiar en
remain permanecer, quedarse
remember recordar (ue), recor-
  darse de; acordarse (ue) de; **—
  me to** recuerdos a
rent alquilar

repent arrepentirse (ie) (de)
representative representativo, –a
republic república *f.*
resemble parecerse (a)
rest descanso *m.;* resto *m.;* lo
  (los, las) demás
rest descansar(se); **— on one's
  laurels** dormirse (ue) en sus laureles
restaurant restaurante *m.*
result resultado *m.; verb* resultar
return volver (ue)
reveal revelar, mostrar (ue)
reverend reverendo, –a
review repasar, revisar
rhythm ritmo *m.*
rice arroz *m.*
rich rico, –a
right derecho, –a; **all —,** bueno;
  — away en seguida; **be —,** tener
  razón; **— now** ahora, ahorita;
  to the —, a la derecha
rival rival *m.*
river río *m.; adj.* fluvial
Robert Roberto
role papel *m.*
Rome Roma *f.*
room cuarto *m.*
round redondo, –a
royal real; **— blood** realeza *f.*
ruin ruina *f.*
rule regla *f.;* **as a general —,** como
  (por) regla general
run correr

S

sad triste
salary sueldo *m.*
same mismo, –a
save ahorrar, economizar
say decir; **— good-bye** despedirse
  (i) (de)

scaled escalonado, –a
scenery vista *f.*, paisaje *m.*
scholarship beca *f.*
school escuela *f.;* **summer** —,
   escuela de verano *f.*
sculpture escultura *f.*
sea mar *m. or f.; adj.* marítimo, –a
seascape marina *f.*
seashore costa *f.*
seasick mareado, –a; **get** —,
   marearse
season estación *f.*, temporada *f.*
seat asiento *m.*
second segundo, –a
secretary secretaria *f.*
see ver; **let's** —, a ver
seek buscar
seem parecer; **as it seems** al
   parecer
seize coger
sell vender
send enviar, remitir
series serie *f.*
serious serio, –a
serve (as) servir (i) (de)
service servicio *m.*
seven siete
seven hundred setecientos, –as
Seville Sevilla *f.*
shade sombra *f.*
shaded sombreado, –a
she ella
sheep carnero *m.*
shellfish marisco *m.*
ship barco *m.*, buque *m.*
shirt camisa *f.*
shirt store camisería *f.*
shop tienda *f.;* **go shopping** ir de
   compras
shore costa *f.*, orilla *f.*
short corto, –a
shout gritar
show enseñar, mostrar (ue); —
   him in le mande entrar

side lado *m.*, **on each** —, a cada
   lado; **by the** — **of** al lado de;
   mountain —, ladera *f.*
sidewalk acera *f.*
signal señal *f.*
since pues, desde (que), ya que
sing cantar
sister hermana *f.*
sit (down) sentarse (ie)
situated situado, –a
situation situación *f.*
six seis; — **lane highway** carretera
   de seis vías *f.*
size medida *f.*
skirt falda *f.*
sky cielo *m.*
sleep dormir (ue)
sleepy: be —, tener sueño
slender delgado, –a
small pequeño, –a
smoke fumar
snow nieve *f.*
so tan, así, tanto; — ... **as** tan ...
   como; — **that** de modo que, de
   manera que
social social
soil suelo *m.*
solid sólido, –a
some alguno (algún), –a; unos,
   –as; algunos, –as
someone alguien
something algo; — **else** otra cosa,
   algo diferente
sometimes algunas veces *f.pl.*
somewhat algo, un poco; un tanto
song canto *m.*, canción *f.*
soon pronto; — **after** a poco de;
   as — **as** tan pronto como, luego
   que; **as** — **as possible** lo más
   pronto posible
sorry: be —, sentir (ie)
south sur *m.*
South America Sudamérica *f.*, la
   América del Sur *f.*

southern del sur
Spain España *f.*
Spaniard español *m.*
Spanish español, –a; español *m.;*
— **American** hispanoamericano,
–a
speak hablar
special especial
spectacle espectáculo *m.*
spend pasar; gastar
spite: in — **of** a pesar de
splendid espléndido, –a
sport deporte *m.;* **sea sports** deportes de mar *m.pl.;* **sports fan**
aficionado a los deportes *m.*
spread extender (ie), extenderse
(ie)
spring primavera *f.*
square plaza *f.*
standard of living nivel de vida *m.*
start empezar (ie), comenzar (ie)
stateroom camarote *m.*, cabina *f.*
stay quedar, quedarse, parar
stenographer mecanógrafa *f.*, dac-
tilógrafa *f.*
step paso *m.*
still aun, aún, todavía
stone piedra *f.;* — **block** bloque de
piedra *m.*
stop parada *f.;* *verb* parar, pararse,
detenerse
store tienda *f.;* **hat store** sombrerería *f.*
story cuento *m.*, historia *f.*
storyteller cuentista *m.*
strange extraño, –a
street calle *f.;* **out on the** —, en la
calle
strip faja *f.*
strong fuerte
student estudiante *m.;* **fellow** —,
compañero de estudios *m.*
study estudiar
style moda *f.*

succeed conseguir (i), lograr
such tal, tanto; **in** — **a manner that**
de modo que
suit traje *m.*
summer verano *m.*
Sunday domingo; **Palm** —, Domingo de Ramos *m.*
sunny soleado, –a
sure seguro, –a; cierto, –a
surprise sorpresa *f.*
sweet dulce; **the sweetest music**
todo lo que hay de más dulce
swim nadar; **swimming** natación *f.*
Switzerland Suiza *f.*
synthesis síntesis *f.*
system sistema *m.*

T

table mesa *f.*
take tomar, llevar; — **along**
llevarse; — **from** sacar (de);
— **leave of** despedirse (i); —
off quitarse; — **out** sacar; —
place celebrarse
talk hablar
talking hablar *m.*
task tarea *f.*
taste gusto *m.;* *verb* probar (ue)
taxi taxi, taxímetro, *m.*
teacher profesor *m.*, maestro *m.;*
profesora *f.*, maestra *f.*
tear down derribar
telephone teléfono *m.*
television televisión *f.*
tell decir, contar (ue)
temperament temperamento *m.*
temple templo *m.*
ten diez
tennis tenis *m.*
terrace terraza *f.*
territory territorio *m.*
testimony testimonio *m.*

than que, de, del que
thank agradecer, dar gracias
thanks gracias *f.pl.;* — **to** gracias a
that *conj.* que; **in order** —, para que; — **of** el (la) de; **so** —, de modo que; *demon. adj.* ese, esa; aquel, aquella; *demon. pron.* ése, ésa, eso; aquél, aquélla, aquello; **that's how it is with** así pasa con; — **which** el (la) que
theater teatro *m.*
their su, sus
them los, las; (*after prep.*) ellos, ellas
themselves se, sí, ellos, –as mismos, –as
then entonces
there allí, allá; — **is (are)** hay
these *adj.* estos, –as; *pron.* éstos, –as
they ellos, –as
think pensar (ie); creer; **don't you — so?** ¿no es verdad?
third tercero, –a
this *adj.* este, –a; *pron.* éste, –a, esto; — **one** éste, –a
those *adj.* esos, –as; aquellos, –as; *pron.* ésos, –as; aquéllos, –as; — **who** los (las) que
thousand mil
three tres
through por, a través de
tight: be — on apretar (ie)
time tiempo *m.;* hora *f.;* vez *f.;* **a good bit of** —, un buen rato; **at the present** —, en la actualidad; **at the — when** por la época en que; **at this** —, ahora; **from — to** —, de vez en cuando; **have a good** —, divertirse (ie)
tired cansado, –a; **get** —, cansarse
to a, hasta
tobacco tabaco *m.*

today hoy; — **as in the past** hoy como ayer
together juntos, –as
tomato tomate *m.*
tomorrow mañana; — **morning** mañana por la mañana
tonight esta noche
too (also) también
too bad! ¡lástima!
too much demasiado, –a
top cima *f.;* **on — of** encima de, sobre
topic tema *m.*, asunto *m.*
total total *m.*
tour recorrido *m.;* **take a** —, dar una vuelta por
tourism turismo *m.*
tourist turista *m.*
toward hacia
tower torre *f.*
town pueblo *m.*, ciudad *f.*
trace rastro *m.*
tradition tradición *f.*
traffic tránsito *m.*
tragedy tragedia *f.*
train tren *m.*
transfer transferir (ie), trasladar
transport transporte *m.;* — **service** servicio de carga *m.*
transportation transporte *m.;* **river** —, transporte fluvial *m.*
travel viajar
treasure tesoro *m.*
tree árbol *m.;* **fruit** —, árbol frutal *m.*
tremendous tremendo, –a
trip viaje *m.;* **take a** —, hacer un viaje
trolley tranvía *m.*
tropical tropical
trousers pantalones *m.pl.*
true: it is —, es verdad
truth verdad *f.*
try tratar (de), probar (ue)

turn volver (ue), girar; — **into** convertirse (ie) en; — **out to be** resultar
twelve doce
two dos
two thousand dos mil
type tipo *m.*, clase *f.*

U

ugly feo, –a
umbrella paraguas *m.*
under debajo (de), bajo
understand comprender, entender (ie)
undoubtedly sin duda
uneven desigual
unite unir
United States los Estados Unidos *m.pl.*
unity unidad *f.*
university universidad *f.*
unless a menos que
unsurpassed insuperado, –a
until hasta que
up to hasta
upon sobre; a + *infinitive*
urbanization urbanización *f.*
us nos, nosotros
use uso *m.; verb* usar, utilizar, emplear
useful útil
usually generalmente

V

vacation vacaciones *f.pl.*
Valencian valenciano, –a
valley valle *m.*
varied variado, –a
variety variedad *f.*
various varios, –as

verb verbo *m.*
verify averiguar, verificar
very muy; mismo, –a
vie rivalizar
vine vid *f.*
visit visitar
volcano volcán *m.*
vow hacer voto, comprometerse

W

wait esperar
wake up despertarse (ie)
walk paseo *m.; verb* pasear; **take a** —, pasearse
wall muralla *f.*
want querer (ie), desear
war guerra *f.;* **world** —, guerra mundial *f.*
warm caliente; **it is** —, hace calor
wash lavar(se)
waste gastar, perder (ie)
way camino *m.;* modo *m.*, manera *f.;* **in this** —, de esta manera
we nosotros, nosotras
wealth riqueza *f.*
wealthy rico, –a
wear llevar
weather tiempo *m.*
week semana *f.;* **—end** fin de semana *m.*
welfare bienestar *m.*
well bien
west oeste *m.*
wharf muelle *m.*
what *int. pron. and adj.* ¿qué? ¿cuál? *rel. pron.* lo que; **—ever** cualquiera
when cuando; ¿cuándo?; **since** —? ¿desde cuándo?; **—ever** siempre que
where donde, adonde, de donde; ¿dónde? ¿a dónde (adónde)?

whereas en cambio
wherever dondequiera
which *rel. pron.* que; el (la) que, lo
  que; el (la) cual, los (las) cuales;
  the one —, el (la) que; **those —,**
  los (las) que
while rato *m.; conj.* mientras,
  mientras que
white blanco, –a
who *rel. pron.* que, quien, quienes;
  los (las) que; *int. pron.* ¿quién?
  ¿quiénes?; **the one —,** el (la)
  que; **—ever** quienquiera
whole todo, –a; entero, –a
whom *rel. pron.* que; el (la) cual,
  los (las) cuales; el (la) que;
  after prep. quien, quienes;
  ¿quién? ¿quiénes?
whose *pron.* cuyo, –a; de quien
  (de quienes); ¿de quién? (¿de
  quiénes?)
why? ¿por qué?
wide ancho, –a
wife esposa *f.*
wig peluca *f.*
win ganar
window ventana *f.;* **car —,** ventanilla *f.*
windy: it is —, hace viento
winter invierno *m.;* **— sports**
  deportes de invierno *m.pl.*
wish querer (ie), desear

with con; **together —,** unido a
withdraw retirarse (de)
without sin, sin que
woman mujer *f.*
wonder maravilla *f.*
work trabajar; *noun* trabajo *m.;*
  obra *f.*
world mundo *m.; adj.* mundial
worry tener cuidado, dar cuidado; **don't —,** pierda Vd. cuidado
worse peor
worth: be —, valer; **be —while**
  valer la pena
write escribir

Y

year año *m.*
yellow amarillo, –a
yesterday ayer
yet todavía; **and —,** sin embargo
you tú; Vd., Vds.; vosotros –as;
  le, lo, la, los, las, ti, os
young: — lady señorita *f.;* **— man**
  joven *m.*
your tu, su, vuestro, –a; **yours** el
  tuyo, la tuya; el suyo, la suya;
  el vuestro, la vuestra
yourself se, te, ti
yourselves se, vosotros, –as

INDEX

(The numbers below refer to paragraphs.)

absolute superlative, **104**
acá and **allá**, **123**
acabar de + infinitive, **66**
accents: rule of, **25**
adjectives: agreement, **13**; common words used as adjectives and adverbs, **99**; comparison of, **100**; comparison of equality, **103**; demonstrative, **47**; forms of, **11**; indefinite, **116**; interrogative, **93**; irregular comparison of, **102**; position, **12**, **97**; possessive, **43**, **94**; relative, **92**
adverbs: common words used as adjectives and adverbs, **99**; comparison of, **101**; comparison of equality, **103**; formation of, **98**; irregular comparison of, **102**; relative, **92**
article: definite, **2**; indefinite, **10**; neuter, **78**; omission of the indefinite, **29**; plural of the indefinite, **77**; uses of definite, **4**
augmentatives, **115**
aun and **aún**, **122**

caer: present indicative of, **46**
command forms: familiar, **39**; negative, **84**; polite, **39**

compound tenses: indicative, **111**; subjunctive, **112**; uses of, **113**
conditional, **60**
conditions, **121**
conjugations: regular, **5**
conjunctive personal pronouns: direct, **37**; double object pronouns, **81**; indirect, **51**; position of, **38**, **83**
conocer: present indicative of, **62**

dar: present indicative of, **26**
days of the week, **16**
deber: with infinitive, **31**; **deber**, **hay que** and **tener que**, **90**
deber de, **91**
decir: present indicative of, **41**
demonstrative adjectives, **47**
demonstrative pronouns, **48**
diminutives, **115**
disjunctive personal pronouns, **61**
¿dónde? and **¿a dónde (adónde)?**, **85**

encontrar: present indicative of, **32**
estar: present indicative of, **19**; uses of **ser** and **estar**, **20**
exclamations, **131**

319

family names, **134**
future tense, **34;** irregular verbs, **35;** probability, **127;** subjunctive, **129**

gender of nouns, **1, 76**
gustar, 45

haber: present indicative of, **54;** **haber de, 91**
hacer: present indicative of, **41;** **hacer** + infinitive, **67; hace, 22**
hay, 22; hay que, 90
hours of the day, **28**

idiomatic present and idiomatic past, **75**
imperative, **38, 39**
imperfect tense: formation and uses, **58;** irregular verbs, **59;** subjunctive, **107**
impersonal expressions, **22, 120**
'in' after a superlative, **106**
indefinite adjectives, **116**
indefinite pronouns, **117**
independent subjunctive, **125**
infinitive: after prepositions, **88;** **poder, deber,** and **tener que** with the infinitive, **31**
interjections, **132**
interrogative: adjectives, **93;** pronouns, **93;** sentences, **9;** words, **33**
intonation, **133**
ir: present indicative of, **26;** present subjunctive of, **74**

jugar: present indicative of, **32**

letter writing: beginning of the letter, **135;** closing of a friendly letter, **135**

months, **16**

negative commands, **84**
negative sentences, **8**
negative words and expressions, **49**
nouns: gender of, **1, 76;** plural of, **3**
numerals, **27, 36**

oír: present indicative of, **62**
ojalá with the subjunctive, **124**
orthographic changes in verbs, **71;** summary of, **119**

para: to express purpose, **21;** uses of **por** and **para, 30, 80**
participle; past participle, **53;** present participle, **86**
passive: reflexive for the, **64**
past tenses, **52**
personal **a, 50**
personal pronouns: table of, **82**
poder: with the infinitive, **31;** present indicative of, **32**
poner: present indicative of, **41**
por: uses of **por** and **para, 30, 80**
possession, **42**
possessives, **43, 44, 94**
prepositions, **30;** compound prepositions, **89;** preposition **a, 50**
present participle, **86;** present participle alone, **87**
present perfect: formation, **55;** uses, **56**

present tense of indicative, **6;** English equivalent of present tense, **7**

preterite: formation and uses, **65;** some irregular verbs, **68**

probability, **127;** probability in past time, **113**

progressive construction, **86**

pronouns: demonstrative, **48;** direct object personal pronouns, **37;** disjunctive (after prepositions), **61;** double object pronouns, **81;** indefinite, **117;** indirect object personal pronouns, **51;** interrogative, **93;** neuter, **78;** omission of subject pronouns, **18;** position of object pronouns, **38, 40, 83;** position of object pronouns with command forms, **40;** possessive, **44, 94;** relative, **57, 92;** subject pronouns, **17;** table of personal pronouns, **82**

purpose, **21, 110**

querer: present indicative of, **26**

radical-changing verbs of the first class, **69;** summary of radical-changing verbs, **118**

reciprocal verbs, **96**

reflexive verbs, **63;** reflexive for the passive, **64;** reflexive in Spanish but not in English, **95;** reflexive to give general directions, **125**

reír: present indicative of, **62**

relative pronouns, **57, 92**

saber: present indicative of, **46**

salir: present indicative of, **62**

seasons, **16**

sequence of tenses, **114**

ser: present indicative of, **14;** present subjunctive of, **74;** uses of **ser** and **estar, 20**

sino and **sino que, 128**

subjunctive: in adjective clauses, **109;** in adverbial clauses, **110;** compound tenses, **112;** future, **129;** imperfect, **107;** independent subjunctive, **125;** in modified assertions, **126;** present: formation, **72;** uses of subjunctive, **73, 108**

superlative: absolute, **104**

syllabication, **23;** practical rule for dividing words into syllables, **24**

tal vez with the subjunctive, **124**

tener: present indicative of, **15;** present subjunctive of, **74**

tener que, 90; with the infinitive, **31**

tenses of indicative: compound tenses, **111;** conditional, **60;** future, **34;** imperfect: formation and uses, **58;** irregular imperfects, **59;** past, **52;** present, **6;** present participle alone, **87;** present participle and progressive construction, **86;** present perfect: formation, **55;** uses, **56;** preterite: formation and uses, **65;** uses of compound tenses, **113**

'than' in comparisons, **105**

time, **28**

traer: present indicative of, **62**

venir: present indicative of, **26;** present subjunctive of, **74**

ver: present indicative of, **46**

verbs: future of irregular verbs, **35**; irregular verbs in the imperfect, **59**; reciprocal, **96**; reflexive, **63, 64**

verdad: uses of *¿verdad?* and *¿no es verdad?* **79**

volver: present indicative of, **32**; **volver a** + infinitive, **70**

weather, **22**

word order, **130**

PHOTOGRAPH CREDITS

page

ii Plaza de Doña Elvira, Seville, Spain *Courtesy, Iberia Airlines*

2 Street scene in Córdoba, Spain *Courtesy, Iberia Airlines*

10 Movie theatre in Madrid, Spain *Courtesy, Spanish National Tourist Office*

18 *top* A colorful hat seller in Acapulco, Mexico *Courtesy, Mexican Government Tourist Department*
bottom Children in costume at fair in Córdoba, Spain *Courtesy, Iberia Airlines*

26 Men's clothing shop in Madrid, Spain *Cifra Gráfica*

34 Church of Los Santos Juanes, Valencia, Spain *Courtesy, Spanish National Tourist Office*

41 Book stalls, Madrid, Spain *Courtesy, Iberia Airlines*

42 Signpost in Madrid, Spain *Courtesy, Iberia Airlines*

48 Street in downtown Bogotá, Colombia *Courtesy, Avianca Airlines*

56 Partial view of a medical center in Mexico City, Mexico *Courtesy, Mexican Government Tourist Department*

64 Market place in Oaxaca, Mexico *Courtesy, Mexican National Tourist Council*

71 La Merced market, Mexico City, Mexico *Courtesy, Mexican National Tourist Council*

72 Central Square, San José, Costa Rica *Jane Latta*

79 Rural scene, Costa Rica *Paul Conklin*

80 *top* Colegiata Church, Santillana del Mar (Santander), Spain *Courtesy, Spanish National Tourist Office*
bottom Children playing "bullfighting" in Spain *Courtesy, Trans World Airlines*

86 Floating gardens in Xochimilco, Mexico *Courtesy, Mexican Government Tourist Department*

93 Columbus Circle, Mexico City, Mexico *Courtesy, Mexican National Tourist Council*

94 *top* Aztec ruins at Teotihuacán, Mexico *Courtesy, Mexican National Tourist Council*
bottom Museum of Anthropology, Mexico City, Mexico *Courtesy, Mexican National Tourist Council*

102 Conversation in a Spanish café *Cifra Gráfica*

110 Avenida Libertador, Caracas, Venezuela *Courtesy, Embassy of Venezuela*

112 Inca ruins, Machu-Picchu, Peru *Courtesy, Varig Airlines*

120 *top* Silversmiths at work in Taxco, Mexico *Courtesy, Mexican Government Tourist Department*
bottom Plaza del Palacio de Gobierno, Veracruz, Mexico *Courtesy, Mexican Government Tourist Department*

128 *top* Teatro de la Zarzuela, Madrid, Spain *Courtesy, Embassy of Spain*
bottom Antonio Buero Vallejo, Spanish playwright *Courtesy, Embassy of Spain*

136 Laguna del Inca, Portillo, Chile *Courtesy, Braniff International Airways*

144 Gardens in Aranjuez, Spain *Courtesy, Iberia Airlines*

151 Gardens of the Royal Palace, La Granja de San Idelfonso (Segovia), Spain *Courtesy, Iberia Airlines*

152 Some of the 6000 oil well derricks in Lake Maracaibo, Venezuela *Courtesy, Embassy of Venezuela*

162 Romería del Rocío, Huelva, Spain *Courtesy, Iberia Airlines*

171 A view of the Magdalena, Santander, Spain *Courtesy, Iberia Airlines*

172 Semana Santa (Holy Week), Seville, Spain *Courtesy, Spanish National Tourist Office*

180 *top* Avianca plane *Courtesy, Avianca Airlines*
bottom Bogotá, Colombia *Courtesy, Avianca Airlines*

188 Carreta monument, Uruguay *Courtesy, The California Institute of International Studies; photo by Juan B. Rael*

200 Dancers in Granada, Spain *Courtesy, Iberia Airlines*

208 Plaza del Congreso, Buenos Aires, Argentina *Courtesy, Varig Airlines*

216 Court of Lions, La Alhambra, Granada, Spain *Courtesy, Iberia Airlines*

223 Façade of The Mosque in Córdoba, Spain *Donald Preston*

224 Miraflores locks, Panama *Courtesy, Panama Tourist Bureau*

1 2 3 4 5 6 7 8 9 0